What people are saying about "Married Man Sex Life" *the blog*... (and the book is even better!)

"My wife doesn't know I read your blog, but she definitely has noticed a change in me. I can honestly say that I've had more sex and more fun with her since I've started reading this stuff." - T.

"The Married Man Sex Life Blog. It is truly excellent and inspirational reading. More than anybody else I've read so far, Athol Kay seems to understand that there needs to be a balance between Alpha and Beta in long term relationships." – Via Reddit.

"Something of a neglected niche online, Married Man's Sex Life writes in a non-traditional (read: realistic) way of keeping your marriage healthy and hot." - Brainz.org Top 100 Blogs.

"As a female reader, your description of what women REALLY want is a huge "gotcha!" I'm a little embarrassed at how well you seem to know me, considering we've never met." -Genevieve in South Carolina.

"Reading your blog helped resurrect our crumbling twenty-five year marriage. You have a way of reaching both male and female readers with equally positive results. Neither my husband nor I had any idea we could be this happy." -John and Jeanne, Selbyville, DE

"Brilliant. This needs to be shared with every single adolescent male growing up in today's society. And most of those who have already grown up, but not "manned up." - M.

"Your blog has helped me bring out the Alpha that my wife (and I) needed. Thanks a bunch, Athol." - Robert and Laura, Las Vegas

"Love your blog and it has been a tremendous help. Just doing a couple of your tricks has made a world of difference." – B.K.

"Anyone who doubts Athol Kay's mastery, only needs to visit his site to understand why he truly is the king of his topic." - Dalrock

"I just wanted to let you know that your blog is awesome. I only stumbled across it a few days ago thanks to your appearance on that top 100 blogs list. It's fantastic! It's like you just switched on the light! So good luck with the book, and keep up the great work! Thanks much!"
- Miranda

"I am getting my husband to read this blog and it's been amazing! Thank you!" – Reader.

"One that has caught my eye and has impressed me no end is Athol Kay's, Married Man Sex Life. Really, although the blog title might be a bit off putting--he really should call it "Wife Management 101"--the blog is definitely worth the read. Why? Because Athol "gets" the big picture." - The Social Pathologist

"Thank you so much Athol, for your astute analysis of my problems. Even without meeting us in person you were able to sum things up so well. Your blog is unparalleled anywhere in the Universe. Wishing you tons of success." - K.B.

"Still reading through all your posts, but yeah, digging it a lot so far. Having a lot of "ah-hah" moments as some things line up and finally make sense. Much appreciated that you are willing to share, very much appreciated." – Ross

"Hey, here's one faithful fan who happens to be female, and I took a break from shy lurking to let you know how much I appreciate your blog, Athol. Once upon a time, I was a doorknob's turn away from being a walk-away wife. Fortunately I put my hand on my computer's mouse instead, and found this phenomenal, real world resource for my husband and me. We've experienced a total transformation in six months, and I'm so glad I stayed. I would have missed seeing a gorgeous Alpha male emerge from the shell of my husband of 25 years." – H.

"I know you helped save my marriage through your efforts. I can't thank you enough. I was almost all Beta all the time, now I know enough to mix it up." – O.

"I accidently stumbled on your blog but I just wanted to let you know after reading a few entries it gave me a huge moment of clarity and just wanted to thank you for putting this stuff out there." – Anon.

The Married Man Sex Life Primer 2011

Athol Kay

For Jennifer

Contents

Contents

Disclaimers

I am not a marriage counselor. I did look into becoming one while writing this book, but discovered I would need two years formal study and the starting money was around $33,000 a year. I figured Jennifer would divorce me if I made that little.

This book is not intended to replace the advice and instruction of your own medical, legal or marriage or other licensed providers. It's certainly not meant to replace advice from plumbers or electricians either. If something requires licensed professionals, use them and follow their advice.

In real life I am a nurse. However I am not *your* nurse, nor am I providing any form of nursing service to any reader.

Readers hold me harmless for negative outcomes based on following any suggestions on this book. Every relationship is different, not everything will work.

Sex is a very primal need. Sometimes the book touches on the darker aspects of human nature. Understanding and discussing these darker elements within us all, is not the same as advocating for them.

Acknowledgments

Some of the ideas in this book are new, but the greater part of them has been based on the work of countless others.

The Talk About Marriage forum – A key place of my learning about affairs and attraction problems in marriage, both why they happen and practical steps to intervene. It also provided a place to start fleshing out some of my early ideas and where the chorus of requests to write a book started.

The "Manosphere" – The collection of bloggers, Pickup Artists, commenters and Men's Rights writers on the Internet. I've ransacked the Manosphere for many ideas. Roissy was particularly helpful in framing the benefits of the Alpha approach.

Dr. Helen Fisher - We've never met, but her insights into the nature of love have underpinned a great deal of my thinking. When I talk about dopamine, oxytocin and testosterone, please consider it a nod in her direction. Any errors on that perspective are mine.

"Mystery" - I would not have found a way to incorporate the idea of comfort building and the Beta traits as a positive thing without his insight. "The Mystery Method" remains an important book.

Evolutionary Psychology – Every time I talk about "The Time Before Writing", know that I'm poaching something from evolutionary psychology. No disrespect is intended by this loose term.

Nursing – Being a nurse has exposed me to the changes behavior medication can make on a daily basis in psychiatric patients. Without seeing that, I may never have really understood much of the Body Agenda chapter. Learning the day in, day out behavior management of difficult patients has been exceptionally useful as well. I've been exposed to hundreds of women and as often the only male nurse, I've been the default male listening ear to their wifely complaints for the last thirteen years. Also working nearly exclusively with women, I far better appreciate the changes in mood from the menstrual cycle...

Personal Gratitude

To be sure, most of the work has been mine, but I have also been enormously helped by others. It's not been the difference between me having a good book or a great book, but being able to finish the book at all. I've been humbled by how many people have offered help and cheered me along the way.

My Blog Readers and Friends – Thank you to everyone that has been so kind and supportive these last fifteen months. The constant encouragement to write a book has truly helped me in this process.

"Bella" – When I asked for help proofreading, thirty people offered. Everyone has helped, but I would like to give special thanks to you, who stayed with the project so consistently and has given me the most helpful criticism and advice. Without you I would have a far worse book. All the errors that remain are mine.

A Patient – I would like to thank a developmentally delayed patient of mine. In the middle of one of my darkest periods, you reminded me of what I stood for. Without you, I might never have realized that being married was in fact my defining characteristic; the source of my personal power. I am, as you said, "The Married Man" simply because I wear a wedding ring. Sometimes it's really just that simple.

My Parents - Warwick and Susan, who met on a blind date and were married for 45 years. I have unwittingly done so many things right in my marriage because of your example. Dad passed away before I could finish writing, and that is the only regret I have from this whole experience.

My Wife – Jennifer, only you know how truly hard this was for me. If I am Frodo, you are my Sam, and you carried me at the end.

Introduction

The Book is a Magic Trick

Let me put my cards on the table and I'll explain exactly how this magic trick works...

The whole book is written intentionally for a male audience. So husbands... I'm going to hand out every scrap of knowledge I know about getting your wife to strip her panties off for you. I can show you how to turn her on so much, she can't help herself for *wanting* you so bad.

Now ladies, come closer and I'll whisper in your ear what the deal *really* is...

...I'm going to teach him how to be a better man. All you have to do is play along and pretend that the book isn't really for you. Cool? Okay, shush, give me some space to work...

Okay guys, now that the women have all mysteriously vanished, we can *really* talk.

Men Want Better Sex, Women Want Better Men

There is a "chicken and the egg" positive feedback cycle with you being a better man and you getting better sex. But all it takes is a little laziness creeping into your relationship and you can hit a patch of not getting enough sex, so you start getting a little moody, so she likes you less, so you get less sex... and then suddenly there's a negative feedback cycle kicking in creating a slow spiraling death towards a sexless marriage; you want more sex and she wants you to be better, and neither one of you get what they want. You just lie there in bed next to each other lonely and confused as to how you got there.

If you're the man, you have to fix the problem. This is not one of those "man up" speeches where you get blamed for everything. You have to fix the problem because you are the only one that *can* fix the problem. She can't, through an act of willpower, make herself *want* to have sex with you. Pay attention to the difference here, it's critical you understand this. *She can make herself have sex with you, she just can't make herself <u>want</u> to have sex with you.*

So when you have sex with her, you will know in your heart of hearts, that she does not really *want* you inside her. Instead of sex with her making you feel loved and accepted, it actually slowly eats you up from the inside. As her husband, the thing you wish most of all is for her to *want* you in the moments you are joined together. Without feeling her desiring you, your relationship will continue to struggle and flounder into unhappiness.

So *she* can't fake it until *you* make it... because *you* can't make it if *she* fakes it.

However as the husband, you may not even want to become a better man for her, but you can force yourself to take action and become a better man. Once you become that better man, she will begin to *want* you again and the positive feedback cycle can resume again. Female sexuality responds to male sexuality, so *you* have to take the lead.

If you are in a low sex marriage and you want more from her, you have to change you to break out of the rut you are both in. Once the positive feedback loop kicks back in again, the relationship can start changing for the better very quickly. I've had couples on the brink of divorce say the love and sex is back in as little as two months.

So *you* can fake it until *you* make it... and when *you* make it, *she* won't need to fake it. She'll *want* you again.

Why You Got Married in the First Place

Let's be real here – maybe you had some good reasons for marrying your wife – but we both know what really counted was you wanting to have sex with her. You might have done that "Pro and Con" thing with a line down the middle of the page, but whatever was on the

"Con" column didn't matter a damn compared to *"I get to screw her!"* on the "Pro" side of the page.

I also know that apart from your hobbies, pretty much everything else in your life is just a hoop that you have to jump through to get back to having sex with her. When you jump through all those hoops and the sex just doesn't happen like you think it should, you get hurt...you get angry...but mostly you're confused.

You're confused because you think you're doing the right things for her, because she probably tells you that's what she wants you to do. Then everyone tells you that women are so complicated and so hard to understand that a regular guy doesn't really have a hope of figuring them out. Then a small army of experts will tell you that your problem is you're not jumping through enough of her hoops! Then when your sex life starts tanking, they all tell you that a declining sex life is normal in a marriage.

Sometimes in the middle of all this she can walk out on you, cheat on you or tell you to leave. So while I am all about getting you laid like tile, there are also serious situations we have to address as well. I'm going to show you how to make the good stuff happen and the bad stuff not happen.

Part One – What She Really Wants

The first part of the book is going to bring you up to speed on how sex *really* works for men and women. There's a bit of biology to brush up on first, because when it comes right down to it, sex is about two bodies coming together to try and make a baby. At least that's been the purpose of sex for millions of years.

This part of the book looks at the disconnection between how women are biologically wired to look for a certain type of mate, but as modern women, they need quite a different sort of man in their life. That biological "wrong wiring" is at the root of the vast majority of marital drama and failure. Better understanding her biological wiring means that you can start to adjust your game plan and start doing things *that she really wants.* Thankfully, it's not all about learning the correct technique of loading the dishwasher.

Part Two – The Male Action Plan

Once you're properly familiar with what she really wants, you're automatically going to start playing a better game by at least stopping some obvious mistakes. But that's not enough for me – I want teach you how to actually switch the balance of power in the relationship from her to you. If she's in charge of your relationship, she doesn't really respect you as a man and that's why the sex is so bad. If you're in charge of the relationship, she will respect you *and that's what turns her on.*

In addition to teaching you the basic principles of The Male Action Plan (The MAP), the second part of the book is going to cover several different long term strategies for sexual success. Some are going to be more important to you than others. Test what works best for you, then run with it.

Part Three – Sexy Moves

This is the fun stuff! The Sexy Moves are all small, practical things you can do to inject sexy romance into your day. This is where I teach you how to kiss her, how to touch her, how to make a move on her, how to date her and (gulp!) maybe even spank her a little. *Women love this part of the book.*

If you want, you can actually dive straight in to Part Three and start trying some of the moves out on her; they are all easy to do and really do work. But you will find them more effective if you read the first parts of the book and understand *why* they work as they do.

Part Four – Errors and Dangers

Part Four also covers critical areas where husbands commonly run into trouble. We can both hope you never have to employ some of these defensive strategies, but knowing you have them in your tool kit is going to make you feel more confident. For example, if you have a clear plan for quickly exposing and dealing with her should she ever cheat on you, she's not likely to ever risk it. Knowledge is power and power is sexy.

Warnings

Now as your official Genie of the Lamp, I do have a couple of warnings for you.

You can't bring back the dead – If your relationship is truly over and the divorce is final, it's usually just best to accept that it's over and move on. You can try if you want, but it's a very long shot.

You can't make anyone fall in love with you – What I'm going to show you will absolutely set the stage for love and sex to flourish, but you can't actually *force* that to happen. You may very well do everything I say in this book and your wife can ignore all your changes and still not be sexually interested in you. As you will see in the chapters on doing The MAP, if she doesn't respond to you, then you will have a very natural progression to leaving her and will be perfectly set up to find a new love who will be excited to have you.

A small technicality – I *can* promise you that you can have a wife that wants you passionately; I just can't 100% assure you that it will be your *current* wife. I wouldn't want things to get awkward between us later on, so throwing that out there now.

Women Have Exceptionally Good Hearing

Also if the women reading were still here to listen to this discussion between us men, I would give them a warning too.

If you give this book to your husband and he does what I say, he will become a far more attractive man. That means not only will he be more attractive to you, he will be more attractive to other women as well. As your husband steps up his game, you may have to step up yours as well.

Part One

What She Really Wants

Chapter 1
Body Agenda

True Love...?

At some point in your marriage, you're going to look over at your wife and wonder what you got yourself into. Marriage which seemed so very traditional and conservative will suddenly seem as risky as skydiving when someone else packed your chute. Why would *you*, a perfectly rational man subject yourself to getting married?

The answer is that we aren't nearly as rational as we like to think we are. When we find that special someone our own body can release hormones and neurochemicals that make us almost uncontrollably romantically fixated on the beloved.

For myself, I have no idea why I married Jennifer. Oh sure I could rattle off a dozen good points about her, but many of those same points were true about other women I knew. In fact before I met Jennifer, I had a friend called Penny who is very similar in looks and personality to my wife, just she's taller. I distinctly remember looking at her one day and trying to figure out why I felt absolutely no romantic interest in her. Everything about her checked off on my secret list of wife material points, I just had no interest in her beyond friendship. I even felt stupid for that lack of interest seeing objectively, she was a real catch.

Then I met Jennifer and it was like discovering cocaine. More Jennifer please. More. MORE! With the exception of what I carried in one suitcase I literally left everything behind in New Zealand to come be with her and that didn't even happen until we had survived a three year long distance relationship. Getting married was just a required task to getting more Jennifer, so I jumped through all the hoops needed to marry her.

So why are we so helplessly foolish in the face of love? Well the answer is *our bodies* may really be the ones running the show...

You Are Not Your Brain

Our large human brain very much sets us apart from the animals. It's our greatest strength as a species and supplies us with the raw cunning to vault us to the head of the class in the domination of the planet. Because of that tremendous strength, most people have the idea that the "real them" is housed in their mind and that their body is just a vehicle to transport them around.

Whether or not it is believed that we are a spirit, a higher being, a soul, a reincarnation or simply a very bright biological computer doesn't matter - all these approaches to thinking about what makes up "the real you" believe that the body is a *tool* for that intelligence. In short, it's believed that we are all self-aware and experience reality as a set of sensations that gets relayed to our brains. Based on those sensations we make choices and are in complete control about what we do.

However, we also know that this really isn't the whole picture. We have plenty of control over our bodies, but we all know there are limits to that control. We can learn to control bowel and bladder and be toilet trained, but we've all experienced some acute moments in our lives where despite our toilet training and express desire to hold something in, our express desire was completely irrelevant and something very much exploded out.

The same thing happens with vomiting. We may even rationally figure out that we just ate something, or drank many somethings, that the body would be better off moving rapidly to somewhere outside of the body. We may rationally think to ourselves *"I really should puke this up"*, but once the vomiting itself starts "you" (meaning your brain) basically become a passenger in the experience of clutching at the toilet bowl and intense stomach contractions.

Likewise with members of the opposite sex, you may meet someone vho quite objectively is attractive and sociable and interested in you, ⸳ you have no sexual interest in them. And of course there is the ᵗening attraction to members of the opposite sex you may even ⸳ dislike, who you *know* are no good for you.

Much of your body just runs on auto-pilot 24/7 and your rational higher thinking brain isn't even required for almost all of it. In fact sometimes thinking about our automatic body functions can interfere with their natural rhythm. One of the first tricks of the trade you learn in the medical field is to pretend to still be taking the patients pulse while you are in fact counting their respiration rate. The reason being that once a person knows you are watching their breathing, they tend to hold their breath or start to hyperventilate. When you take someone's pulse they tend to mentally focus on the fact that your hand is on their wrist and their breathing remains normal.

In a very real sense humans are no different than animals who all quite happily have all their bodily functions work quite nicely without a high school diploma or Internet connection. We are a truly gifted species intellectually, but even that is a result of DNA hardwiring intelligence into our bodies.

The Rational Brain is a Late Adaptation

Riding roughshod over evolutionary science for a moment, the key understanding is that the uniquely human highly rational brain is in fact a late adaptation to the human animal from perhaps only a few millions years ago. It's something that evolved as an advantageous tool for the human animal to use. Somewhere back in "The Time Before Writing" humans with bigger brains started out performing whatever was around at the time and slowly the big brains started taking over and running the show.

Perhaps the human animal could have evolved to have poisonous spit, or razor sharp tusks or night vision as a means of trying to grab a bigger piece of the pie. We didn't, instead we evolved our superior brain to do the same job. So in this sense your brain, what you may think of as "you" - *is a tool for your body*, rather than your body being a biological machine to allow "you" to walk around and get places. So in a very real sense "you", are your body and "you" are not nearly as fully in charge of yourself as you may think you are.

When it comes to sex, we have a multitude of biological programming hard-wired into us that very much sets our interest in the opposite sex. What we find sexually attractive in others is usually beyond our rational control. In fact our minds may very much wish to be attracted to some group of traits or someone in particular, but our bodies can choose for sexual interest in other traits or someone else entirely. This is why a woman can swear she wants to love and have a relationship with a "Nice Guy," but then finds herself drawn into sweaty entanglements with a "Bad Boy."

The Rationalization Hamster

Obviously with things like trying to hold our breath forever, or not use the bathroom, we can only really delay the inevitable a little before we gasp for air or wet our pants. Our rational brain has only a tiny amount of influence but no real control over autonomic body functions. But with behavioral choices that have a moral component, our rational brain very much plays a part in deciding what we do... at least on the surface of things.

Say a delivery truck transporting bread leaves its door open and you are passing by. If you've just had a hearty breakfast, you are very likely going to pay that open door minimal attention as you believe "stealing is wrong." But if you are very hungry and your family is hungry, you are going to be interested in all that unattended bread. There is a conflict between you understanding that stealing is wrong and you wanting to steal the bread; this conflict can be solved however, by finding a convenient rationalization to justify stealing the bread. Something like *"Stealing is a less serious wrong thing to worry about than the very serious issue of my children starving."* Now armed with this rationalization, you can happily steal the bread... because only an immoral person *wouldn't* steal the bread in your circumstances.

Hunger is well understood as a clear motivation for behavior. Truly hungry people will do nearly anything to get food and they clearly understand the motive at work. When it comes to sexual desire however, most people are not fully aware of what exactly is motivating them, so a rationalization for their sexual behavior can take place without the person being even aware that they are rationalizing; they can even be fooled0 *themselves.* This sexual mental sleigh-of-hand is called The Rationalization Hamster. More fully it is called The Female Rationalization Hamster because female sexuality can have great swings in her sexual interest during her menstrual cycle, so women tend to require greater use of rationalizing sexual behavior (or lack thereof) than men do.

As a common example, a wife who doesn't want to have sex with her husband often announces that she has a headache. She's rationalizing why she doesn't want to have sex and her Rationalization Hamster pops out a perfectly good excuse... she has a headache... which is convenient in that she gains task avoidance of the unwanted sex, but she's not so sick that she is required to actually get up off the couch and seek medical attention. Unless her husband has an MRI scanner in the basement, he can't actually prove she doesn't have a headache, so he's forced to accept her version of things. He could call her a liar about the headache of course, but that would just be picking a fight with her with no proof of her lying. So her lie about the headache works!

When it comes to illicit sex with an affair partner, there are strong social sanctions against cheating on a loved one, so the rationalizations required to overcome the sense of wrongness are much greater. A wife may love her husband and not want to hurt him at all, but she also may want to cheat on him with Mr. Studly next door. Thus the job of The Rationalization Hamster is to make up as much mental bullshit as possible until she can be comfortable with herself cheating on her husband. It's sort of a cloaking device for a conscience.

"Yes of course cheating on a husband would be wrong, but in this case my husband hasn't really been paying attention to me and he hurt my feelings by not picking out the china pattern I wanted for the reception and I'm just so lonely and neglected. He also dated a friend of mine when we were broken up before and I think he just did that far too quickly, so I'm really not even sure he really cares for me anyway. Plus I just feel so special and loved when I'm with Mr. Studly, so how could anything so special really be wrong. In fact I deserve this experience since I'm always putting everyone else's needs before my own. It's finally my turn to be happy!"

Meanwhile the husband may be a great husband but just have a vague dislike of Mr. Studly that he can't quite place.

In the middle of affairs the Rationalization Hamster goes into absolute overdrive spinning everything like a White House press secretary in the middle of a scandal. It's what allows rational and kind people to do the most illogical and horrible things to the people that love them the most in the world.

Body Agenda

So while our brains can have a very acute sense that having kids is labor intensive, expensive and... well, that the little brats can be quite annoying at times, our bodies tend to be quite keen on trying to make more of them. Our bodies have their own agenda for making babies that they keep sneaking into our consciousness for action. Potential sex partners are sized up as possible mates and the environment is assessed for the suitability for bringing children into the world.

Generally as long as there is an adequate food supply and reasonable shelter, the environmental conditions for making babies are met. As an example, much of modern human courtship behavior involves "going out to eat" and trying to "get the girl home," thus meeting the two primary environmental needs for getting the green light for baby making activities.

We are so used to the easy use and availability of birth control, having sex with the goal of making a baby is actually quite rare compared to the modern normal sex activity of just doing it to have sexual pleasure. As an example my wife and I have had sex around 5000 times in our marriage, but based on how quickly she got pregnant, we've probably only had "make a baby sex" about a dozen times if even that. Nevertheless our bodies don't really know the difference between sex for fun and sex to make babies. To our bodies all sex is about making babies and raising them and our bodies evaluate what is sexy based on what is going to meet those goals.

What is Sexy?

Once you start looking at human sexual behavior with the mindset that whatever is good for making and raising babies is sexy, everything regarded as sexy starts making perfect sense.

It can be physical:

Fit, healthy bodies are sexy because they pass on good genes to the baby.

Beauty is sexy because beauty is an indicator of health and good genes.

Bigger boobs are sexy because they indicate higher fertility and a woman with them has a better chance of having a baby.

A 0.7 waist-to-hip ratio on a woman is sexy because it is a key indicator of the likelihood of a full term pregnancy and the successful delivery of a baby.

Youth is sexy because younger people make healthier babies.

Strong is sexy because sometimes you need to beat off invaders or move something heavy to improve life for baby.

Lots of semen is sexy because that stuff just rocks for making babies.

Tall is sexy because it shows good health and nourishment. For a woman, this means her baby is likely to be healthier. For a man, this also indicates that he is likely to have a stronger social presence.

It can be material:

Rich is sexy because all that money is money that can be spent on raising baby.

A house is sexy because baby will have somewhere safe to live.

It can be trait-based:

Smart is sexy because baby will be smarter and better taught. Plus high intelligence is related to good semen production and motile sperm.

Foreigners are sexy because cross breeding-passes on a better immune system to baby.

Being good with kids is sexy because an active father is good for raising baby.

Courage is sexy because sometimes baby has to be defended from predators.

It can be social:

Having multiple women interested in the same man (a.k.a. Preselection) is sexy because if multiple women are interested in a man, it's probably because they all want to have his babies and are willing to compete for him.

Listening is sexy because it means you can communicate and form social bonds, which means you'll probably stick around to raise baby.

Fidelity is sexy because it means both parents will be focused on raising their baby.

I'll say it again... *what is sexy is anything that is good for making or raising babies.*

Hormones are Feelings

We all have feelings both positive and negative, but what is not fully grasped by most people is that our feelings are not simply abstract things, but have a real world physical component as well. Our bodies produce a vast array of hormones that act as physical messengers of emotion and feeling. Take away the hormones and your feelings vanish as well.

In a very quick summary of the work of Dr Helen Fisher, in terms of sexuality and relationships, there are three main hormonal systems that are at work.

Dopamine – This creates the "in love" feelings of excitement and the Obsessive Compulsive Disorder-like mental obsession on the person of desire. This is the thing that makes you crazy about the other person and makes you wonder why they aren't calling you. As an important aside SSRI anti-depressants can interfere with dopamine and have the very well known side effect of blunting sexual desire. Per Dr. Fisher they can also diminish the ability to experience romantic interest as well.

Oxytocin / Vasopressin – these are the pair bonding hormones; oxytocin more for women and vasopressin more for men. These hormones create that warm companionate love. It's cuddly and caring. These are the same hormones that are released into the parents in a great torrent after the birth of their children.

Testosterone – this creates the general sex drive, and both men and women need testosterone to get horny. Men have much higher amounts of testosterone than women do, but that should not be taken as an idea that men have a much higher sex drive than women do. Men use testosterone for a large number of things in their body compared to women, while women tend towards using the majority of their testosterone to trigger sexual interest. Men and women both have a fairly similar sexual drive.

It's very important to understand that these three hormonal systems operate independently of one another. It's very possible to feel a huge crush on a co-worker (dopamine), while feeling warmth and contentment with your wife (vasopressin) and just a raw lust for the barista at Starbucks with the perfect boobs (testosterone).

There is also a general perception that romantic love (that's the dopamine) fades away in a marriage after a few years and it turns into a more easy going cuddly type of companionate love (vasopressin). The truth is it doesn't – these are two separate systems. Some married couples do experience that plummeting of romantic feelings but many long term couples also experience in-love feelings coming and going over the years while a pair bonding persists the whole time. Also in arranged marriages it's clear that one can completely skip the opening romance and head directly into marriage and pair bonding takes place anyway.

Testosterone is the hormone that powers the base physical sex drive and is why men can get turned on by strippers. Men can have no romantic or companionate feelings for a woman, but if she's naked and jiggling inches from their face, they usually experience sexual arousal.

Why Cheaters Act Like Crack Addicts

Have you ever watched something about a sex scandal on TV and found yourself wondering why the cheater did something so stupid? In the wake of cheating there can be wrecked careers, tens of thousands of dollars just gone, shattered families and public humiliation. Often it's all for a handful of sweaty moments that seem hardly worth it to an outsider. It's really best thought of as the same process that drives an addiction.

From Wikipedia...

"Dopamine is commonly associated with the reward system of the brain, providing feelings of enjoyment and reinforcement to motivate a person proactively to perform certain activities. Dopamine is released rewarding experiences such as food, sex, drugs...

...such as cocaine, nicotine and amphetamines, directly or indirectly lead to an increase of dopamine in the mesolimbic reward pathway of the brain."

In short, if anything "feels good", it's because your body gave you a little shot of dopamine. Whether it's a great meal, hot sex, cocaine or being in love doesn't matter, it's a dopamine based reward system making you want to do it again. Importantly though, the same hormonal system that can make you rush to the altar can make you override your vows and sacrifice everything to be with your lover.

I Love You But I'm Not In Love With You...

Having your wife tell you "ILYBINILWY" (I Love You But I'm Not In Love With You) is about the largest red flag there is that your relationship is in trouble.

A woman can have minimal "in love" feelings for the husband she is pair bonded to and just coast along for *years* with no apparent cause for concern. I know of marriages where the wife clearly craps all over her husband and has done so for years and years, but the marriage continues on unabated anyway. She might quite dislike him even, but she has no real thought of leaving him.

It is of course quite easy to be faithful if no one else wants to have sex with you. But once a new man enters the picture who flips her dopamine on, things can unravel between a wife and her husband very quickly. The obsessive romantic thinking effects of the dopamine response can overwhelm the strength of the pair bond. The woman gets torn between the two men she is chemically drawn too. It's not an easy emotional state to survive in for long.

So when a wife tells a husband ILYBINILWY that invariably means there is a guy she is in love with that has entered the picture. Not only that, but she is usually actively trying to find a way to transition herself from being in a relationship with the husband to being in a relationship with the lover. In hormonal terms she is saying *"I oxytocin you, but I dopamine him".* In blunt terms though what she really means when she says ILYBINILWY is some combination of: *"I'm leaving you for him", "I'm thinking about having sex with him", "I'm having sex with him but I want to live with you still is that ok?",* and *"I think I might be pregnant and don't know whose baby it is".*

ILYBINILWY is also used as female code for some combination of *"I have no clue how to make this decision"* and *"Are you going to fight for me?"* The other reason a wayward wife can say ILYBINILWY is as a delaying tactic to avoid the husband acting pre-emptively to end the marriage or take other action against her. Think of how hard it is for a man to toss the mother of his children and love of his life out of the family home... all while she weeps real tears and tells him she "loves him" still. She's just not in love with him... and... cue up the

Rationalization Hamster... *"(sobbing) This is all so hard... I didn't want this to happen!"*

Often the purpose of the delaying tactic is to actually dupe the husband into unwittingly assisting in the transition of the wife's primary relationship from the husband to the lover.

What it Means When She Says "I'm Bored".

When a wife tells a husband "I'm bored" it is also a red flag but not nearly as bad as the ILYBINILWY one. What it really means is *"I need some dopamine, can you get me some?"*

What she's announcing is that she is experiencing a lack of stimulation and excitement. The opportunity is there to provide her with some sort of interaction and play that *does* stimulate her. If you fail to stimulate her enough, she may take matters into her own hands and find a source of stimulation.

One easy way of creating some exciting drama is by picking some sort of fight with you. I'm not saying a fight is fun or pleasant for either of you, but it is certainly very stimulating and you're usually giving her your full attention while yelling at each other. Then afterwards while you're still somewhat keyed up from the yelling, you can have hot make up sex with her. Some women also pick fights just to get their man worked up into having "angry sex" with them and really pounding them in the sack.

The other way of creating some drama and getting a dopamine rush is by looking outside the relationship. *"I'm bored"* can start coming closer and closer to sounding like *"You aren't listening to me, I keep telling you I'm getting bored of you and you do nothing about it."* A husband who fails to listen and pay attention to this clear red flag may be in for some nasty surprises in the future.

Concealed Ovulation

If a human female was similar to other primates, when she ovulated her ass might turn bright red and swollen, there might be an intense aroma wafting from her vagina and she might make some sort of vocal call that alerted all male humans in a mile radius that she was able to get pregnant. Now as amusing as that sounds, imagine what life would be like if women *actually did that.*

For the majority of the month, husbands could probably completely ignore wives. As in, not even live with them. As in, *"I'm hanging with my buddies at the bar for three and a half weeks, text me if your ass starts turning red."* Or he could simply spend three weeks... well listening for that sex call women did and "following his nose" so to speak.

But for those two days of ovulation, he would have to absolutely stick to her like glue. Everyone male would know she was fertile and keen for sex. We'd probably be allowed to not come into work on those days and just stay home and have sex repeatedly. We'd be calling our boss *"Her ass is turning red and all I can smell is vagina. I can't come in today".* Your boss would believe it too, since in the background he could hear your wife making that screeching call repeatedly.

But women have the entire ovulation process pretty well hidden and it's purposely confusing to both her and her husband. Usually a woman doesn't wake up in the morning thinking *"Oh wow, I'm ovulating, I'm going to need the four inch heels and a Brazilian wax",* they just wake up and think *"Ooooh I want to wear the red dress today. I feel great!"* This is why women struggling to have a baby wander around taking their temperature half the month waiting for the sudden increase in body heat signalling it's time to get some baby batter from her husband and get a bun in the oven.

A woman's moods and sexual interest can swing up and down because of her Body Agenda. Her body doesn't want him to know when she is ovulating and could become pregnant. Plus the body also wants to confuse her a little as well; if the body can get her a little bit sloppy and silly, then she might slip up and get pregnant. This is why asking a woman what she wants is often frustrating for both of the couple as she may have no real idea what she wants either. Women can be confused by their own moods as much as the men in their lives are.

Because ovulation is concealed and somewhat random, it forces a male partner to hang around to ensure paternity. Her sexual interest might stop and start a little during her cycle and the male has to be constantly available to have sex. Any one sex act might be the one that gets her pregnant, so it creates the need for a primary partner to pay her attention and create a serious committed relationship. This is quite excellent for holding a regular male partner around to help raise children.

The other reason ovulation is concealed is so she can cheat. There's no possible way a male can watch his primary female partner 24/7. Everyone falls asleep or needs to use the bathroom eventually, so despite a very high level of attention a husband gives a wife, she will always have some wiggle room to disappear briefly for something quick and dirty. Because ovulation is concealed, there's no sure way for the husband to know whether or not she was perfectly faithful even when he was watching her like a hawk.

The evolutionary purpose of this cheating is that while her primary male partner may be a good provider and pleasant companion, another male could offer her significantly better genes to impregnate her with. It's a try and have your cake and eat it too proposition. A woman may have sex with her partner thousands of times and with a lover maybe only a handful of times, but if any of that handful of times results in a pregnancy to the lover, it's an extremely significant outcome.

The link between ovulation and cheating is highly significant in that when she ovulates, a woman experiences a large spike in her sexual interest. Ovulation lasts only a few days, usually no more than two, but it is the highest point of sexual interest for a woman. Even quite low sex drive women can perk up and play for sexual attention during ovulation. It's when a woman is most likely to cheat on a partner, she is most likely to orgasm and in plain simple terms when she likes sex the roughest.

If you pay consistent attention to a woman, it's usually easy enough to discover when she is ovulating. There won't be a blatant change to her dress code from "demure angel" twenty-six days a month to "slutzilla" for two days a month. She'll generally stick to her basic appearance, but she just ups the ante slightly. Some more exposed skin, a little more attention to her makeup, a little more jewellery. Her interactions with men will be a little more attentive and flirty, with something like extra touching on the arm, eye contract and smiling.

Hidden Female Sexual Impulsivity

Women are just as sexually interested as men are, but it's typically hidden beneath the surface of their behavior. If you believe that women aren't as sexually interested as men are, then you have been fooled... which is precisely the point of the general female sexual strategy.

The reason women use this strategy of hiding sexual interest is because of a combination of three things:

(1) Women have a high social cost for being overtly sexual. This social cost has become less acute in the last few years with the rise of the hook-up culture, but it is certainly true historically and one shouldn't be surprised if the historical values return at some point in the future. The branding of a woman as a "slut" or a "whore" is a serious affront to her. Most men want women who will remain exclusive to them to assure his paternity for any children she has, so a woman that sleeps around lowers her sexual value. A women that sleeps around impulsively *before* marriage, gives an indication of a sexual impulsivity that will likely continue *after* marriage. Therefore most women do make an effort to not gain the reputation of being a slut to maintain their chances of marriage.

(2) Women are highly sexual and cheat as often as men do. Assuming heterosexual sex, every time a man cheats, a woman cheats as well. *It's just math.* So under the projection of *"good girl who's not so interested in sex that I'll cheat on you,"* is what can be a very turbulent sea of desire, especially when they ovulate. A woman interested in a man other than her partner can at times quite aggressively seek him out (though usually he needs to make the first move on her), and enthusiastically have sex with him. Then depending on the circumstance either seek to stay with her current mate, or attempt to jump ship to the new one. The results of DNA testing prove that anywhere between 2% to 30% (this number varies wildly by social group) of all children are fathered by a man other than the wife's husband. The general statistic of around 10% seems to be a rough average. Women cheat just as much as men do; they are just way sneakier about it in comparison.

(3) A woman's sexuality can often lie somewhat dormant until triggered by her response to a sexually attractive man. Many women can go months or years feeling only moderate desire, then once exposed to someone who interests them turn as hot for sex as a male virgin getting felt up for the first time. The intense desire for high quality males to have sex with, lies latent in all women. A woman risks an enormous amount of resources and effort in having a baby, so having top quality semen to start the process off is a critical concern. This need for a high quality male is what drives the fairly common story of a quiet "sexless" wife suddenly going sexually berserk over a new man, despite her frustrated husband having spent years begging her for sex.

Sperm Warfare

Having discussed concealed ovulation and how women are designed to be able to deceive their man and poach another man's genes on the sly, we come to the way the male body attempts to counter that female strategy. Men have ways of fighting back and trying to stop another man getting his partner pregnant.

One defense against another man's sperm is the way the penis is shaped. A penis being thrust into a vagina actually creates a mild suction and will slowly draw out any other semen present. Long and vigorous sex will create greater suction. A larger penis probably creates greater suction than a smaller one. It seems counter-intuitive, but if a wife's infidelity is discovered or suspected, a husband can become both extremely angry and wildly sexually aroused as well. It's a natural biological reaction to seek to immediately enter her and thrust very aggressively, unconsciously seeking to displace the other man's semen by pumping it out. This is what makes women find rough sex enjoyable, it's a signal of the male being sexually powerful.

Having just terrorized every man with less than a monstrous sized penis that he is inadequate as a lover, it's best to consider that it's in a sense like getting excited over the length of the barrel of a gun. *Ooooh so big.* Yet the penis is simply a delivery system for the more important thing – semen.

A primary purpose of men is to be walking semen factories. Each day a healthy male will make millions of sperm. This is why teenage boys lean on everything and can hardly stand up straight. Making 100 million sperm before breakfast is work. Women coast on juggling a single – maybe two – eggs a month which just seems lazy by comparison. The goal for a man is to ejaculate as much as possible into a fertile female and make a baby. Interestingly you cannot fool your own body. Your Body Agenda knows the difference between masturbation and sexual intercourse. Wikipedia...

"Sperm samples obtained via sexual intercourse contain 70-120% more sperm, with sperm having a slightly higher motility and slightly more normal morphology, compared with sperm samples obtained via masturbation. Sexual intercourse also generates a 25-45% increase in ejaculate volume, mainly by increased prostate secretion."

This is all done unconsciously; a man's own body can adjust the volume of semen and the sperm content of the semen depending on whether or not he is masturbating or ejaculating inside his woman. Also a male will unconsciously adjust the amount of sperm in his semen depending on how long it was since he last had sex with her. The longer it was since the last sex, the more sperm he gives her.

The male typically has no idea when the female will be ovulating and able to become pregnant, so the biological point of sex as far as the male is concerned is to constantly try and "top off" a female's reproductive tract with sperm. Sperm can survive for up to five days inside a female, so the plan is that as long as he can keep her topped off with his sperm swimming around inside her, he'll eventually get lucky and get her pregnant.

The other reason a male wants to keep a female topped off with sperm is that not all sperm are actually designed to make a run at the egg. Sperm come in three basic types: runners, blockers and killers. Only 1-2% of all the sperm are "runners" designed to make a break for the egg and fertilize it. The rest of the sperm split into two basic groups of "blockers" and "killers". The blockers act like a defensive line in football, they form chains of themselves and attempt to block up the females reproductive tract and deny access to any other male's competing sperm. The killers live up to their name too and patrol around looking to attack any other male's sperm as well.

If hearing the names "runners," "blockers" and "killers" sounds like sperm play a game of football against other sperm, you have it completely right. On a biological level, the *Male Body Agenda assumes that the female he is having sex with will be unfaithful.* By constantly seeking to top off a female's reproductive tract with sperm, he assures himself a standing army inside her ready to repel another male's sperm if she cheats on him.

A wife can avoid having a standing army of her husband's sperm inside her by simply denying him sex. A couple can have fairly frequent sex, but if she avoids sex with him, or just gives him handjobs or blowjobs in the three or four days before she ovulates, the husband is rendered defenseless from a sperm warfare perspective if she meets a lover for sex. There's no standing army of the husband's sperm to fight off the lover's sperm. Importantly because the lover is not likely to have many attempts at sex with the wife, his ejaculation will be extremely large and flood her vagina. The husband is at a decided disadvantage.

It's important to wave the flag again that this sort of planned deceit on the wife's part can happen completely unconsciously; the Rationalization Hamster can likely supply several excellent reasons as to why she avoided her husband's semen in her vagina for a few days before she ovulated. Plus obviously the hook-up with the lover was just an appalling lapse of character. She's not that kind of girl. In fact she's just realized from that hook-up how very empty sex without love can be and she now knows that deep down she really loves her husband and wants to make it work with him. So perhaps some good came of the whole thing. The Rationalization Hamster is holding off on telling her she's pregnant for a bit...missed periods sometimes just happen you know. (See how the Rationalization Hamster works?)

Sperm warfare also explains why if a husband is denied regular sex with his wife, he typically becomes fixated on the lack of sex with her to the exclusion of every other issue in the relationship. After five days of no vaginal sex, all his sperm inside her are either dead or have dripped out of her. In a "get her pregnant" sense it's like he's never had sex with her. He wants her topped off; instead she's completely empty of his sperm. She is therefore providing him with a very strong expression of disinterest in him. She may *say* that she loves him, but he will typically experience her actions as a deeply concerning rejection.

As a variant on this, if a wife has sex with a lover, she will often return to her husband and immediately seek sex from him as well. The husband may be quite surprised by her initiation of sex and her highly sexual intensity. What is happening is her Body Agenda is seeking to actively play the sperm armies against each other in a survival of the fittest game to find the winning sperm. If the husband is unaware of the lover, he likely just experiences this as a wonderfully intense sex experience that likely extends over several sessions. For those involved in the Hotwife or Cuckolding lifestyles, this return of the wife after being with a lover for immediate sex with the husband is a point of purposeful enjoyment.

Semen is Good for Women

Not all women cheat, but like men, they are designed for the possibility to do so. As long as a husband is attractive to her, a wife will typically bond to him securely and remain faithful to him, but the effects of her husband's semen does have greater effects than simply the ability to get her pregnant.

Semen is known to contain several hormones: testosterone, estrogen, prolactin, luteinizing hormone and prostaglandins, all of which then pass through the vagina's walls into the bloodstream. These hormones can make her both happier and more interested in sex. There have been studies done on the use of condoms showing a link between condom use and depression compared to women that have sex and don't use condoms. When the semen is blocked from her vagina, she misses out on the positive mood enhancing effects of the hormones in the semen. Plus the testosterone in the semen triggers her sex drive further.

Or like the old joke says, grumpy women really do just need to get laid. Plus there's an element of being able to fake it until you make it as well. If a lower sex drive woman has frequent sex, eventually her sex drive can increase from exposure to all the extra testosterone.

The husband's semen volume is an important marker to a wife that affects her attraction to him. This is so basic that even men watching porn movies seeing a tiny dribbling cumshot feel disappointed watching it. Big arcs of jetting semen are clearly superior to a little dribble. So imagine how a wife's Body Agenda reacts to that happening inside her vagina. Clearly a great pulsing flood creates a vastly better standing army of sperm than a little dribble, so it's sexier.

There's also a question of semen quality. A fitter and healthier male will have a better quality of semen. Again, his wife's Body Agenda is going to know this and it's going to affect her attraction to him. A couch potato swilling alcohol, smoking and eating terrible food will make absolutely terrible semen. When he has sex with his wife, he will send her a clear signal of his poor quality as a mate and poison her attraction to him.

Attraction is Not a Choice

While who we have sex with is a choice, who we are attracted to is not a choice. We are deeply and unconsciously influenced by our bodies to even simply be able to experience attraction, so our own Body Agenda is controlling who we get attracted to.

As an example – a man seeing a wonderful pair of naked breasts will have a completely uncontrollable positive interest in them. He may choose to gaze on them or look away, but he can't control his interest in them. There's no rational thought passing through his mind when he looks at cleavage thinking *"Oh wow, I'm looking at cleavage. I should probably like that and get aroused."* You simply see the cleavage and drool. The rational part of your brain says stuff like *"I'm going to get called in to Human Resources again if I don't stop drooling at her tits."*

A woman will have no control over the way her body tells her to react to a man either. There's even evidence that a woman can unconsciously assess a man for his genetic compatibility to her by sense of smell. Things like his body shape and semen volume and quality affect her unconsciously just the same. A wife may even very much desperately want to feel attraction for her husband, but if his body and semen simply revolts her Body Agenda, it's not that she *won't* feel attraction for him, it's that she *can't.*

Female Appearance is Important

A woman's physical appearance is extremely important in mate selection. It's absolutely not superficial for a man to focus on the physical health and body shape of a woman. In fact, of all the factors making up a woman's sexiness it is the one that is weighted the heaviest.

There is a huge body of evidence that suggests feminine physical beauty is a well agreed upon thing across cultures worldwide. It all comes down to quite measurable things like: waist to hip ratio, skin tone, health and length of hair, symmetry, good immune system, good teeth and so on. All these things are positive indicators of the woman's ability to have a good pregnancy, give birth to a healthy baby and then manage to stay alive to raise it to adulthood. As I've said before, whatever is sexy is whatever is good for making and raising babies.

So when a male looks at a female, his brain literally looks her over and sums up her baby making ability and then decides whether or not to inform the rest of his body that a healthy, sexy female is in proximity to him. Men have no control over sexual attraction, it's simply a response to stimuli.

Birth Control

As an aside, birth control is always problematic in that you are interfering with what a few million years of evolutionary fine tuning has planned as the way sex works. The best possible sex is two highly fertile people going at it without interference. Of course endless children appearing is regarded as highly problematic, so the majority of us turn to birth control in some fashion.

For a married couple you're looking for the version of birth control that causes the lowest number of negative effects. All birth control will have some sort of side effect or risk and there is no one size fits all solution. Generally I advise trying the easier options first before trying a surgical one. Bad surgical outcomes on your sexual organs can result in a very poor sex life and cripple your marriage. *For myself, a vasectomy would be the very last thing I would try.*

Because I am asked so frequently... Before we had kids Jennifer and I used a combination of the rhythm method and condoms during her fertile period. Since the kids we've had her on birth control pills and she's had very minimal side effects, so we've stuck with that. If

Jennifer had issues with the pill we would have likely started looking for a different option. Possibly we'd go back to condoms as I actually find them mildly erotic, though more likely something like a copper IUD as Jennifer doesn't like the condom "scrunching" inside her.

The Time Before Writing

Most importantly, the biological wiring for determining what is sexy is unchanged from 10,000 years ago. We are still evaluating potential sex partners now, through much the same eyes as our tribal ancestors on the ancient savannah did. But we're also highly social creatures as well and we're trying to court one another in the Information Age. In a sense we're all still cavemen, we're just dressed in jeans and have cell phones.

The next chapter delves into the disconnection between what women are biologically designed to respond to in a man, and what they need in a modern husband.

Chapter 2
Alpha and Beta Balance

The Time Before Writing

Back in the Time Before Writing, it was easy to understand what type of men a woman would be drawn sexually to. Women were attracted to bigger, stronger, faster and more powerful men. Women were especially attracted to men willing to fight and defend them from outsiders or natural predators. A man with a long pointed stick that was good at killing other men (or lions) is a vastly superior mate for a woman than a man who specialized in getting maimed in combat. The warrior caste has always had its appeal to women.

The traits that make a man a good warrior overlap strongly with traits that make him a good hunter. Good hunters return to the women with precious fat and protein-based food. Plus in times of acute shortages, a good warrior could simply dispossess a weaker man of his property and food. So a good warrior/hunter was also a good provider to a woman.

In a world devoid of effective medical treatment, the health of male partners is also a prime interest to women. There's no point getting pregnant by a sickly man and risking a sickly child that may die young, so the hunters and warriors with good physical conditioning would appear attractive to women.

In the rough and tumble world of The Time Before Writing the difference between the haves and the have-not's were not simply degrees of wealth, but the difference between survival in minimal comfort and a life of extreme poverty and famine. So a more socially prominent male partner was much better than a less prominent one. Women's attraction to men of high social status is called hypergamy and has been well documented by sociologists since around 1940. In short, given the choice between marriage to the lord of the manor or his butler, the lord of the manor gets the clear advantage.

Also, for the overwhelming majority of human history, men clearly dominated women socially. That domination came through the physical strength of men being clearly greater than that of women and while such use of force now is agreed on as being quite wrong, it did result in social domination back in The Time Before Writing. It's the social domination that women have a positive sexual response to in particular. A male that is socially dominant over men as well as women is especially attractive to women. Men on the other hand, don't respond to socially dominant women with feelings of attraction.

As an overly dramatic example of the rough world of The Time Before Writing, if two men square off against each other in a fight over a woman and one kills the other outright, there is clearly no point in a woman offering physical resistance to the winner. He did, after all, just kill someone significantly stronger than her, so her physical resistance would accomplish nothing and very likely place her own life in danger. Plus if her current male protector and provider were just killed, she needs a new one as quickly as possible and an objectively "better" male is immediately available and interested in her. On one level it's a coldly rational move on her part to submit to the victor and become sexually responsive to him. On another level, her own body likely doesn't even offer her a choice in the matter and produces a hormonal cocktail to offer minimal resistance and even bond to the victor.

Importantly, in both animals and humans, most male versus male conflicts do *not* reach the point of death for one of the fighters. What happens in the overwhelming majority of fights between males is that it continues until one of the males submits to the other. Whether that is by fleeing the fight, "tapping out" like an MMA fighter or just cowering, there is a display of social submission that ends the fight. For the most part men fighting each other these days are generally not very socially acceptable, but it is understood as something that does occasionally happen. However continued violence by the dominant male after the weaker one has offered submission is regarded as extremely unacceptable. It's one thing to knock a guy out, but it's quite another thing to beat an unconscious person further.

In The Time Before Writing, when a man approached a woman for a sexual relationship, he would come with enough physical and social dominance to ward off other men who wanted her. Her natural response is also to submit to a male approaching her with cool confidence; it's both for her safety and because her own body recognizes him as a dominant and therefore attractive sexual partner. She doesn't have to like him as a person to find her own body becoming aroused by a dominant man as it's an inbuilt response.

Incidentally, this is why when you lose a fight in the playground as a kid, all the girls start giving you a wide berth and pay more attention to the guy that whipped your ass. They really can't help it. So in quick summary, the things that women are hard-wired to find sexually attractive in men are physical health, physical power, social power and interpersonal dominance.

The Information Age

Of course in modern society, much of what makes a good male warrior makes for a terrible citizen, employee and husband. While physical health remains a good thing, hair trigger violence and coercion by intimidation quickly gets a man in trouble. Jails are full of men that would have been good choices for husbands in an ancient tribal culture. (In fact, the sexual attraction of women for jailed men is well known and famously violent offenders can get a good deal of female fan mail.) But a husband jailed for a third drunken fistfight is an appalling thing for a modern wife to have to deal with.

Interpersonal dominance by a man over a woman is now deeply frowned on, particularly in the workplace. Back in The Time Before Writing a man faced with a woman seeking dominance over him may simply have threatened or committed violence until she displayed submission. A male retail clerk simply cannot do the same to his female manager and get away with it. The consequences of such a thing would be extremely costly to him, so male employees typically perform the work requested of them by their bosses, male and female alike, without even considering violence.

Likewise, the skills that make someone a good warrior or hunter don't apply terribly well to most white collar occupations. It matches up pretty well to something like being a firefighter, but much less so to being a computer programmer, accountant, teacher, supermarket manager or pizza delivery guy. Warriors really suck at working in cubicles.

The entire social hierarchy has vastly changed and in many ways has rendered the old traits that attract women obsolete. Warriors go to jail. Warriors can't hold a job and be a good provider. Men that routinely seek physical aggression over women to gain compliance fall afoul of Human Resources and domestic violence laws. Men who fight other men have to find a way to do it without violence, otherwise even if they win, they lose.

What modern women *say* they want in a male partner is someone that can be a productive member of modern society and will support them in their own interests as well. So according to what women *say*, an ideal male partner would be someone that can hold down a job, pay attention to her, provide child care, help out around the house and provide emotional support and so on. These are all very different skill sets than our warrior has.

The point is that all these skills that women say they want really are valuable and do create comfort for the woman, but they don't generally create sexual attraction to the man that has them.

Alpha and Beta Male Traits

Now we come to the essential disconnect between what a woman is hard-wired to be sexually attracted to and what she needs to create comfort in a modern relationship. I call these two differing skill sets Alpha Traits and Beta Traits.

The Alpha Traits are those that worked in The Time Before Writing. The old physical and social dominance abilities based on the warrior and hunter skill sets. The Alpha Male Traits are devoted to physicality, assertiveness, leadership, social dominance, healthy genes, raw sexual energy, power and at times even violence. The positive version is that of an inspiring protector and the not so positive version is simply a thug. These are the male traits that women are biologically hard-wired to respond to that get panties wet and trigger sexual attraction. The thugs still get panties wet just as the high school quarterback does, but they are scary to be in a relationship with.

The Alpha Traits do seem to very much align with the dopamine response in women. Alpha Males are exciting, fun, intense and engaging. Not only do they spark a woman's sexual interest, they spark her romantic interest as well.

The Beta Male Traits are those needed for a modern relationship. These are often about the ability to be socially submissive and in a loose sense a "Nice Guy". The Beta Male Traits are devoted to things that are good for raising children in the modern age like having a work ethic, building the nest, kindness, parenting skills, listening, holding a job, controlling anger and sexual energy, being artistic, verbal skill and creativity. The positive version is the man that provides for and supports his family; the negative version is the man that gives away all relationship power to the woman and turns himself into her "pussy whipped" servant.

The Beta Male builds relationship comfort and this seems to very much align with the pair bonding hormones oxytocin in women and vasopressin in men. It's all about comfort building and interpersonal warmth. It is a critical point to understand that Beta activities will make a woman like you around, but not fall in love with you.

The Betaization of Husbands

The failure to understand the need to have both of the skill sets of Alpha and Beta Traits lies at the root of a wife's declining romantic and sexual interest in her husband. For example, when a young woman meets a young man, he likely has much of his "warrior" or Alpha mindset still in place and therefore creates a good deal of attraction in her. He isn't a thug, just somewhat mindlessly demanding and assertive with her. The first time he asked her out he didn't really ask her, he just told her to meet him at a local restaurant. She told him he was a pig for talking to her like that, but she went anyway. Plus he had good physical health, surfed competitively and she loved watching him. So when he asks her to marry him, she excitedly agrees because he has a wonderful Alpha profile and she is in love with him. Sex is frequent and hot.

But after five to ten years of marriage the situation might be quite different. There's a job that he now really needs to keep, so rather than just blow it all off and go surfing like he used to, he's grinding it out at the office. He's older and thirty pounds fatter. Then there are the kids who he loves of course, but they take up a lot of time and in general he defers to what his wife wants to happen with them. His wife certainly doesn't have time to just sit and idolize him from the beach either; she has a job of her own and the house to keep up. She's started complaining about him not doing everything correctly and he does try to please her, but it doesn't really seem to make any difference. There's always more complaining. The sex has dwindled to a trickle, mostly because his wife says she is always tired.

As you can see in that little snapshot, the husband started with a high Alpha profile, but as he started "doing everything that he should," he stopped doing the Alpha things entirely and substituted them with nothing but Beta activity. This switch from Alpha to Beta is called Betaization. As a result of being Betaized, his wife started losing attraction to him and the sex declined between them. She did however feel quite comfortable in the relationship, hence her assuming the role of being the dominant partner in the relationship and being willing to chew him out over household chores. Those that are socially equal typically don't yell at each other – that is usually something that only the socially dominant does to the socially submissive.

This unwitting transition from a mostly Alpha profile to a mostly Beta one is very common for husbands. The trap for men is that all mainstream media advice on relationships strongly encourages husbands to make this transition and often his wife and family request the same as well. Furthermore most things that are Beta are actually useful and good: helping out at home is good, being an involved father is good, holding a job is good. But frequently the big picture gets lost in everything that needs to get done and the man loses what attracts his wife along the way. The wife is of course usually completely unaware of her role in his decline and is typically bewildered by her lack of interest in her husband. She never planned to neuter him, fall out of love and detest his sexual advances. Most couples just assume that romantic feelings are short term and that failing sex lives a few years into marriage are normal.

Finding the Alpha Beta Balance

The man needs to develop both Alpha and Beta traits in a long term relationship and show them appropriately. Without the Alpha the woman loses attraction and wants out of the relationship, but without the Beta the woman isn't comfortable enough to stay in the relationship.

Most men typically do better with one or the other of these traits, and in times of pressure (like a break up) act more and more from their position of natural strength. Natural Alphas get bigger and louder and become scarier and even less reliable. Natural Betas do more stuff for the woman and bore her to death with their neediness even faster. So more often than not, men's natural reaction to relationship stress just intensifies the relationship problem.

So if you're too Beta the solution is to add Alpha. If you're too Alpha the solution is to add Beta.

Also the menstrual cycle affects what women are more attracted to throughout the month. For about three weeks of the month women respond more positively to Beta Male behavior. But when she is ovulating, Alpha Male behavior is more attractive. Importantly, while ovulation is only a small part of the month, this is when she is at her horniest and will make her most critical sexual decisions. Husbands who fail to display Alpha traits especially during ovulation run a higher risk for being abandoned, being cheated on, or raising children they think are theirs but aren't.

Personally, I fall along the lines of being more naturally Beta. For the majority of my life I've not been readily confused with being a macho man warrior type. My marriage has always been decent, but I've seen many improvements by learning to up the Alpha stuff as we've grown together.

There can be a misunderstanding that Alpha behavior involves some sort of purposeful aggression towards the wife like yelling, hitting, property destruction, issuing humiliating demands, public shaming, or demeaning her. Some of these things are Alpha in the sense that they are seeking to enforce social dominance over her, but they only act in the man's interest in the very short term. Violence towards a woman seriously undercuts the positive Beta traits and will ultimately destroy the relationship. While thugs do attract some women, I certainly do not advise that approach to relationships as most women give thugs a very wide berth.

Ultimately the best Alpha display is that you're just going to make your way in the world with confidence and succeed at whatever it is that you're going to do. Opinions of the rest of the world be damned, you're your own man. And like a huge truck on the interstate, you just create a huge hole in the air that makes following you easy. Alpha isn't about being a bastard who makes people obey him. Alpha is about making people want to follow you and pulling the attraction of women.

Beta isn't about being a weak man that struggles to please a woman. Beta is about purposely creating a place to raise a family and creating comfort in your presence.

There are some natural conflicts between Alpha and Beta traits, but also some overlap.

Bad Boys...

Clearly many women are attracted to Bad Boys, while Nice Guys frequently lament that women pay them no sexual attention. The Alpha and Beta Traits explain these issues very well.

A Bad Boy is someone with a very high Alpha profile, but minimal Beta Traits. These are the guys who can coast in relationships on the natural attraction women have for them. They typically have a very masculine appearance in dress, demeanor and body shape. But while Bad Boys certainly do pull the women, their relationships tend to be short as eventually the women become uncomfortable with the lack of comfort building support that the Beta Traits bring to the table. (For some Bad Boys the temporary nature of their relationships isn't a bug, it's a feature.)

With a Bad Boy, there's always plenty of excitement and sizzling sex for the woman as she is highly attracted to him. She probably knows from the beginning it's not going to last, but she is drawn to him anyway. It's one thing for a woman to have sex with a passing professional sports player, a gang leader or the leather-jacket-wearing Harley guy who hangs at the bar. It's quite another thing for her to consider raising a family with any of them.

When a Bad Boy is in a relationship and it starts to fail, typically he becomes even more extremely Alpha with the woman. These relationship breakups can be quite nasty for the woman as he gets louder and more aggressive with her, or simply just reveals a lack of empathy for her and removes her from his life as an annoyance. It's one thing to feel like a Bad Boy's "sexy bitch" when the relationship is good, it's quite another to be smacked around like a bitch and dumped like a used whore.

...and Nice Guys

A Nice Guy is someone who typically has a high Beta profile, but minimal Alpha Traits. A Nice Guy will pull women, but he pulls them differently. He "makes sense" on an intellectual level he is very comfortable to live with. This is the sort of guy that everyone tells a woman is "a real catch" if she marries him. He's also a great partner for a woman who has been damaged in some way by prior abuse or is licking her wounds after a divorce with kids in tow. He's going to provide a high level of comfort, which after a woman has been through a period of extreme discomfort she is going to find very appealing. Thus the Nice Guy can play the role of emotional ER for a woman freshly dumped by a Bad Boy.

This Beta Male comfort seeking in women fuels the female side of the mail order bride industry where women in poorer countries seek to jump ship to a richer one. The men who use these services typically do not present as Alphas, they are just lonely men willing to assist her in coming to a life of a better standard of living and comfort in exchange for her sexual companionship. Of course those involved in mail order bride seeking do experience it as a search for love, but the men clearly present a very strong Beta profile to these women as a way of attracting them.

However, Nice Guys are just too comfort creating and it all backfires on them. At some point a woman gets her fill of comfort and starts wishing for sexual attraction. Without a display of dominance, eventually she starts reducing her sex with him until it becomes nothing. Ultimately Nice Guys are just too sexually boring to the average woman for her to remain completely focused on one.

Important Concept – When a relationship starts to flounder, the Nice Guy typically tries even harder to be nice to the woman. He tries even harder to please her, submits to her more, buys her expensive gifts and caters to her more. Unfortunately this is all the exact opposite of what the woman is looking for and the relationship gets worse as she becomes even less attracted to him. Increasingly irritated with his attention she starts to consider ending the relationship, and queues up the "I love you, but I'm not in love with you" speech.

Growing Into Wholeness

Both men and women struggle with finding the right inner balance of Alpha and Beta in their relationships. The ideal for women is that the sole man they are involved with has both Alpha and Beta traits, but it can take many men a great deal of time to learn and balance both sets of traits. So if a woman cannot find both Alpha and Beta in a sole partner, she may elect to try and find her own balance of both traits from more than one man.

What is often seen in young women is a ping-ponging between Bad Boys and Nice Guys – she gets a dose of crazy sexual attraction from the Bad Boy, but then she needs the comfort building and she seeks it from a Nice Guy and leans on him for emotional support. Then the cycle repeats over and over until the music stops at around age thirty-five and she's scrambling to find a chair anywhere.

Sometimes women establish themselves in a relationship with a good Beta male, but meet their Alpha needs for sexual excitement through an additional male presence. That may be fairly benign if she gets her Alpha thrills through reading romance novels or obsessing over the Twilight books and movies. But it could also be through the excitement of taking an actual lover and having risky and intense sex with him.

Women can also attach to a heavily Alpha man and simply lack emotional comfort in the relationship. They can turn to a male friend and forge a deep emotional affair as a way of balancing out their need. Infidelity in women can easily start not from the need for sex, but from the need for intimacy. She may not even be sexually attracted to her male friend, but still have sex with him as a way of securing his continuing emotional connection to her.

For men it's largely the task of working on the weaker area of their personality to find the balance. An Alpha Male needs to "grow up" a little and tone down the antics slightly, become a little more socially conscious and more of a team player. Beta Males need to "grow a pair" and start bumping back on the rest of the world rather than just taking it lying down. Either way works as a route and it's a process to get there. You already know what your weak area is, so work on that for easy gains.

This chapter has covered Alpha and Beta as general concepts. The next two chapters will expound a little more on examples of what are the good versions of the Alpha and Beta Traits.

Chapter 4
The Alpha Male Traits

Alpha = Attraction = Dopamine

The Alpha Traits are the things about a man that typically create attraction in women. Female attraction is the involuntary response to Alpha Male Traits that is built into the Body Agenda of women. Alpha Traits spark a dopamine hormonal response in women and it's the dopamine that makes them experience the feeling and impulse of attraction. *Attraction is not controllable.*

Physical Body, Semen and Genes

The first aspect of the Alpha Traits is the physical body of the male. Women are drawn to well muscled and lean male figures. It is quite possible to bulk up too far and find that women become repulsed by excessive muscle. The closer to looking like Michelangelo's "David" he is, the better his attraction building is.

The point is that women look for a good source of semen, and therefore genes, for a potential pregnancy. Having a firm, fit and attractive body is a walking advertisement for those genes. Fit men ejaculate both more semen and better quality semen.

I have generally covered the importance of physical health in the Body Agenda chapter so let's not repeat that and simply close with this - *it's almost impossible to underestimate the importance of good physical health and fitness in attracting women.*

Peacocking and Preselection

Adding onto the physical health of a man is his appearance of being socially desirable and appealing. Male peacocks have enormously long beautiful tails, and when interested in a female peacock they fan them out behind them and shake them to attract her attention. The larger and more beautiful the tail, the more likely she is to mate with him. Thus the pickup artist strategy of "Peacocking" gets its name.

Peacocking refers to wearing clothing that act as a Display of High Value (DHV). Peacocking can be wearing clothes that are expensive and tailored to give a greater impression of wealth, or by wearing clothes that make a statement about a high profile occupation, like a business suit or doctor's lab coat. Though obviously wearing a lab coat to a bar is horribly out of place.

Peacocking can also be the purposeful breaking of dress codes in such a way that it implies that the male is greater than the need to conform to the social arena. The boss of the company for example, might be completely comfortable popping into the office in jeans and T-shirt, while a junior manager would feel vastly under-dressed doing the same thing. It can also just be wearing something that is flamboyant and interesting that pulls female attention. Clothing always sends a message, positive or negative, about the man and women respond to that.

Preselection is another strong tie to how attractive a man looks. A man with no women paying him attention appears less attractive than a man with multiple women showing him attention. It could very well be the same man, but the effect of the difference in women paying him attention is the difference in his *perceived* attractiveness.

Preselection explains the effect that many men notice of going from absolute droughts of female attention to floods of attention, with no real major changes in their skill with women. Simply put, once you pull the interest of one or two women, the rest tend to follow suit quickly. Newly married men that struggled to find women to date them and were tickled pink to find someone that wanted to marry them will frequently find that they have a greater ability to pull female attention now that they are married. Simply having a wife makes their "peacock's tail" bigger and prettier so to speak.

It's important to realize that women see and respond to attractive male appearance via Peacocking and Preselection the same way men typically respond to a woman dressing highly provocatively or taking her clothes off.

Male Interests

Women are also attracted to men that have stereotypical male interests. Things like watching sports, doing dangerous things with cars and watching things being blown up float towards the top of the list of stereotypical male interests. Note that the women themselves may not be interested in these things, but they are attracted to men who are interested in them.

Women may even complain about their husbands watching football for example, but they don't find them sexually repulsive for doing so. The complaint isn't that he watches sports, but that he watches too much of it and doesn't do the other things that she wants him to do. Should a husband grow seriously interested in watching a show about flower arrangement and knitting, his wife may not complain about him watching it, but she would find herself less sexually interested in him.

Even more attractive than a man who enjoys stereotypical male interests as a spectator is one that actually participates in them. It's one thing to like listening to hard rock; it's another to be in a band. It's one thing to like watching motorsports; it's sexier to drive in a race. It's one thing to watch football on TV, it's another to run into the end zone and make a touchdown.

Male interests are important because they reflect that a man is actually a biologically wired male who comes across as masculine. There may be nothing wrong with a man doing feminine things if he wants to, but in a relationship the woman typically wants to feel more feminine than the man and she looks to him to be masculine.

Most wives don't want their husbands visiting strip clubs. But most wives would probably experience him visiting a strip club with much less concern than if he came home with a gift for her of *"this great eyeliner that I found on sale at the mall."* That would tend to signal potential gayness or cross dressing rather than heterosexuality. A husband who turns into her best girlfriend loses her sexual attraction as a consequence.

Alpha Male of the Group

Because the difference between having a socially dominant male as a mate in The Time Before Writing was often the difference between surviving and not surviving, women are strongly attracted to socially dominant men. That difference in social dominance can be as simple as the difference between being a retail clerk and a retail manager, or the manager and the regional director, or further up the food chain to the company CEO. The more social power and authority a male has, the more attractive to women he becomes. A man can even be quite ugly but with enough power still be able to pull female attention.

Within each social group there is always a social leader referred to as the Alpha Male of the Group (AMOG). A group's ultimate leader does not have to be male, but far more often than not a male is a group's ultimate social leader. Within a family unit either the husband or wife is the leader of the family unit. If the leader is the husband he creates attraction for him in the wife, but if she is the leader she loses some attraction for him.

Very often people like to say *"It's an equal relationship,"* but it's usually a bunch of baloney when push comes to shove - someone is usually the stronger of the two personalities and in reality runs the show. If it's the wife saying *"It's an equal relationship,"* it usually means she is in fact the one in charge but doesn't want to frame herself in conversation as actually being in charge, because that would essentially force her to not respect him as a man. The husband being the less dominant one in the relationship is then required to agree with her about the equality, or suffer the consequences of his insubordination.

It's not terribly politically correct to frame a male-led household as better than a female-led one and there are obvious concerns about how this can be abused by the husband. However these are essentially no different than the same concerns of a relationship where a female is dominant over the male. I'm sure the reader knows of several men living in a state of constant fear for displeasing their wives and the resultant tongue lashing that would follow. Not to mention how studies show that women are no less prone to resort to violence than men are in relationships. Leadership and husbandly dominance ideally works on the principle of evoking the desire to follow. If a wife submits, it's through her own consent and right to do so. For the majority of wives, a husband acting with leadership creates and sustains her sexual attraction to him, which is of ultimate benefit to both of them in the relationship.

Likewise, the ability to exercise reasonable discipline and direction over the children in the family frames a husband as the social leader and makes him more attractive to his wife. A husband's failure to be effective with the children will reduce the wife's attraction to him.

Cool and Confident

One of the key signals that a male has social dominance is his confidence, thus women are highly attracted to displays of confidence in men. A basic confidence display is the willingness to approach women, especially highly attractive women, and display calmness in their presence. That calmness can be successfully extended to expressions of mild disinterest in the woman, implying that he has become used to being with even more beautiful women than she – which would imply that he had a very high value as a man, which then triggers her interest in him.

A typical fan meeting a celebrity in person usually becomes highly excited and can become quite giddy and silly, while the celebrity is usually much less excited and "cool." That coolness is a statement of higher social value as it says *"I'm not excited to be meeting you."* Cool men have always created attraction in women. The underlying message is that *"I am not going to react to you."*

The other side to social confidence and dominance is when the confident male creates situations where the female is forced to react to him. In other words, *"I am not going to react to you, but you will react to me."* The simplest way of achieving that is by leading a conversation that delights the female and draws her attention to him. The cornerstone of leading these conversations is a combination of being "cocky and funny" where the male playfully abuses his position of social dominance and gets away with being a "naughty boy". This can be anything including mildly teasing her, telling outrageously funny or interesting stories and becoming the center of attention, leading her in short games of fun (like looking at the couple two tables over and making up funny fake background stories about them) or simply talking about something passionately enough to draw her into his frame of reference.

Highly confident men will also take more risks than a less confident man will. Low confidence appears no different in the eyes of women than cowardice and men who shrink back from action lose attraction. Highly confident men do things and appear brave and attractive to women. Highly confident men aren't boring to women, as they will at least manage to do something of interest. The link between boredom and low dopamine issues in women has already been covered, but it does not hurt to review that men who "do nothing" are very boring to women and they quickly tire of them. Wives bored of their husbands may very well stay married to them, but their vaginas go offline.

Sometimes those things that highly confident men do are quite dangerous, and women usually experience a great deal of discomfort about men doing these activities. Whether that is going into a combat zone, hang-gliding or motorsports isn't usually important, but what is important is the rollercoaster of emotion it sets her on when he does it. It's extremely non-boring for a wife to worry that her husband could be potentially seriously injured or killed and the accompanying relief afterwards totally feeds whatever sense of emotional stimulation she needs to experience. She may feel discomfort at the activity he does, but she gains attraction to him for his doing it.

There is obviously a scale of risk here as well. It's one thing for a woman to experience a sense of nervousness as her husband races a 100cc Go-Kart and feel impressed watching him. It's quite another thing to know that he's being dropped behind enemy lines at night and will be out of communication for a week... or forever.

A One Track Mind

The final Alpha Male Trait is pretty primal. Alpha Males want and expect to have sex frequently and with women who are happy to comply with their sexual demands. It's possible to misunderstand that being Alpha is about forcing women to do something they don't want to do, but the entire point of being Alpha is that women find Alpha men attractive and actively want to be seduced by them. A physically fit, well dressed, confident, powerful man knows that women find him attractive, so he naturally expects their pleased compliance with his advances.

Physically touching women in both sexual and non sexual ways is a display of confidence and dominance. Typically social touch is initiated by the socially dominant person rather than the less dominant one. Your boss at work is far more likely to pat you on the back, than you are to do the same to them for example. With large gap in social standing it becomes even more extreme. If the President wants to give you a bear hug it's fine, but if you try it on him there would be half a dozen very twitchy Secret Service agents intervening. Simply touching a woman before she touches you is making a statement of social dominance.

Touch will usually be non sexual – a tap on the arm, a handshake and a pat on the back being some of the most common ones. But an Alpha is interested in escalating the physical interactions towards sexual touch fairly quickly. With each step towards sexual intimacy, it's Alpha to be willing to push for more as far as she lets you. Alphas understand that not every interaction will lead to actual sex, but remain obviously capable to close the deal if she is interested in doing so.

A woman may not always be interested in sex, but if she is interested in having sex, she wants a man that will clearly be able to follow through and give her the sex she wants. A man that declines sex when a woman asks for it creates a very negative response in her towards him; typically she will find him much less attractive as a result. That marked reduction in attraction can lead to her treating him quite differently in the future. If it was to be their first sexual experience together, she will usually write him off as a total loser permanently.

It's also Alpha to not care about getting sex from any one particular woman. Alphas are generally attractive to women, so any one woman that gives any difficulty granting sexual favors can simply be replaced with another who is willing. This can create a sense of stress in a wife, as a husband with high Alpha qualities, clearly has a much better chance of finding affair opportunities than a husband without them. Jealousy can be an emotional rollercoaster and lead to a more intense connection and sexual intensity as well. She also may just find him highly attractive and lay him like tile regardless of his potential for other women.

It is somewhat of a dark tactic, but this dynamic of multiple women finding Alpha males attractive is a very tangible thing for gaining leverage over a particular woman. So as this book progresses we will return to this approach as a key element of change. However dark or immoral it may seem on the surface, pulling the interest of multiple women isn't anything other than the natural consequence of being a good quality man. In the current sexual marketplace, not being a good quality man leads a husband to endless sexual denial and/or eventual divorce. A man has no option but to better himself constantly... or risk being cast out.

Chapter 5
The Beta Male Traits

Beta = Comfort = Oxytocin

The Beta Male Traits are all about creating relationship comfort and typically stem from the needs of raising children in a modern society. Back in The Time Before Writing women still needed comfort building, but that comfort was supplied simply by having a dominant male they could attach to. The reason women are wired to be attracted to Alpha males, is that for 99.9% of human history an Alpha male supplied the comfort a woman needed.

However, modern living creates comfort quite differently and modern child-raising comes with an array of needs that are vastly different to that in The Time Before Writing. The skills and abilities in men that meet those needs are the Beta Traits. Typically Beta Traits are aligned with creating a pair-bond by her body having a hormonal oxytocin response to her partner.

It's a cruel trick of biology to both sexes that women are wired for attraction to ancient Alpha unconsciously seeking modern Beta, but that they can actually have a Beta partner and not really want him because of his lack of Alpha. The solution remains as always, that a husband has to balance both Alpha and Beta to sustain a marriage.

Dependable Provider with Money

Having a reliable source of income is a foundational Beta skill. The more money you can bring in, the better. Quite often having a high income matches up with some sort of socially prominent job and can be Alpha. For example, a doctor is a prestigious vocation and Alpha, but the income a doctor makes is Beta. In simple terms, the more money you make the greater comfort an attached woman and her children can live in.

A man's current income may be low, but the potential for greater income in the future is also part of the Beta appeal. In short, given a choice between two identical males, a woman will choose the one with the better income.

In recent decades the earning power of women has increased greatly, so the need to have a man supply wealth is less important than in the past, but it is still an important factor. Men unable or unwilling to provide are often abandoned by their partners.

One of the more obvious things that make men sexy is having a coherent career. Whatever it is in particular isn't all that vital, as long as the man can show some kind of general story arc of making more money and generally gaining more power in his work environment.

Money isn't everything, but below a certain level of income, it sure feels like it's everything. When all is said and done, more money is generally better than less money. The guy with a $100,000 income is going to go home with the pretty girl, and the guy making $25,000 gets to go home with her designated ugly fat friend a.k.a. "The DUFF".

This is an incredibly harsh way of looking at the world, but it plays out this way time and time again. Once upon a time, having an income was all a guy needed to have in order to land a wife and she was completely dependent on him for that income. Times have changed and generally women earn similar incomes to men, but having a decent income still rates as an important signal of social worth.

We all don't get to be CEOs or astronauts, but as long as you aren't failing by ending up working retail, serving coffee or flipping burgers when you're age 30+, you're generally doing okay. To be sure, some professions have a generally higher status than others, but what you do may not be as important as how you do it. You may be better off being an amazing teacher as opposed to a really awful lawyer for example.

Undamaged Career Potential

This may be mildly off topic for older men, but on the off chance that younger unmarried men read this book, this section is critical. One of the ways you can seriously damage your overall earning power and career arc is by being stupid in your education. You pretty much can't hurt yourself by your high school choices other than getting crappy grades, but once you're at the college level you can cripple yourself for years to come by bad choices.

Before you go to college, know that you are being sold a ticket to an outcome. The college doesn't care about the outcome; they only care about the sale of the ticket. So if the college can convince 500 people to enroll and graduate from Tulip Arranging, earning $60,000 per student, but only two jobs for Professional Tulip Arrangement exist, leaving 498 people with a completely useless degree... well that's not really the college's problem. The college's problem would be finding an artist to build a statue of a giant tulip with the extra $30,000,000 revenue and making damn sure that the brochures for the next class will be extra glossy.

Then the poor saps that graduated from Tulip Arranging have $45,000 worth of loans and only Starbucks is hiring. They can't afford to return to college ever again and remain trapped into serving coffee until they die. Trying to meet women when you're in debt and working a service counter anywhere just sucks.

The problem is that a large number of college degrees and majors don't seem to be for anything other than filling out the coffers of the college. See, if you go through med school, nursing school, or law school, all of those schools are a direct line to having an actual job at the end of it. If you go through med school, it's pretty damn obvious that you'll work your ass off as a doctor at the end of school. That's the whole point. But if you have a degree in English, or History, or Psychology or basically any of the liberal arts majors, there is no direct line to a job. You can complete your entire degree and still not know what you want to do at the end of it.

Then you head out into the world and work for a bit and discover what you like, and you may or may not have to head back to school to do that. All in all this turns into the most appalling waste of time and money right in your most fertile and attractive spouse seeking years.

Given the choice between a twenty-five to twenty-six year old male that has a smart education and has been working in his chosen field for a few years with a minor promotion, or a twenty-five to twenty-six year old male that has a useless degree and is serving coffee, it's a no brainer what a savvy female is going to be more interested in. And by savvy I mean perky tits.

And let's not discount not even going to college. Plumbers, electricians, and carpenters can all make good money without even going though "higher" education. You just need to have a plan and play it out. Sometimes the "smart people" can make appalling decisions while the supposedly less smart people just have more common sense and finish strong. That's $400 to stop the leaky pipe on a Sunday for an hour's work. Think about that.

If you want to learn about Tulip Arranging, do it on your own time as a hobby. Don't waste tens of thousands of dollars and years of your life educating yourself for a job that may or may not be there and pays crappy money anyway.

Nest Management

One of the most important things for raising children is the creation of a home. Wealth ties in directly to buying a bigger, better home, but there are also a great number of tasks involved in managing a house and keeping it well maintained.

One aspect of home maintenance is the exterior of the house: keeping the lawn mowed, the gutters clean, and the house painted and looking generally appealing from the road.

The second aspect of home maintenance is the internal upkeep of making sure things aren't broken and that everything inside the house works. Dripping taps, doors that don't close properly, drafts, broken windows, and a fridge that has no inside light are all things that can be fixed and made functional again.

The third aspect of home maintenance is the general cleanliness of the inside of the home: carpets cleaned, floors mopped, trash removed, piles of magazines and newspapers dispensed with, laundry done and so on.

Beyond heavy lifting needs, there's really no reason why either husband or wife would be any better at any one of these tasks, but for the most part husbands tend towards the exterior aspects of home maintenance and wives the interior. Essentially, working productively at any of these aspects is Beta because it creates a comfortable and functional home. How the division of labor works between the husband and wife isn't terribly important; what is important is that the end result is a pleasant home that is a good place to raise children.

The more a husband does to maintain the home, the greater level of comfort he builds in his wife.

Cooking

There is a very common perception that cooking is a female skill. It is true that women do the majority of the cooking in most relationships; it's not a feminine skill but rather a life skill. Men are usually quite happy to man the BBQ grill and cook outside for example. Plenty of well known chefs are male and don't present as "weak men" but are aggressive competitors in their own arena. Sharp knives and high temperatures don't equal "feminine". I do of course lean towards "Iron Chef" rather than cake decorating as an approach though.

By knowing how to cook, a husband lifts some of the burden of cooking off of the wife and affords her greater relaxation and comfort. Most wives assume the duty of cooking and planning meals and simply dread the endless *"What's for dinner?"* questions and expectations of being fed. When a husband becomes simply another mouth to feed, he starts being viewed as a dependant by the wife. If he's viewed as a dependant, it can trigger a sense of being his mother in her mind and that can switch off her attraction as well. By cooking with some degree of frequency, the husband creates a mindset of teamwork and mutuality in the relationship.

The act of cooking and supplying a family with a meal feeds into a very primal set of programming. Think of a hunter returning to a tribal village with a fresh gazelle kill - he's bringing the women food. Roasting a chicken from a supermarket may be a less dramatic event, but it's still bringing a woman food.

Going out to dinner for a date is essentially the modern version of bringing a tribal woman some fresh meat. Many women see a man buying them dinner as directly influencing them towards giving sexual favors. This is why women on first dates can mentally scan a menu for something that doesn't say "vaginal intercourse", but instead says "handjob"... like a chicken caesar salad. Likely cave-girls suffered through the same torment as their modern counterparts and mentally wondered to themselves, *"Which part of a gazelle equals a handjob?"*

Likewise, most women express jealousy directly to another wife if her husband cooks well. It's of course extremely inappropriate for a female friend of your wife to say to her *"I'd really like to have sex with your husband,"* but it's usually perfectly fine to say to her *"I'm so jealous of your husband cooking. I wish my husband cooked."* This of course is often done in the presence of her husband as well and amounts to an enormous Preselection effect as she openly announces her interest in the chef husband and snubs her own.

Cooking can also feed back into Alpha-ness by the husband setting the tempo and directing the meal. There's plenty of opportunity to be in charge and direct assistance from the rest of the family. It's all as simple and telling a child to set the table, the second child to prep some vegetables and telling everyone that dinner is ready and they need to come to the table now. Larger more complex meals can require copious planning and direction. Your wife doesn't have to squeak "Yes chef!" at every turn or course, but she likely will respond very well to your leading the team in making an unusually important meal.

Cooking is a foundational Beta skill that creates loads of comfort in women. Women tend to automatically assume that any man that can cook is capable of being a fully functioning adult and isn't going to trash a house on a daily basis.

Fidelity, Integrity and Trust

The more likely you are to leave a relationship the less comfortable your wife is. Whether that leaving is threatened by your death from a dangerous profession, being jailed for illegal activities, abandoning her for another woman, or simply just going crazy and vanishing on her, it doesn't really matter. What you are doing is threatening the removal of the supply of her comfort.

A husband's interactions with other women can be very concerning for a wife. There is the risk of him leaving her for a new woman and ending her supply of comfort completely. She would be forced to seek child support as a means of enforcing a supply of any Beta comfort to continue. Even with court ordered child support she would be living at a marked reduction in the support that he would have been giving her, so being more obviously trustworthy and faithful to her is an enormous comfort builder in a relationship.

There is also the risk for a wife that if her husband gains a woman on the side, then her husband's resources would begin being split between her and the other woman. That would mean less time for the husband to spend fathering her children and maintaining their house together. If he fathers a child with the other woman, even if the relationship fails with the mistress, the husband could be forced to pay child support for the next eighteen years for zero benefit and serious cost to the wife.

There is always a risk for disease in extramarital affairs and the other woman may turn crazy and seek to harm the wife at some point as well. The threat of a husband engaging with another woman emotionally and forming a deep relationship is extremely serious to a wife, so much so that many wives experience less concern about a husband having actual physical sex with a prostitute than creating an intimate but as yet non-sexual relationship with a true rival for his affections.

This Beta trait of fidelity is in tension with the Alpha trait of always being ready for sex. Passing up sex with another woman is a failure on the Alpha front, but illicit sex outside the marriage risks being caught and a very negative reaction from his wife to defend her supply of comfort. Many wives can appreciate that a husband has sexual interest in women in general and respond to that with positive attraction to him. However, turning that interest into reality and cheating on her can utterly destroy her comfort level in the relationship. Gaining a point of Alpha for a loss of three or four points of Beta is a serious net loss.

Creating a pattern of fidelity will increase a woman's comfort in the relationship. Once trust is broken it is often like Humpty Dumpty and very difficult to put back together again. A single act of cheating can effectively end a marriage.

Showing Appreciation

Appreciation for the wife and her contributions to the marriage and family is an important comfort building skill. Many women feel utterly taken for granted in their relationship and feel like they labor endlessly for no recognition. Ultimately, these statements or gifts of appreciation are statements that the wife has a high value to the husband.

This can appear to be in dramatic tension with the Alpha approach that the male is the attractive one that has high value and that the female needs to respond to that. That would be a misunderstanding; what this does ideally is show appreciation for her positive response to him. If a man is an attractive husband and the wife responds positively to him because of that, it is good sense to provide positive feedback for her positive response. In a more extreme example, if he's being a crappy husband and she is being a good wife, if he has an ounce of good sense he will put her on a pedestal and start composing poetry to her.

It is foolish however to shower appreciation and gifts on a wife that is in fact not acting appropriately towards you, as this simply rewards her bad behavior. If you have a two year old having a temper tantrum over getting candy and you give them candy to shut them up, you're going to get more tantrums to get more candy. Likewise, if your wife frequently declines sex and you pander to her constantly trying to get sex, then you're establishing that her giving you no sex results in you rewarding her. You are in effect training her to continue to deny you sex in the future.

The Beta trait of appreciation creates a positive feedback loop in your wife that her positive actions will net her a positive response from you. If a woman likes to please you, she won't feel happy unless you tell her you are pleased by what she did.

Failing to recognize her good efforts to please you in effect punishes her for trying. If you had a dog that was trained to fetch the newspaper and every time it went and got it, you smacked it on the nose with the newspaper, it would eventually decide to stop fetching the paper for you. If you punish good behavior, the good behavior will eventually stop. Ignoring good behavior is the same as punishing it, as very frequently good behavior is done for the purposes of gaining positive attention.

In summary, a remarkably simple and effective Beta trait is just saying *"Thank you," "I liked that," "You did that really well,"* or *"The house looks great."*

Affectionate Caring

Being physically affectionate, gentle, kind, patient and attentive to a wife creates a great deal of comfort in her. The simplest explanation for this is that all these traits are pleasant to her, but they are also ideal for caring for an infant as well. Thugs are not good with babies, but Nice Guys are. Showing the ability to be nice creates relationship comfort for the wife.

Men tend to feel emotionally connected by doing something together. Two men can have minimal conversation but still feel very connected to each other as long as they are working on a shared task together. Women seek to create community and feel emotionally connected by talking. It's not an uncommon situation to have a husband "ignore" his wife because he can't experience the same sense of needing to talk each day. Most women faced with this need to talk and his apparent lack of listening will intensify their volume and verbal insistence that he communicates better. Men just experience this as nagging and therefore as toxic.

By creating a pattern of listening to her, a husband can supply the depth of verbal intimacy that the wife is seeking. It makes her feel comfortable and engaged with him. If she does not feel that emotional engagement from him, that makes her feel vulnerable because she feels that she is more committed to the relationship than he is. Many wives stumble into affairs because another male figure does nothing more than start listening and talking with them frequently. The emotional connection comes first and once emotional intimacy is established, she feels driven to experience that as sexual intimacy as well. Wives that would have no difficulty turning down highly sexually attractive strangers, can yield to someone they feel emotionally intimate with despite a lack of apparent hotness in the lover.

Physical touch is also important. This is not touch designed to automatically lead to sex, but simply a physical expression of the intimate relationship. Words are not always a requirement to expressing love. Touching women creates a response in them that releases oxytocin into their bodies. Oxytocin creates a sense of emotional warmth, closeness and trust. Stroking, kissing, hand-holding, and backrubs all work well.

This physical connection is also good for babies and children. There is the well known effect of "failure to thrive" in babies that are supplied with adequate food and shelter, but are left untouched. Without physical touch, the babies suffer slower growth, greater illness and can even die.

The ability to interact well with children is also a critical skill for husbands to develop. That includes discipline, education, direct care and playfulness. The discipline tends to feed into the Alpha trait of social dominance and has been covered earlier. Education and mentoring is an important trait, since the husband that can help with homework or spends the time showing his children how to do something, is more useful to a wife than one that doesn't. Children who learn skills go on to have better chances at reproductive success as adults.

Being able to provide direct child care assistance is also a positive Beta trait. Most wives feel forever "on duty" and being able to rest while a husband cares for the children is a positive thing. Being able to demonstrate skill with children in the presence of multiple women nearly always results in a positive verbal response from them, creating a Preselection effect as well.

Where most men clearly excel over women in dealing with children is in their ability to play with them. To be sure mothers are usually better with infants playing peek-a-boo, but once into the toddler age, fathers that play with children have the clear edge. Most especially with boys, roughhousing is considered enormously fun by children and is almost solely done by fathers. One rarely sees a mother kneeling in a sandbox building something, but a father will get in there and start scooping and building like one of the children. Women tend to observe a child's play and intervene if something is unsafe, while men tend to actually get in there and physically play as well. Plus dads frequently push the limits of "what mom would allow" in terms of roughness and safety, which is of course what really excites the kids.

In any case, the sound of her children shrieking with laughter very much positively influences her feelings for the man creating the laughter. Should more children arrive, he would no doubt be a good father for them as well, so her sex drive doesn't switch off.

Sexual Technique

When a woman orgasms, her endocrine system releases a flood of oxytocin which hormonally primes her for social bonding and trust in the man that made her orgasm. A wife that is frequently orgasmic with her husband becomes more bonded to him, trusts him more and feels a real sensation of emotional warmth and comfort in him. Though it may be surprising to those wishing to rely on a solely Alpha Male approach to women, having an excellent sexual technique is in fact a Beta Male Trait.

The lack of sex and orgasms a woman has in a relationship with a Beta Male Orbiter who is "just a friend" is in large part why she can use him as an emotional tampon and then discard him at will. The Orbiter never gets to have sex with her, so she never orgasms with him, so she never gets the flood of oxytocin with him, so she never attaches to the Orbiter. Just as soon as her emotions have stabilized and a man she is actually interested in wants a relationship with her, the Orbiter will be shunted back into the background of her life.

This Beta trait is in contrast to the Alpha trait of a male always being sexually impulsive and pleased to bang any available female. The Alpha Trait really cares nothing for a woman's sexual response other than her compliance and willingness to submit to him. It's all about him getting his penis into her vagina and ejaculating into it. This somewhat coarse sexual approach relies on the element of social dominance creating the dopamine response in her rather than sexual skill creating it.

It's easy to see how a woman could very much be excited by her man just overwhelming her with his passion and taking his pleasure from her, at least as an individual act of sex. That's the sort of thing that is in every other Hollywood movie and in romance novels all the time. However, if that is the plan for every sexual interaction, sooner rather than later her lack of orgasm is going to become an issue.

The Beta Trait however, does care about her pleasure sexually. Giving a male an orgasm is fairly straightforward, just get hold of the penis and jiggle it about a bit. In comparison to the male orgasm, the female one is fairly difficult to achieve. Thoughts of the G-Spot and A-Spot aside, most women orgasm via clitoral stimulation and the clitoris is fairly small and not really close enough to the opening to the vagina in nearly all women. Plus the clitoris starts trying to hide during sex as well, it's like "Where's Waldo" but with wetness and awkward despair.

Research shows that women are more orgasmic with attractive men, but being willing and competent to bring a woman to orgasm is a test of reproductive fitness of sorts in and of itself. The man that has the patience and tactile finesse to make her orgasm very probably has the right sort of temperament to also be good with raising children.

Unfortunately, there is a sort of chicken or egg issue here. In a low sex marriage, a wife may be disinterested in her husband and acting less bonded to him, so the solution is to make her orgasm more frequently. But she may well decline sex because of her low interest in him. The solution is to spark attraction via Alpha traits and being sure to make her orgasm, repeatedly if possible, when sex does take place. Many people experience a post-orgasmic glow that can last for a few days after sex. It's the oxytocin in women and vasopressin in men creating that effect. Technically, these really are drugs.

Of extreme concern though is a wife taking a lover. Once she experiences repeated orgasms with her lover, she can quickly bond to him and form a serious emotional attachment to him. Even a single instance of sex can create a powerful connection. Many people (male and female) experience an emotional connection to people they've had a sexual relationship with, even only as a one night stand, decades after the original event.

The goal here of course is in developing both the Alpha and Beta Traits in you so that your wife never considers risking losing your relationship. There will always be better men than you somewhere in the sexual marketplace, but if you're maximizing your good points and minimizing your not so good points, you may very well be the best man she can attach to and love. In the next chapter we discuss exactly how that sexual marketplace works.

Chapter 5
Sex Rank

Pick a Number From 1-10...

Sex Rank is a somewhat harsh way of looking at the world, but ultimately it is an honest one. Based on how sexy they are, everyone can be loosely assessed as having a number from 1 to 10 and that number is called their Sex Rank. Just admit it, we've all done it, looked at a woman and had a number pop into our head. She's a 7, a 9, a 4... whatever. When a man rates a woman, he's focusing a good deal on physical beauty as a primary factor in her sexual attractiveness.

Women of course do exactly the same thing to men, but when they do it, while physical beauty is a factor, it is much less of a factor to women than men. Women find wealth, social status and more (the whole range of Alpha and Beta Male traits) appealing and sexy. So women can also mentally rank men on a 1to 10 scale of sexiness as well.

Sex Rank is best viewed as a metaphor; it's hard to nail down exactly what is a male 6 vs. a male 7 for example. We could possibly come up with a chart and point system for everything to map out what exactly makes up every level of Sex Rank, but then we'd all just get into a big fight about the chart, disagreeing over the fine points. Some people find different things sexier than others. What makes someone a 6 or a 7 is essentially instinctive knowledge built into your own Body Agenda.

Both men and women rank each other continually and for the most part without conscious thought. In this way men are engaged in a constant battle for their place in the pecking order with each other. There's only so much room to be a 10, only so much space to be a 9... and so on down the ladder. Also women are in constant competition with other women to be the most appealing. Women may wear makeup to be attractive to men, but primarily to be more attractive to men than other women are. It's about staking a claim higher up the Sex Rank ladder.

In a monogamous society, people of equal Sex Rank will tend to pair off with each other. 10s will couple with 10s, 9s with 9s, and 8s with 8s... all the way to 1s with 1s. Basically an 8 won't settle for a 7, and a 7 won't settle for a 6, so a male 7 and a female 7 will just meet each other and feel a surge of mutual interest and pair off.

Finding a female's Sex Rank is fairly easy. You just hold up her photo and ask a bunch of guys how hot she looks. While women clearly have more value than just beauty, female Sex Rank is very heavily weighted towards physical beauty. The interest men have in the physical attractiveness of women is often chided as being "shallow", but in reality this interest is of critical importance. The male Body Agenda is constantly looking for a healthy woman with good genes and the ability to successfully bear and nurture their child.

Women have to take more factors into consideration when assigning Sex Rank to a man, as men are more complex to rate with wealth, power, appearance, social status, physicality, aggression and language skills all being factors toward their final Sex Rank. Yet I'm sure as soon as you meet someone you can probably mentally peg them as a number, or at least "less hot than me", "as hot as me", "hotter than me", which is ultimately the point.

Divergent Sex Ranks Lead To Relationship Failure

For both genders, the sexual competition to be at the top of the pecking order never stops. A woman who was an 8 at age twenty-three when she married, but then packs on the pounds, smokes, drinks and generally ages very badly may turn into a worn out 3 by age forty. A women who was a 4 at age twenty-three may lose some weight, get her teeth fixed, dress better, exercise consistently and advance a career, and turn into a solid 5 by age forty. It's all about your sexiness relative to the average sexiness of your gender regardless of your age. In terms of raw sex appeal, it takes a beautiful forty-year-old woman to match a quite plain twenty-year-old woman.

If the Sex Rank within a couple starts to diverge, then stress is placed on the couple. Consider what would happen if two 6s marry and the woman becomes health focused and dresses to impress consistently, and blossoms into a 7. At the same time her husband starts as a 6 and then struggles to work and turns into a couch potato, hits 350 pounds and falls to a 2. What was a balanced male 6 to female 6 relationship is now a badly imbalanced male 2 to female 7 relationship. No one is going to be surprised when the woman falls for another man that is a 7 and leaves her husband without much fanfare.

As a critical point - the more divergent the Sex Rank, the greater the relationship stress. A male 5 with a female 6 relationship may be an "imperfect marriage" but can survive if the couple has a strong moral basis. A male 4 with a female 6 marriage is likely to just fold, or be only tolerable to the wife if she has affairs on the side. A male 3 with a female 6 relationship is doomed, as other men will brazenly approach the wife for a relationship knowing they are far more attractive than the husband.

One of the classic examples of divergent Sex Rank leading to relationship failure is when a wife suddenly starts aggressively working out and makes serious progress towards weight loss. As the weight loss is progressing the husband is usually excited and acts as a cheerleader for her...after all, he's getting a sexier wife because of it. But when the weight loss gets coupled with a new hairstyle, sexier clothes and perfect makeup, she starts pulling the attention of men with a higher Sex Rank than her husband. Once she makes a serious connection with one of them, she announces to her husband that *"I love you, but I'm not in love with you"*, right before she leaves him.

Displays of Low and High Value

A Display of Low Value (DLV) is any display of behavior that would indicate that the male has a low Sex Rank, or would indicate that he should now be perceived as having a lower Sex Rank. A male DLV can be a display of lack of income, bad dressing, physical weakness, social clumsiness and fear. A male performing a DLV reduces sexual interest in observing females. For a female, a DLV is looking bad.

A Display of High Value (DHV) is any display of behavior that would indicate that the person has a high Sex Rank, or would indicate that he should now be perceived as having a higher Sex Rank. A male DHV for a male can come from such things as a display of wealth, good dressing, physical fitness, achievement, social skills or dominance. A male performing a DHV is what creates sexual interest in observing females. For a female, a DHV is looking hot.

Preselection

Female Sex Rank as I have said is fairly quickly assessed; most men can assess a woman's physical sexiness in less than two seconds simply by looking her over. It takes far longer for a woman to assess a man's Sex Rank as unless he hands her his resume, she would have little idea about his earning power, social status and occupation. So as a time-saving measure to fill in the blanks, women rely on the prior assessments made by other women of the quality of the man. This is the Preselection effect that I covered in the Alpha Trait chapter and as it's a key effect on Sex Rank it is worth returning to it for a moment.

A woman looking at a man standing by himself sees *just a man*. A woman looking at a man standing with another woman sees a man who has enough latent attraction to pull the interest of another woman, so she assumes he has some additional value. A woman looking at a man surrounded by women sees a man that has attracted multiple women and *she just assumes* he must have very high value.

Having women with a high Sex Rank being interested in you adds greater fuel to the Preselection effect. A quite unattractive appearing man with highly attractive women hanging on him would still be perceived as highly attractive to other women looking at him.

Preselection is a very strong effect and confusing to many men. It's often surprising to newly married men how frequently women approach them or show greater interest in them now that they are married. The explanation is simple, before they had a girlfriend, but now that they have a wife, they have greater evidence of Preselection and hence greater pull on female sexual interest.

Using Preselection does lend itself to dark tactics. A husband who can clearly pull the attention of other women will demonstrate a high Sex Rank to his wife. She may be acutely unhappy that he can do so, but she will nevertheless be highly emotionally engaged with the obvious Preselection her husband is achieving.

Female Sex Rank Is More Fluid

Because so much of a woman's Sex Rank is appearance based, it's possible for her to swing her Sex Rank up and down on a day to day basis. Tabloids love showing glamorous movie stars all dressed down and without makeup. What looks like a perfect 10 on the big screen suddenly looks like a frumpy 5 trying to nip into a convenience store for cigarettes in stained sweatpants.

The other way a woman can alter her Sex Rank is by increasing and decreasing her sexual response. Men have markedly reduced sexual interest in women who dislike or respond poorly to sex. So a woman who clearly sends out the vibe that she has low sexual interest will reduce her Sex Rank. The opposite is also true and if she makes it clear that she likes sex and has a high sex drive, she will increase her Sex Rank.

Within a marriage the frequency of sex acts is a primary measure of sexual interest. Simply turning up the sexual response can net a woman an extra 1 to 2 points at will. The same woman who is a 6 with sex once or twice a month becomes a 7 when she ups it to once or twice a week, and becomes an 8 at being willing whenever hubby wants it. It may only be his perception of her Sex Rank – others may see a 6 or a 7, but if he's being laid like tile he probably sees her as an 8.

Once you throw in effort with clothing and general fitness, the ability of a woman to swing her Sex Rank up and down can become quite impressive. A female 6 can probably turn herself into a 4 just by dressing badly and holding out on sex, and turn herself into an 8 by sexing it up with her dressing and being playful good fun in the sack on a frequent basis.

Male Sex Rank is More Stable and Can Grow Over Time

A man on the other hand, has sexiness based on factors that are harder to develop and maintain. Since these factors are external and social status based, there is more effort involved to perform them. Men get Sex Rank points for stuff like becoming a lawyer, or earning $100,000 a year. But if a woman puts on a red dress and announces she wants to be ridden hard she gets lots of male attention instantly. In the last few decades the physical appearance of men has become more of a factor as has the wealth and status of women, but overall the stereotypes still hold.

Men tend to have a particular Sex Rank and then have to work extremely hard or totally slack off to change their number. A guy might go from a 7 to a 9 by becoming a doctor, but that takes seven years of work and usually a mountain of debt. A woman might do the same simply by hitting the gym hard for a few months, wearing makeup with more finesse and showing a little more skin. What a woman can achieve with a dazzling red dress, men can only achieve with a Ferrari.

The good news for men, though, is that once they attain Sex Rank positive factors they tend not to lose value over time. If you've created a large business that influences your Sex Rank positively, unless that business folds you're going to maintain that Sex Rank. Women however are slowly going to lose Sex Rank with the fading of their beauty and once out of their fertile years their Sex Rank will plummet even further.

Female Calibration to Male

Women's sexual activity can increase or decrease based on their attraction to a male. So the same woman "with a low sex drive" with her low Sex Rank husband might suddenly discover her "sex drive just increased somehow" if Brad Pitt started asking to screw her.

For men complaining about wives who have low sexual interest in them, some of that drop in her sexual interest may reflect the drop in the husband's Sex Rank. He got fat, or laid off, or sick, or weak and he's less attractive to her, so her sexual activity with him drops.

The woman will generally tend towards calibrating herself to the man's Sex Rank. So a female 6 with a male 8 will "turn it on" and spruce up to her best and find that she feels horny. But stick the same female with a male 4, and she'll "turn it off" and just feel a low libido. It's important to note that this calibration is unconscious in nature and she is likely unaware of her behavior changing. Of course if she does become conscious of her behavior changing towards her husband, her Rationalization Hamster will come up with several perfectly good reasons for it. Something like being unhappy with his inability to stack the dishwasher right, thus ruining her mood for the evening would be ideal.

Orbiters

Often high Sex Rank people attract large numbers of people to themselves, and often those that are attracted have a lower Sex Rank. An Orbiter is someone that has a low Sex Rank who attaches themselves to a higher Sex Rank person of the opposite sex, in vain hopes that they will one day return their sexual interest in them. They rarely do.

A nice example of orbiting is Taylor Swift's *"You Belong With Me."*

"But she wears short skirts, I wear t-shirts
She's cheer captain and I'm on the bleachers
Dreaming bout the day when you wake up and find
That what you're lookin for has been here the whole time"

In the song the cheerleader girlfriend is a 10 and the focus of the song is the boy who is probably an 8. As he is two ranks below the cheerleader girl, she craps all over him in their relationship. He's crazy about her, but it's just painfully one-sided. The boy is supposedly the cheerleader's boyfriend, but she treats him as her Orbiter.

Taylor's character in the song is a 6, and she's just crazy about the boy who is an 8. Unfortunately she has about as much chance with him as he has with the cheerleader. Consequently he craps all over her by not even realizing she could have feelings for him, and simply uses her to prop him up to sustain the emotional battering he gets from the cheerleader. Taylor's character is the Orbiter of the boy.

Of course all three of them have no way of knowing that high school Sex Rank doesn't always equal real world adult Sex Rank... but try telling teenagers that.

Individualized Sex Rank via Biology

This is all very unromantic, but there is at least one special exception that does seem romantic with Sex Rank. We've all experienced meeting a lot of what appear to be very similar people with the same general attractiveness, but sometimes individual people stand out from the crowd and just hold our attention.

A whole team of people might agree that ten women standing in a line are all a 7, and you might agree. Except one of those ten women just doesn't seem like a 7, well objectively yes, you can see a 7, but you can't really look at her objectively... *there's just something about her...* to you she's a *de facto* 9.

What's happening in these cases is that there is an unconscious awareness of a positive match up of each other's DNA for making healthy babies together. There have been studies done showing that women can assess a man's immune system compatibly with hers by sense of smell. Women can literally sniff out good mates. Among other things, this sense of genetic compatibility is a trigger to experiencing feelings of being in love.

As an example of this effect, let's look at my wife. Jennifer is very pretty, but very short and as a rule I didn't really feel attracted to short women before I was married. I really strongly preferred women in the 5'7" to 5'9" range and Jennifer is just 5'0". (Step stools are a sex toy at our place... true story) Also she is a brunette and I have a strong preference for blondes. As an aside she had bleached blonde hair when I met her and I was totally unaware of this when I asked her to marry me. Thankfully she highlights it blonde still and it's a point of humor for us now.

On an objective level, I would peg Jennifer as a natural 8, but *I experience her* as sexier than that. I can't "just cuddle" in bed for example. Oh I can try and "just cuddle", and I really do mean to just cuddle and we start off just cuddling... but I'm pretty soon doing the "rearrangement dance" and then I'm lightly glazing her ass with pre-cum as we spoon. Then she starts giggling and yada yada yada you're welcome baby... you are welcome. I can't help it with her. She just smells so damn good.

Also while I don't exactly see myself as beastly in appearance in a Beauty and the Beast equation, Jennifer definitely responds to me as if I had a higher Sex Rank than I objectively deserve. So she tends to calibrate her sexual response higher to me than she objectively should. In a marriage, sexual chemistry is extremely important. If each feels the other is a prize catch that will create positive cycles of attention and love between them

That natural sexual chemistry stems from a good genetic compatibility for having healthy and attractive children. So Jennifer and I sex it up lots and are blessed with two attractive and extremely healthy daughters. This is how nature works. Science can be very comforting sometimes.

Old Boyfriends

The downside to that special connection is that prior romantic partners probably have a good chance of having that special genetic compatibility as well. Plus there is an emotional content to that prior relationship that doesn't always vanish. Your wife's old boyfriends are far more likely to induce her to cheat on you, or even poach her back completely, compared to a random new man she happens to meet.

The new cliché way of losing your wife to one of her ex-boyfriend's is by them reestablishing contact via social networking sites like Facebook. Your default assumption should be that your wife's old boyfriends (or Orbiters) that message her or leave comments on her status are in fact still sexually interested in her. Given too much allowance, they may seek to enlarge the level of contact with her. Romantic feelings can rekindle quickly and once she is emotionally engaged to them again, if they make a play for her she will be very tempted.

Sex Rank issues with her old boyfriends are more serious than with random men she knows. If you are a 7 and the ex-boyfriend is a 6, then advantage you. If you fall to a 5 and the boyfriend stays a 6, then advantage ex-boyfriend. Even if she falls from a 7 to a 5 with you, she can perk it up with minimal effort for the ex-boyfriend's benefit straight back to a 6. I'm not saying it's an automatic packing of her bags as soon as you drop lower than him, but it is a strong influence on her behavior.

Importantly, old boyfriends who have had sex with your wife have a much higher chance of influencing her to restart a relationship or have an affair with them. Having crossed the line into sex with him once, it's easier to do it again. At some point he managed to trigger her attraction enough to get her seriously interested in him. So no matter how badly the relationship ended, he can still probably flip at least some of her switches. Ex-boyfriends, especially ones that were at all...Alpha, dangerous, bad or edgy...can lodge in a woman's mind forever.

As a counter point, one thing to watch out for is *you* obsessing about her ex-boyfriends. That communicates fear and weakness and is a Display of Low Value. High status males don't need to worry about their females wandering off to find someone better. Basically ignore the entire topic unless one of her exes shows up on her radar again. Then watch carefully and be mildly annoyingly present as required.... by which I mean cockblock. Only if you start seeing something inappropriate do you need to start making clear demands to end the contact.

Unbalanced Sex Ratio

One of the things that can also affect Sex Rank is how many members of each gender are available in any one social group. The gender with the lower number of members gets a natural boost to their Sex Rank, while the group with too many gets a reduction in theirs.

As an example, I spent a few years in a youth group of about forty girls and twenty-five boys. Assuming we dated within the youth group, simple math would suggest that fifteen of the girls would have gone dateless and been lonely. The least attractive of the boys could have paired off with one of the average girls. Even as a painfully shy and utterly clueless young man, dating was fairly easy going once you tried the spectacular technique of simply asking for a date.

In places where there are far too many men and too few women, the advantage is reversed. I have an Alaskan friend that says all a girl needs in Alaska to pull men is *"all her teeth."* Alaskan boyfriends don't get dumped, they just lose their turn.

Marriage Does Not End Sex Rank Issues

The most vital point for a husband is to understand is that the wedding was not the finishing line and this very much dovetails into the issues brought up in the Marriage 2.0 chapter. Staying sexually attractive to your wife is a lifelong requirement these days. Sometimes the very reason your wife is rejecting you sexually is that she is less attracted to you and she has simply calibrated her sexual response to you down.

If you were both 8s, but now you're a 5 and she's still an 8... guess what... *she's not attracted to you*! She feels she has sold herself short and that's why the sex has dropped to a mere trickle.

In a world of other men and ex-boyfriends who have minimal compulsion to respect your relationship with your wife, you should just expect that men will approach her. Obviously you should have a reasonable expectation that she will simply refuse them. But there's no wisdom in displaying to the rest of the world any weakness in your ability to charm your own wife. You most certainly should not show it to her either.

Understanding Sex Rank as Leverage

Once the dynamics of Sex Rank is understood – the essential point being that the hottest member of a couple is the one that holds the balance of power and sets the tone of the relationship- we can actively use that as a tool to gain the things we want from that relationship. This leads us on to Part Two of the book and taking practical steps towards trumping you wife's Sex Rank and pushing towards a point where she must become highly sexual responsive to you, or risk losing you.

Part Two

The Male Action Plan

Chapter 6
The Male Action Plan

Introduction to The MAP

Up until now I've been explaining the way the sexual marketplace works and what women respond to in men. Having reached this point in the book, I hope readers will already be starting to understand their weak areas and can see what they need to work on. From here to the end of the book it's all very practical advice. If you have no interest in actually doing anything to improve your sex life, you may as well stop reading now.

The Male Action Plan, or The MAP for short, is a proven approach to getting you a better sex life. Simply put, The MAP gives women what they actually want and then they respond to it. In a more precise sense, The MAP gets you to model behaviors that trigger her body to release dopamine and oxytocin. Once those two hormones are strongly triggered in relation to you, her own body creates a positive emotional and sexual response to you that she has little control over.

Importantly, The MAP is not about changing her, it's about changing *you*. (If it was about changing *her* I would have called it The Female Action Plan, or The FAP.) If you've ever tried begging, pleading, or rationalizing for getting more or better sex from your partner, then you know how remarkably ineffective that is. To be sure you may get one more begrudging sex act to shut you up once in a while, but then she just returns to her baseline disinterest in you. There's also little pleasure gained in sex with a woman that clearly does not want to have sex with you. Nagging might spread her legs but it won't make her wet and put her hands on your ass as you take her. A core element of doing The MAP is to stop begging for more sex and to start making yourself sexier. You're not pushing her into having sex with you; you're pulling her sexual interest to you so she wants to have sex with you.

The MAP also focuses on modeling the positive of both Alpha and Beta male behavior. Most men find they are more naturally good at one or the other. If you're better at modeling the Alpha traits, then you will make the fastest gains by working on the Beta traits. If you are better at Beta, then learning the Alpha traits will get you the fastest gains. The MAP also requires you to maximize your physical fitness as best you can.

By gaining physical fitness and showing better versions of Alpha and Beta traits, a husband will increase his Sex Rank. Once he has a higher Sex Rank than his wife, she will find herself increasingly attracted to him. The purpose of trumping her Sex Rank is to purposely destabilize the relationship and force her into choosing either a more sexual relationship, or have her risk losing her husband to another woman. I won't pretend that this is a polite method of saving your relationship, just an effective one.

There is a timeline that I cover in the next chapter as to how you doing The MAP will play out, but each man doing it will have to find his own sense of male balance. For example it's not a case of getting physically fit and *then* working on the Alpha and *then* working on the Beta as a planned sequence. The MAP is something that needs to be worked on consistently in all three areas. If you are endlessly Beta, you don't just stop being Beta to work on the Alpha. You're trying to create the best composite balance you can. More than likely though, you will find that working on your weakest area first gets you the fastest gains.

If you're already excellent in one area, there's likely little reason to try and develop it further if you have other areas that are weak. If you're already in fabulous physical shape, training harder to become in even better physical shape is likely of no benefit compared to potential gains from learning how to help out around the house, make more money or say no to her making ridiculous demands of you. It's all about balance.

Critical Point – The MAP may not work in your current relationship with your wife. You may very well spruce up perfectly and become more appealing to women in general, but your own wife may turn her nose up at you. You really can't control another person's reactions to you. You can *influence* her reactions and make her more likely to choose you, but you can't force those reactions. Should you push harder and start heading to the door, there will be another woman willing to take your wife's place and give you the love and sex you desire. This may seem like an exceptionally cold approach to relationships, but it is simply realistic. If a wife doesn't want to have sex with a sexy husband who is a good man, *then there is no pleasing her*. Her husband's torment will last as long as the marriage does.

A Sexless Marriage Cheats You

I am of the firm belief that in sexless marriages, the spouse who denies sex is cheating the other out of their marriage agreement. I use the word "cheating" quite purposely and see it as minimally different from an "affair." The marriage agreement is one of mutual sexual exclusivity and meeting each other's sexual needs. A spouse who goes outside the relationship for sex denies the cheated on spouse their half of the marriage agreement. A spouse who denies the other reasonable sexual access cheats the other out of their half of the marriage agreement. Either way the marriage is under enormous difficulty.

Seeing as I'm good with crass examples... If you became the customer of a cable TV company and they came and hooked up your neighbor's house, or refused to hook your house up, but they still demanded payment, how long would you tolerate that? You would immediately demand the company stop billing you for the neighbor's cable and come hook it up at your place, or you would threaten to immediately stop being their customer. Whatever you do though, you shouldn't keep passively paying the cable bill hoping the cable company will give you cable one day.

Why Men Get So Agitated About Not Having Sex

The clinical definition of a sexless marriage is sex ten or fewer times in a year, or about once a month. Personally I think the clinical definition is so far below a normal level of sexual functioning that it really clouds the issue. Getting sex once or twice a month from your wife is a slow torture to a sexually healthy man. Most men become increasingly anxious to have sex with their wives *within a few days* of the last time they had sex. Going back to the Body Agenda chapter, we remember that the husband's goal is to load up his wife's reproductive tract with sperm, thus maintaining a standing army to repel any other sperm that isn't his. After five days of no intercourse, his entire army of sperm is dead or flushed out of her. So after five days of no sex with his wife, it's from a male Body Agenda point of view *like he's never had sex with her at all* and his anxiety level increases accordingly.

Having sex less than twice a week is a red flag in basically physically healthy young couples. I'm not looking at this from a psychiatric *"Is this diagnosable as sexual dysfunction?"* point of view, simply from an *"Are you happy being married to her?"* and *"Are you going to get cheated on or otherwise divorced?"* point of view. By having vaginal sex with her husband less than twice a week, a wife is telegraphing her sexual disinterest in him and refusing to allow him to effectively colonize her reproductive tract with sperm. She does this to keep her options open.

If your wife offers frequent blowjobs or handjobs, enjoy them but be careful that she's not just distracting you. An interested wife will desire frequent vaginal intercourse and be glad to get your sperm into her vagina. But if you suspect she's interested in another man and she's nearing ovulation, pay attention to excessive offers of blowjobs or handjobs. A woman unconsciously blocking her husband's sperm for several days before ovulation is a red flag that could indicate potential cheating.

If a husband gets vaginal sex on Monday, a handjob on Wednesday and a blowjob on Friday, that would seem like a pretty good week of sex to many husbands and they would likely feel happy and satisfied. But if the wife then meets her lover on the Saturday, none of his sperm from Monday would still be inside her to fight off his. If she gets pregnant on the Saturday and on Sunday morning wakes her husband up with a surprisingly energetic session on top of him... he might never know the truth. She might suspect it, but her Rationalization Hamster would probably just advise her that it was just one time and not very likely, so not to worry about it.

For many husbands in very low sex marriages, having their wives start to give handjobs and blowjobs are signs of *improvement.* By all means accept them and just stick with doing The MAP and the vaginal action should return to the menu as well.

How Sexless Marriages Play Out

Assuming one partner wants sex and the other doesn't, marriages tend to play out towards one of four basic outcomes.

One – Endless Misery. The first outcome is that essentially nothing changes in the marriage. It stays locked in the cycle of one partner denying sex and the other miserable and desperate to get more sex. Without either spouse making a serious change in behavior, this is the default outcome because the cycle of denial and begging will continue forever. The spouse being denied sex may very well claim they are unhappy and that the relationship is intolerable, but they stay in the relationship and tolerate it nevertheless.

Two – Extramarital Sex. The second outcome is that the partner denied sex simply gives up on gaining sexual access to their spouse and seeks sex outside the marriage. Whether the sex is via a lover, random hookups, escorts or some really high quality porn doesn't matter. The extramarital sex might even be known to the spouse denying sex and may be actually encouraged sometimes. It's not wildly uncommon for a wife that has no sexual interest in her husband to tell him to find a girlfriend for example. Generally the request is framed as *"Go meet your needs, just don't mess with what I want from you or embarrass me about this."*

Three – Divorce. The third possibility is that the spouse who is denied sex may simply get tired of being taken advantage of and leave the marriage by divorcing. Almost always there's an affair partner lined up to replace the low sex desire spouse before the exit is announced.

Four – Sexual Marriage. The fourth option is that the low sex partner actually becomes more sexually interested and sexual activity resumes at a level that the more interested spouse can enjoy. Obviously this is the end point that The MAP intends to create.

Without effective change in one of the spouses, the first option of endless misery for the high sex spouse will continue forever. By taking the first option off the table, the denying spouse is ultimately going to be forced into making a decision between the other three options. So what The MAP does is start to force the issue towards one of the other outcomes.

Critical Point – Before you start doing The MAP, I'm assuming you are probably in the default outcome of sexual denial and unhappiness for you. It might be a bad relationship, but it's a *stable* relationship. You and your wife might both be unhappy with each other, but you both know the roles you've mapped out for each other and play them well together. By you removing this default option from the choices your wife can choose from, *this will destabilize your marriage*, so things may get worse before they get better.

In putting The MAP into practice, it is very important to see this as a process and not a rush to judgment. If you push too hard too fast and don't give your wife time to adjust to the changes you have made in yourself, the marriage can destabilize so much that it fails. It can take six months to two years to get you into a position where an ultimatum may need to be made; thought ideally an ultimatum is never even needed because the situation resolves itself naturally over time.

For example, assume a male 6 is married to a female 7 who is hardly interested in him sexually anymore. Should the husband announce that she can either be cheated on, get divorced, or start having with him sex four times a week, the conversation will likely not go nearly as well as he might imagine and he will not like the result at all. She might just laugh at him and accept the divorce option. You should never issue an ultimatum unless you are the higher Sex Rank of the couple.

But if our male 6 just starts doing The MAP and six months later he is a 7, she is very likely starting to respond to him more positively anyway. A year into doing The MAP, he might be an 8 to her 7, so now she is starting to feel excited about him and a little nervous. Attracting a woman *better than her* is now a possibility for him, and rather than having idle thoughts about divorcing him, she worries just a little that he might divorce her. More than likely she starts exercising, dressing better and initiates sex with him more frequently trying to increase her Sex Rank to keep pace with his - *all without him forcing the issue to an ultimatum.* The key is to work for constant positive progress.

Stop Tolerating the Intolerable

I get many emails that all essentially ask the same question with minor variations. It goes something like this:

"I've been married for [years] and for the last [awfully long time] I've had a problem with my [husband or wife] and the [huge intolerable relationship breaking problem] and they refuse to do anything about it. I've tried [all manner of things] to try and get them to change [the huge intolerable relationship breaking problem] but they still refuse to do anything about it. How do I fix this?"

As you can probably guess, the huge intolerable relationship breaking problem that people write to me about is usually a lack of sex. I'm getting emails from both men and women as many as sixteen years into a sexless marriage and some are heartbreaking to read. As I said earlier, my viewpoint on sexless marriages is that they are just as serious as having a full blown affair in terms of its insult to the partner wanting sex but not getting it. I've had many emails where a woman has said it's to the point where she just wants to hear that her husband is gay because that would explain things better and soften the blow to her ego.

Marriage is at its heart, a sexual relationship. Without the sex it's just a legally binding friendship, which is a needlessly complicated way of having a friend. The basic agreement of being married is to meet each other's sexual needs and not to run round getting them met anywhere else. Both affairs and sexless marriages break that relationship agreement.

The main difference between discovering that your partner is having an affair and finding that the sex is just being slowly turned off is how you as the injured party react. If you discover you're being cheated on, the shit typically hits the fan instantly. There's yelling and shouting, crying, threats and angry squealing of tires in the driveway as people "take space". With threats of divorce and other drama, it all comes to a head very quickly.

But most times when one spouse cuts the other off sexually, the sex tapers off gradually and there isn't usually a critical incident. Over time the high sex spouse just takes it with quiet suffering, save for the pleading for sex or requests to visit a doctor to see if anything medical is going on. Then they wait and hope that magically the sex returns, and when it doesn't years can pass by. The pain and hurt can mount up for so long that you can build up a tolerance for a level of suffering that no mentally healthy person would consider tolerable.

Ironically, this gradual slide into a sexless marriage uses exactly the same principles as The MAP does, just in reverse! There's usually no ultimatum given by the low sex spouse – "I've decided that I will not have any more sex with you in this relationship. Either stay with me and never have sex again, or leave now." If you heard that in your second year of marriage you would probably rebel and leave. But if she can manage to taper off the sex to nothing over two years, you might just start getting used to it. If she's smart, she will throw in a few nights of hypersexual behavior to rock your world, just to keep you hooked into her with hope that a regular sex life will one day return.

Medical issues aside, when you are cut off from sex by your spouse, the marriage is in critical condition because one spouse has started actively working against the marriage. This is a serious and legitimate issue. You have the right to feel angry and hurt by it. It's okay to take action to address this issue.

Stop Talking and Start Taking Action

Now as the denied partner, you may feel like you've been banging your head against the wall for months or years in asking for her to change. You have been pleading, begging, asking, and telling her how intolerable the intolerable relationship breaking problem is. The trouble is these are nothing but words and extremely ineffective at getting what you want.

By sticking around and endlessly focusing on the problem of lack of sex, your actions and behavior are making it clear that the problem is in fact not intolerable... *you're sticking around and tolerating it.* Even worse, the louder you squeal about the issue, the deeper commitment to option one (sticking around and suffering) you make to your partner. You're making it clear that you are completely engaged in this relationship and are utterly fixated on your partner.

The solution is to take action that makes it clear that the problem is in fact intolerable. While you don't know whether you will make a move towards option two (extramarital sex), or option three (divorce), option one just isn't acceptable anymore. You need to stop pursuing the dead end of sex with your wife and start preparing yourself to pursue things with other women in general. So you work out, upgrade the clothes a little, open up a dating profile, just go "out" a little without providing the details, smile, be happy, friendly, carefree, text some new friends, socialize... *play*.

The goal is to stop chasing and pursuing your wife, and generally make it clear by your actions that you are no longer going to be held as her emotional hostage. Show that you will be capable of moving towards a life without her, and that you have discovered the will to do so. Once you have that attitude down, there is a reasonable chance that her level of interest in you will significantly change for the better. Don't actually cheat on her; just make it clear you have the potential to move on without her. This sounds like a dangerous anti-marriage ploy, but I figure after a marriage has been sexually dead for no good reason for a year or more, it's essentially over and you're justified in taking such bold steps.

Stop Begging For Sex

The other reason you need to stop begging for sex is that it actively turns off a woman's sexual interest in you. Begging and pleading is a submissive display and frames her as the dominant one in the relationship. As most women respond sexually to male dominance, advertising the exact opposite is a turn-off.

The goal here is to make yourself more appealing so she is attracted and responds to you, rather than you having to try and endlessly jump through her hoops in pursuit of her. You don't *beg* for sex from her. You can and should still ask for sex, and if she agrees then great, you have sex with her. But if she declines sex, act like it's no biggie and move on with your day. But pressuring her into sex will put her shields up and make her increasingly defensive about it. Never force a woman to think about the reasons why she doesn't want to have sex with you because she might decide on a definite answer. Whatever that answer is, will be The Mother of All Cockblocks.

Realize She May Have No Interest in Solving the Problem

The wife who denies you sex may have zero interest in solving the problem of a sexless marriage. After all, that might damage the carefully balanced relationship she has created, where you do exactly what she wants all the time and she doesn't have to do anything. This is why begging her to give you sex is pointless because giving you sex would be counterproductive to the relationship she worked so hard to create. If she rewards you with too much sex, she might accidentally make you sexually satisfied and that would reduce your motivation to continuously jump through her hoops, in vain hope of getting the sexual scraps she allows you.

If you're the husband, you would obviously feel terribly cheated in an arrangement like this. It's very easy to frame everything as being her fault and believe she is the one who must change for the marriage to be happy or even to continue. While that sounds quite logical, the trouble is that it gives all the power to change and improve the situation to her, and she may have no interest in changing the relationship where you cater to her endlessly. That's what "low sexual interest" means. And let's face it... many men have tried asking for more or better sex until they are blue in the face and jumped through all her hoops, and they have still not seen the changes they hope for. So let's just be done with that strategy.

You Be the Change

My approach is that husbands need to find out how to become sexier in the eyes of their wives, and that being sexier will trigger greater sexual interest in them. So rather than trying to ask her to change, you need to change for the better and she will either respond or she won't. If she responds to you the way you want, then that's a big win. If she won't respond then you are in a better place to find another partner who will treat you with the interest you want. There's a real shortage of worthwhile men willing to commit to a marriage compared to women who want to be married. Compared to a divorced woman finding a new partner of value, divorced men finding new partners is not terribly hard. You probably hold better cards in your hand than she does.

Of course, the best outcome is that the wife does respond and the couple resumes their sex life. I won't lie and say that this plan is a 100% lock on that outcome, but if you turn yourself from a 6 to an 8, there's a great chance that your 7 wife will start drooling over you, love every minute of you inside her and be happier in your marriage.

Most wives crave their husbands becoming more attractive and appealing, but cannot get themselves unstuck to communicate that effectively. One of the most common ways men find my blog is through their wife suggesting they read it...or maybe leaving it opened on the computer for him to find it. Women always want a better partner and you know they just love to think they are changing us for the better.

No Quick Fix

As I've said before, if you're a decent Beta, the solution is to add Alpha traits, not reduce Beta Traits and add Alpha. It's not a zero-sum game where you can be either Alpha or Beta, but not both. You can and must be both. The Alpha traits "turn her on", but lacking the Beta traits eventually "turns her off."

It's actually quite a long journey to really change yourself in this way. There's a lot of "two steps forward one step back" that happens. Much of Alpha-ness stems from physicality, and that can take 1-2 years of exercise to really pay off fully if you have let yourself go, so it's a process. If you're changing little by little, then you're changing the status quo and destabilizing the relationship little by little. To restablize the relationship, she will have to change little by little as well. Everybody has a natural resistance to change– even if it's a positive change and one you'll both ultimately enjoy. Just be "comfortable with your discomfort" and keep plowing ahead.

As an example, I've been on a number of health kicks over the years. In terms of physical exercise for Jennifer and me, usually I start seriously exercising first, and start feeling better and sexier. Usually about three weeks later, she starts exercising more too. Up until then she "resists" exercise. I don't even ask Jennifer to work out - I just start exercising and wait three weeks. And if I stop, she stops.

Coming back to the idea of Sex Rank, assume you both married as 7s, and along the way you dropped to a 6. Now that you've learned some Alpha stuff and have progressed, maybe you're moving past 7 and heading towards being an 8. If you're heading towards 8 and she is still a 7, that's actually a little scary for her. It's one thing to be the more desirable member of a couple, but it's another to feel like you need to step it up a bit. There's a natural temptation to want to drag the improving spouse back down to your level, though that can just as easily turn into trying harder on her part and getting her to an 8 as well. (Which is exactly why my wife starts exercising after I start.)

Correct Your Weak Area First

For me the Beta traits come easily and I've had to struggle to learn the Alpha ones a lot later in my life. People often assume that I'm a natural Alpha, but what I'm writing about now has taken the better part of the last six years of my sixteen year marriage to develop. I've struggled with the political correctness issue of male dominance for over a decade and have only come out of the closet and publicly said I'm willing to be dominant towards my wife in the last two years. Jennifer was willing to accept it all along; the problem was me thinking it was morally offensive.

Ideally you have a strong hand of Alpha and Beta cards and then play them depending on the situation. I can cook dinner, throw a slumber party for tweens, change a diaper, feed and burp a baby, match an outfit for a middle school girl and do laundry like a dream. But I can also shut the slumber party off at midnight with a deep rumble, cut allowances out until compliance with chores is appropriate, order Jennifer to stop working and rest and have on many occasions initiated sex simply by making eye contact and pointed in the direction of the bedroom. It's all about having options and being able to give her a shot of dopamine or a shot of oxytocin. Politically incorrect or not, Jennifer likes this treatment from me, so it works for us.

In terms of physical fitness, if you weigh 240 pounds and you really should be 180 pounds, that road to losing 60 pounds is not going to be overnight or effortless. If you can't hold a job, turning that around can take one or two years before you find one, settle your crap down and get to a first promotion or better hours. If you dress like a slob, that extra $1,000 to $2,000 to transform a wardrobe can take a while to earn and spend. If you're terrible at keeping a house together, you may have a year's worth of DIY projects ahead of you.

As a rough guide, give yourself a year per point of Sex Rank. So going from 6 to a 7 is about a year; then 7 into 8 is a second year. It's a gradual but serious effort. There is no one killer move that makes her vagina explode with fluids at your approach. It's about you becoming a better man. Good sex is just the consequence of being sexy.

Whoever has the Higher Sex Rank is in Charge of the Relationship.

The effect of the higher Sex Rank half of the couple being in control of the relationship is actually best seen by women who suddenly lose a great deal of weight. In the cases where fairly unattractive couples are together, they can have a fairly even relationship, but if the woman suddenly loses a great deal of weight and begins dressing better and showing off her body, the relationship is usually doomed.

If two 4s are married and then the wife loses sixty or seventy pounds and starts paying attention to clothing and makeup, it's possible she could morph into a 7 or an 8. Her 4 husband is toast. If he doesn't do everything she demands, she could simply leave the relationship for a better man. She probably already has multiple men interested in her who are more attractive than her husband. The further apart the Sex Rank numbers are, the stronger the destabilizing effect is.

Your plan is to up your Sex Rank by improving your body and your Alpha and Beta skill sets in order to purposely destabilize your relationship with your wife by trumping her Sex Rank. That does sound like a cruel threat, but remember that a woman can easily add an extra point or two to her Sex Rank simply by increasing her sexual frequency and being more exciting in bed – which is your goal. Having a high sexual interest and drive is sexy in and of itself. The same wife that's a 6 when she puts out twice a month is a 7 at twice a week, and an 8 at "whenever and however you want me." Bonus points for mixing it up with games, toys and being a little kinky in the sack.

Of course if her Sex Rank trumps yours, you've got nothing to use as leverage to change things. You're giving away your power in the relationship and you can find your entire relationship reframed for her benefit as a result. Of course if your Sex Rank goes up, and hers stays the same but she doesn't turn into Miss Sugarpussy on you... well you're going to be getting better interest from other women.

Over the long term, a man who basically applies himself to any sort of career and personal development while maintaining physical fitness, becomes sexier than his similarly aged wife does. An average twenty-year-old-man is over shadowed by the raw appeal of a twenty-year-old-woman. At thirty it's more balanced. A forty-year-old-man generally has far more appeal than a forty-year-old woman. All things being equal a single forty-year-old-man can date and remarry with ease, but a forty-year-old-woman will have a much harder time of it.

There Are Limits

Adding more than a couple of points to your innate Sex Rank is extremely hard - if you're a natural 6 getting to 7 is some effort, getting to 8 is quite hard, 9 is just out of reach without someone else footing the bill or being on a reality TV show to make you hot. Going from 6 to a 10 isn't even in the cards at all. I'm just telling it how it is...The MAP is all about the possible.

Attractive to all Women, Means...

A risk of doing The MAP is that you will pull the interest of a woman more attractive than your wife, or multiple women of equal or lesser value. Okay so maybe that's the lamest "risk" statement ever, but bear with me. You may not even be actively looking for these women, but they will eventually show up and make it known that they are available to you. Now if you weren't banging supermodels before you read this book, you probably aren't going to be banging supermodels after you read it, but you certainly can find attractive women who could see themselves having sex with you starting to express interest in you.

Say you were a 6 and you had an old female friend that was a 7 that you struck out on and got the "Let's just be friends" (LJBF) speech. You've stayed in friendly contact for many years via Facebook or whatever. Now that you're an 8, Ms. LJBF has started looking at you a little differently. One day she calls you out of the blue and suggests getting together to "catch up", when you've always been the one to call her. The light will go on in your head that she just expressed interest in you. In fact she just asked you to meet privately with her... so maybe now you can have her. It's easy to say that you would never cheat on your wife, but it's another thing to have someone you've hungered for press themselves against you as you finish "catching up." A lifetime of wanting can turn into quite a kiss.

Even if your wife responds to your improvement and increases her own Sex Rank to keep pace with yours, other women will still respond to you with a far greater interest anyway. That may be a whole new experience to get used to and decide about. My general advice is to be very cautious about exploring that behind your wife's back, as years of marital progress can be undone in a few careless kisses and text messages, let alone progressing to a hotel room.

Like I just said, it's easy to denounce cheating in abstract before the event. When someone unexpected hits on you, try not to be taken by surprise. Know that as you do The MAP faithfully and make yourself a better and sexier man, you will become more attractive to women in general. Tests will come to you whether you want them or not.

Your Wife May Want You to Change

While your wife may not have any interest in changing herself to be more sexual, she is very likely highly interested in seeing you change. Women want to be sexually responsive to men, so she may in fact be purposely waiting on you to make positive changes before she changes herself. She may in fact be quite agitated that you haven't "manned up" for her. As a point of frustration to you both, *she can't tell you that* because you're "just meant to know" and by asking you to be dominant towards her it ruins her fantasy of you taking charge of things. If she asks you to be dominant towards her and you start acting dominantly, you're doing what she asked you to do... so in reality she's the dominant one, which she doesn't want to be. So therefore she can't tell you.

Your own wife is probably one of the easiest women you know to get a positive response from by running The MAP. After all, she was into you enough to marry you, so there has to be some sort of baseline interest, and that should peak if you are the best version of you possible. She's also heavily invested in your relationship and it's the path of least resistance to see you blossom into a sexier man. Her other option if she wants a sexier husband is to attempt the very risky strategy of divorcing you and trying to find a new husband that is better than you.

If your wife is a 7, and you can turn yourself from a 6 to an 8, all she has to do is wait for you to hit 8 and then look nicer and have lots of sex with you. That doesn't actually sound like all that bad of an option for her. But if she divorces you, she takes a hit to her Sex Rank as a "used goods and prior relationship baggage" penalty and it's going to be a very long shot for her to find a male 8 who would want her – even finding a 7 might be difficult. In fact she may be faced with the horrible possibility that in the aftermath of the divorce, you finally get your act together and actually become the 8 she wanted, while she is faced with the prospect of either giving up sex on the second date to 6s or living alone. Ugh.

Also she's extremely proximal to you, and simple proximity can make a huge difference in getting her moving towards taking her clothes off and lying down with her legs apart. Living in your house together is a natural way of isolating her and creating privacy for her to be sexual. So as bad as things might look between you now, your wife is still the easiest woman you know to work on getting hot sex from.

I also expect that as you perk up your Sex Rank, she will follow your lead to keep pace. Ideally there isn't even a "fight night" where everything turns into a dramatic confrontation – you just up the sexy and she follows suit.

However, she may not respond positively and you will be faced with the possibility that the marriage will have to end in order to move on to the sex life you need and deserve. If it goes down the divorce route, you are still better off seeking new sex partners as an 8 than as a 6. Either way you will win from the process of making yourself more attractive to women.

Failing to do The MAP is a Risk

Failing to work on your sex appeal is a serious risk all by itself, as you run the risk that your wife may simply decide to take her own action that's against your best interest. She may simply divorce you or cheat on you. Seeing around 8-10% of all children have a misidentified biological father, being cuckolded is quite possible too.

Critical Point – Women like sex just as much as men do. If she is not having sex with you because she is not attracted to you, it does not automatically mean she has a low sex drive. If you are less sexy than your wife and you plan to just coast along, do not be surprised if you find out one day that she has a lover she is passionately involved with. You sure as hell don't try and keep her with you by offering or allowing her sex with other men. That's like being in the express lane in the wrong direction. Chump be thy name.

Men who are highly attractive have firsthand knowledge that women are definitely not the moral angels that they may like to present themselves as. The good girl image is nothing more than the social equivalent of the biological concealed ovulation strategy which was covered in the Body Agenda chapter. Women very much like sex with men they find attractive and can be exceptionally devious and insistent on getting it.

It is extremely politically incorrect to say so, but all women have a component of slut in their makeup. The trick is not to fear it, seek to sanction it, or flee it, but to adapt to the presence of the slut in your woman and harness it for your mutual enjoyment. But if you don't pay her active attention to account for her slut influence, you might find that it gets up to all sorts of mischief.

Summary

As cynical as my advice may seem, the only person you can really control is you. As long as you take positive action, you will end up with a positive sexual outcome regardless of your wife's decisions and behavior.

This is a process with no rush to an ultimatum. Divorce is amazingly serious with kids and houses and money and careers all tied up together. Unpicking all that is a mess. But if you're basically being shorted on the love and sex front, you are ultimately being screwed over. Sometimes enough is enough and you see the whole thing as abusive towards you. You can't have an agreement for an exclusive sexual relationship, do your part, and not get a reasonable amount of sex in return.

Another thing to consider is that when you're about two or three months into doing The MAP, your wife should be noticing some positive changes in you. If you can prove that you're heading in a positive direction and have some momentum, she's quite possibly going to be your biggest ally in your quest. Her inner slut wants to see you turn into a stud. If only her stud.

So maybe she responds to you, maybe she doesn't. I can't promise that she will. Either way though, you win in that she either responds to you and you have a proper marriage, or she doesn't and you're positioned to move on and find new love with someone else. This is a deeply pragmatic perspective, but there we go.

I'm not saying that doing The MAP is easy either. If your feelings for your wife overwhelm your ability to get into action, or you believe the good in your marriage outweighs the bad, your own Rationalization Hamster will always find a way to keep you locked in endless misery.

Chapter 7
Get Control of Your Health

A Secretly Disappointed Princess

For some strange reason Princess Leia was totally not into Jabba the Hutt. She had the skimpy bikini thing on for him; he clearly had money, power and bondage equipment and usually this sort of thing works for a girl. But the thing where she kissed her brother in Episode IV was simply uncomfortable in retrospect compared to the repulsion she felt for Jabba.

Jabba also has this totally Alpha opening line as well, *"Soon you will come to appreciate me."* I dare you to try that one on your wife later tonight...trust me, it's a closer. It's so powerful it's illegal in three States and Canada. Just look her in the eye, drop your voice an octave and unload it on her. Rumble a *"Soon you will come to appreciate me"*, and somewhere deep in the female brain the anterior ravishment cortex is going to fire and it's all on from there. You know it's working when she dissolves into a fit of giggles. That's normal, just plow ahead and don't stop for air. If you can keep a straight face, afterwards when you get out of bed and walk to the shower offer a *"You have pleased me."*

But I digress... very obviously the reason Princess Leia didn't feel attraction for Jabba was that he was the size of a small truck and smelled like the wrong end of a Bantha. (Okay, I'm done with Star Wars metaphors for the book, I promise.)

Sex is Physical

So what about you? Maybe Jabba the Hutt is an extreme metaphor, but the thought holds. You can have money, power, fancy boats and personal wait staff, but being physically in shape is also a major Alpha Trait as well. Women aren't as body oriented as men are in terms of what is attractive, but they certainly do look.

What if one of the reasons you don't have tremendous sex with your wife is that your physical fitness is so low that it's actively repelling her from you? Oh sure, she can love you no matter what, but that isn't the same as having a tingle between her legs every time she looks you over.

If you're overweight, I figure you already know it. And like everybody else, you know there's really only one basic solution – eat less and exercise more. The only time diet and exercise involves rocket science is on the space shuttle missions. What you will find is that even moderate exercise has its benefits. Weight training will especially benefit you. Even losing ten pounds will result in you feeling better and sexier. And like I've said before, good sex is just a consequence of being sexy. Your whining that she never initiates sex is silly if you are clearly not physically attractive. Why would she ask to have sex with you if she finds you unsexy? Queue up the *"I love you, but I'm not in love with you"* speech...

I am by no means some sort of ultra-hunk. I'm a regular guy. But I very much find that my wife responds better to me when I am in the best physical shape I can be. Usually about two or three weeks after I start exercising, she "just decides" to start too. So it's a fun together thing as well. If you we're a natural Sex Rank 7, but fell to a 5 because you employed Homer Simpson as your personal trainer while your wife stayed a 7, well you've left the front door open a bit wide, don't you think?

If you've let yourself go to pot, you should absolutely not get all upset and issue demands and ultimatums for more sex right now. That may go very badly for you. What you should do is plan ahead and drop the weight. You don't have to turn yourself into a professional bodybuilder, just get into decent shape.

I'm not going to go into detail about how to lose weight and get in shape, because that information is endlessly available on the Internet and in other books. It's really not my job to wake you up in the morning and drive you to the gym. You already know exactly how to get yourself started on fitness routine; you just have to go do it. *So go do it.*

Physical Fitness Creates Confidence with Women

If you do nothing else to improve your sex life with your wife, and I mean *if you do nothing else*, you should work out. Some sort of physical exercise is just foundational to almost all of the Alpha Male Traits. It's awfully difficult to radiate that sexy confidence of beastly power when you're hooked up to an oxygen tank to keep you from passing out, for example. Back in the Time Before Writing, the physical strength and ability of individual men created a pecking order of social rank. That sense of physical prowess still has an effect in modern social situations. Jocks being more socially dominant than nerds doesn't end at high school.

Most men experience something called Approach Anxiety when trying to approach an attractive female with the intent to gain her sexual interest. With exceptionally attractive women well beyond a man's Sex Rank, he might have no hope of sex with her, or even intention to *try* and talk to her, but he may experience acute anxiety simply by being in close proximity to her. His anxiety might be so high, that even if she makes physical contact possible between them, he might be unable to physically touch her. The classic example of this is the website hoverhands.net, devoted to photos of men with their arms around beautiful women, but all with their hands mysteriously hovering a few inches away from actually touching them. Thus "hover hands."

Most men assume that Approach Anxiety is caused by interpersonal fear, stress, or the possibility of emotional rejection by the woman. But the *physical* symptoms of the Approach Anxiety reaction are exactly the same as that of the "flight or fight" response. As daft as it sounds, when a man approaches a woman in hope of gaining a phone number, what really makes his heart race is adrenaline. The male Body Agenda automatically assumes another male will potentially arrive and threaten a *physical* fight over the female.

This is why physically poor men have such enormous inability to approach women and seek to start a sexual relationship. Simply by walking up to an attractive woman, his Body Agenda assumes he's going to get his ass kicked, so he avoids it. Modern laws about violence don't register into the male Body Agenda.

By increasing physical ability, the Approach Anxiety fades and you can approach women with a greater confidence. It's the man with a confident approach that women respond to positively. A male approach of high confidence implies physical ability and therefore, social dominance to the Body Agenda of women, so they feel attracted to the male that approaches them that way.

As an aside – another way to overcome Approach Anxiety is to not allow yourself any hesitation in immediately talking to a beautiful woman that interests you. You have approximately a five second delay between thinking about maybe approaching a woman and your body kicking in the adrenaline to start the Approach Anxiety/flight or fight reaction. If you can *immediately* start conversation with her, there's a good chance that no man will show up and be violent with you for approaching his mate. Without an aggressive male to fight, your Body Agenda relaxes and cuts off the adrenaline response. If you wait more than five seconds though, you've left it too late for this to work.

Women are Turned On by Strapping Men

Often a group of people can shake their heads in confusion at a woman having sex with an asshole/loser and wonder "what does she see in him?" Usually the answer is something like "nice abs and a tight ass." Women love physically fit men.

If you're a husband, the deal is that the only man she should sleep with is you. So all the brawn she'll ever get is meant to come from you, and if she can't get it from you, then where can she get it? If the only thing Brawny she gets to hold in her hands is a roll of paper towels, then that's a problem.

Oh sure, I know, not your sweet angel, she can't possibly think like that, but have you ever looked at the covers of romance novels? These are not science geek bodies they have plastered across the covers. I believe the word we are looking for is "strapping". There are strapping men on the covers of romance novels, usually semi-naked, displaying their brawn, looking serious and not making particular eye contact but just gazing yonder. Women buy these novels all the time. This is a huge industry and those strapping guys aren't there by accident.

Increasing Testosterone

Part of the natural leaning towards Alpha Traits in men stems from their high testosterone levels. However, in addition to getting older, becoming both married and a father typically results in a decline in testosterone levels. This natural decline in testosterone can play a part in the falling off of Alpha traits and you can become overly Beta in your marriage. A method of combating this is to take steps to increase your testosterone level. Here are a few easy and simple methods to do that.

Eat Better – Having a balanced diet with fruits and vegetables has a positive effect on testosterone production. Plus the proteins in eggs and whey allow the adrenal glands to keep testosterone levels even.

Decrease Body Fat – Fat contains an enzyme that actually converts testosterone to estrogen. Obviously men do need some amount of estrogen, but getting obese is going to cause a shift in the balance of power from testosterone to estrogen. Perhaps you'd like a purse to go with your spare tire.

Eat Meat – Don't go vegetarian, that's really for chicks. Meat helps increase testosterone levels and so can nuts as well. Have some peanut butter. Be careful though, since there is also evidence that going to a high-protein low carb diet will actually hurt testosterone production. Balanced diet, hear me? *Balanced diet.*

Lift Weights – Do exercise and lift weights. Don't work yourself into complete exhaustion and over-train, just keep up a steady level of exercise and your testosterone levels will increase. Weight training is particularly good for testosterone levels.

Limit Alcohol Intake – When your body is working overtime to get the alcohol out of your system, it isn't working to create testosterone. Three drinks will basically shut production of testosterone off until the alcohol is cleared.

Sleep Better – Well duh. Everything goes better with sleep.

Get Sexually Turned On – Get hard! Being turned on and physically erect leads to increases in overall testosterone levels. No reason why a little porn can't be helpful. (I generally advise cumming inside your wife as much as possible though. It actually delivers testosterone to her that gets absorbed through the vaginal walls and makes her sex drive increase!)

Omega-3 Fatty Acids – Seriously, try this. It costs about $10 for a three month supply of Fish Oil from any supermarket. What do you have to lose?

Engage In Competition – Do something competitive once in a while. You increase testosterone from this, especially if you win!

Dominate Someone - Just like winning a competitive game can increase your testosterone, taking a leadership position in social situations can increase testosterone levels. Perhaps a playful spanking of your wife…

Weight Training is Key

It's very difficult to overestimate how important weight training is with sparking female sexual interest. Because social dominance is sparked by physical ability, and more correctly, combat ability, having muscle mass is basically a good thing.

Given a choice between either a man with excellent cardio ability like a runner or a man with excellent muscle mass like a boxer, most women tend toward the one with muscle mass. From a female point of view, there's no point having a male protector whose best ability is to run from combat, when a male that can actually win combat is available. Women tend to choose the men that specialize in the "fight" response rather than the "flight" one.

Women have long been known to get excited over "a man in uniform." The uniform really isn't the issue, it's more the fact that the man in the uniform is willing to put up a fight and not be combat avoidant.

Martial Arts

If you have the time to spend learning a martial art, then that can also be a profound influence on female attraction. The combination of physical conditioning plus actual combat skills creates a true sense of personal confidence that women very much respond to. Unfortunately, the time spent training in this way can be fairly sizable so this is not always a reasonable option for married men to start up. Again – balance is everything.

Male Enhancement Products

They don't work. Save your money. Your dick is your dick.

Health and Semen Production

As I keep repeating, physical exercise is key to an awful lot of male sexuality. Along with that is diet, both to support the exercise and keep you growing and uninjured, but also to support the manufacture of sperm and semen. We men really do get fixated on the size of our penis, but the reality is that semen is more important. It's like how the gun doesn't kill you; it's the bullet that you really worry about. A man may well be a life support system for a penis, but then the penis is just a hose for semen to shoot from.

I'm sure you've all seen bazillion ads for male enhancement "MegaSurge3000" or whatever the names are of the latest cum creation product. They all promise to make you shoot cum like a horse getting a prostate massage. I can't promise any of that beyond getting generally a bit better ejaculations and better health, but I can say what I'm going to show you next is what I really use. It does in fact make me feel better and more virile. Plus it's all pretty easy stuff to have and cost effective.

Control What You Drink - Get the hell off soda. Soda is liquid Satan. I'm not going to harp on about it, because we both know you already know this. Food coloring + High Fructose Corn Syrup = diabetes on a layaway plan. The problem is replacing it and not just folding and going back to soda. Likewise, alcohol needs to be in moderation. I've got no issue with a few drinks a week, but obviously you know that you can't down a few drinks a day and not get hurt by it eventually.

My solution is simple. Crushed ice and juice cut 50/50 with seltzer water. It's fizzy like soda, it's still sweet enough, and overall decent juice is vastly better than soda. Seltzer is also very cheap and it makes the juice go a lot further. Try it.

Basic Supplementation - I'm 40 and the joints creak a bit these days. I find a joint complex that has Glucosamine, Chondroitin and MSM is the best for me. Without taking it I tend to hurt in the knees in particular and then I have to stop exercising, which blows.

Multivitamin. Look for one that says "Men". Importantly don't take them on an empty stomach as it can more easily cause you to feel nauseous that way.

Omega-3 Oil Supplement. This helps with testosterone as I said before, but I also find that without Omega-3 supplementation I get depressed, especially in winter. Plus it helps for joints and heart.

Protein Supplementation - I use a Whey Protein supplement mixed with milk. (I've always been confused as to why it's okay to drink milk from the female of another species, but it's not okay to ask for a drink from a female of your own species.) You don't need to find something with a muscle bound hulk on the front of it unless you want to pay 30% more for the privilege. I use a Whey Protein from my local grocery store for $10 a can and it lasts me about two weeks. Great for a quick breakfast or post workout snack. My only advice is to look around for something similar and make sure you get a decent list of amino acids on the back label. That's what is going to make muscle growth and repair more effective. I don't advise buying soy based supplements unless you are female, as it can spur female hormone production and is likely the opposite of what you want here. Soy is not for boys.

The purpose of the protein supplementation plus multivitamin and generally keeping your fluids up is all to support your body getting all the building blocks it needs to produce sperm and semen. If you have any kind of nutritional shortage of what semen is made from, obviously your semen production is going to be limited somehow. So while I offer no magic pill that makes you squirt gallons, you very likely will experience an increase in semen production if you take in a healthy diet.

Having a large volume of ejaculate is a very positive signal of sexual health and fitness. I'm sure even as a man, watching a porn video where the male does a tiny little trickle of cum at the end is disappointing. Having a large volume of semen is going to make you feel more sexually confident and make your own sexual pleasure more intense when you orgasm. For the women, a large volume ejaculate is a great sign that you are a good partner to have sex with.

Are You Poisoning Your Wife Against You with Bad Semen?

I just talked about the quantity of the semen, but now let's move on to semen quality. Before a woman opens her legs for a man, her Body Agenda is hard at work determining whether or not she should do that. You might get in once, but having crappy semen is really going to cut down on repeat visits. And trust me, if you're pumping pond scum semen into her vagina, her Body Agenda will know and shut down against you. If you are in bad physical shape and eat and drink crap, you can kill your own sex life dead by poisoning her against you.

The easy way to know if something is good for a man's basic health is to simply have a peek at whether or not it is going to be good for his sex drive and semen/sperm production. One very obvious "duh" is smoking. If you smoke you know you need to quit smoking because of lung issues, but smoking also impairs sperm count, sperm motility, reduces sperm lifespan, and may cause genetic changes that affect the baby. Some studies also find that men who smoke have lower sex drives and less frequent sex.

Marijuana use can result in significantly less seminal fluid, a lower total sperm count and abnormally-behaving sperm. Also in terms of flavor, much has been written about pineapple juice making semen taste better. Caffeine and nicotine will make it taste much worse as well; they are... *poisons.*

The entire purpose of sex for women is to get semen into their vaginas. It is not a very large leap of understanding that men should focus on creating good quality semen. I don't believe any research study is possible on female reaction to unhealthy or healthy semen deposited in the vagina (seriously who would sign up for that as a test subject?), but a woman's sense of smell is acute enough to pick out genetically compatible mates. Vaginas are exceptionally good at receiving medication as well. So all in all, vaginas are a highly sensitive instrument and they very likely make assessments of male semen that we as yet can hardly fathom.

SSRI Medications Can Kill Off Sex

One of the most important things in having a wonderful sex life with your wife is having a functional penis. It's important that blood can flow in, it can get hard, it can stay up, you can come to orgasm, and you can squirt a good amount of semen into her. It's also important that you have some amount of sexual desire, in that it's fairly normal that your first reaction on meeting an attractive woman is *"I'd like to tap that."* Ideally you should also be experiencing that *"I'd like to tap that"* reaction with your wife quite frequently. This is a normal response and nothing more than a display of positive male health.

As a man, there is a real sense that your entire body is a life support system for your penis. From a biological point of view, that's your prime directive; whip it out, plug it in and make more little humans. Plus it's fun. So your penis is like the canary in the coal mines. If it stops working or starts failing for any reason, you find out why, and stop doing whatever is causing it... *immediately.* If you want to loosely summarize my approach to male health, the rule is: *If it's good for your penis and semen, it's probably good for you as a whole.*

One thing that can clearly interfere with sexual functioning is SSRI anti-depressants. SSRIs have well known common and potentially severe sexual side effects and coming from the belief that "it's not a bug it's a feature," many of them are also now used to treat premature ejaculation. Essentially Mr. Trigger Happy goes on an SSRI, and becomes less trigger happy because the SSRI nerfs his desire, excitement and sexual sensation. Because the drugs can be *intended* to reduce sexual excitement, you should have a reasonable expectation that you will experience some diminished sexual ability. Some people they are effectively neutered by the SSRIs.

For more people the sexual side effects of these drugs are short term, but some unknown percentage of patients will develop Persistent SSRI Sexual Dysfunction (PSSD) and the sexual side effects can continue on six or more months *even after the drug is discontinued.* Does sexual function return sometime after that six month mark? I've got no clue, no one seems to have even asked the question, or done a study on it.

In writing this book I have had several friends reveal to me that their own marriages have been all but ended over the non-existent sex life and in some cases, childlessness resulting from SSRI induced sexual dysfunction. Considering how easy it can be to get a SSRI script, I can only imagine the agony of being scammed out of an active sex life forever over these meds if they were not truly needed.

These medications can also affect more than the sexual drive. Emotional changes can occur as well. From Dr. Helen Fisher's website...

"It is well known that these medications can cause emotional blunting and dysfunction in sexual desire, arousal, and performance in upward of three of every four patients. But we are writing now to add that we believe these side effects have even more serious consequences than currently appreciated, due to their impact on several other related neural mechanisms....

...Due to their impact on the sex drive, these medications can also jeopardize other brain/body mechanisms that govern mate assessment, mate choice, pair formation and partner attachment. For example, female orgasm has many functions. Among them, it aids sperm retention and enables women to discriminate between self-centered as

opposed to dedicated partners—partners who might be more likely to help them rear their young. Female orgasm may also help women choose men with better genes, as women are more orgasmic with men who are healthy and symmetrical, markers of good testosterone load. Female orgasm may also enhance feelings of attachment, because it stimulates the release of oxytocin and prolactin. As these drugs impair or eliminate female orgasm, they interfere with delicate biological mechanisms designed to aid mate choice and partner attachment. As these SSRI medications impair male orgasm, they also jeopardize a male's ability to court, inseminate, and attach to a potential partner."

Or in plain English... if you or your partner is on these pills you are chemically castrating yourselves to some degree. If you can't get an erection and frequently have sex with your wife, you are literally shouting at her Body Agenda that you are a poor choice of mate. One can only hope she doesn't listen. Likewise, if your wife is on these medications herself, they may play a very large part in her sexual disinterest in you.

Should either you or your partner be on an SSRI medication, do not stop taking them and please seek medical advice as to whether there are better alternatives for you to take. One of the more common non-SSRI anti-depressants is Wellbutrin and it is often used to either replace an SSRI or added to the medication regime where sexual dysfunction has occurred because of the SSRI.

Personal Hygiene

Some guys miss the whole personal hygiene thing. You have a body and that body can get a little stinky. That is a huge turn off to women. Work out, get all sweaty, then rinse it all off. Sounds stupid to have to mention it, but some of you just need to be told.

Particularly the washing up needs to happen "down there" if you have any hope of getting blowjobs. You may think you smell just fine, but in the words of Fat Bastard, *"Everybody loves their own aroma."* Her vagina doesn't have a sense of smell, so as long as you don't smell terrible all over she can lie back and think about shoe sales for the two minutes it takes for you to be done. (Yeah yeah, I know, you only need two minutes because you're *"so intense."*)

Her nose does have a sense of smell though and when it's nuzzling into your crotch she's going to get a heady whiff of whatever has been happening down there. Two-day-old underwear with urine stains aren't going to cut it. If you've spent half the day getting hard over the busty chick in the cubicle next to you and there's something approaching a pint of drying pre-cum swill in your pants, that's going to smell *bad.* Women have sensitive noses, far more sensitive than those of men. Faced with smells as strong as these, she's just going to uncontrollably gag as soon as something goes in her mouth. Wives hate that.

Even if the last person you had sex with was *her,* if that's not cleaned off with soap and water and is just left *au naturale,* within 24 hours your cock is going to smell like you have a fetish for bare-backing cheap zombie hookers. So please, wash your cock.

You Can Do This

Seriously you can do this; just go work out. You don't have to turn yourself into a Chippendale Dancer, just be a physically put together version of you. I know I'm not going to turn into an Olympic athlete, and probably neither will you. In fact, after a certain point getting bigger and bigger starts turning women off. Just work out regularly and get in shape.

She already married you, which means the deck is pretty well stacked in your favor. She's already shown she can be sexually responsive to you and she's probably just drawn to you by sense of smell because your genes and hers match up so well for making babies. More likely than not she's already set up, on a biological level that she has no rational control over, to be in love with you and attracted to you. You might be quite average physically, but you probably aren't average *to her perception* of you. At some point in her life she just looked at you and felt *"There's just something about him."* Exercise, general fitness and health just make that entire aspect of your relationship click.

But you can completely blow that natural advantage by being in bad shape. Half the time when she's ticked about something minor it's just a symptom of a lack of sexual interest in you. If you were a strapping version of you, do you really think the way you stacked the dishwasher is going to be quite the same drama as it would be if you were a pasty weakling version of you? No way in hell, not if her vagina gets a vote.

So get rid of some of the bad pounds and put on some of the good ones. Stand taller, live longer and come harder. Don't love being on the bottom because you don't have the upper body strength to be on top.

Chapter 8
"Instigate, Isolate and Escalate"

Pickup Artistry 101

The basic core for seducing women is to *"Instigate, Isolate and Escalate"* on them. There's no fixed order you have to do it in, but all sex comes from these three factors. I'm a firm believer that a married man needs at least an *idea* of how to still date and seduce a new woman or three as part of running The MAP. You shouldn't actually cheat on your wife as I've said before, but the possibility of other women being interested in you, coupled with an actual ability to seduce them, changes the marital dynamics quite drastically in your favor. It's very empowering.

And more to the point, you have to know how to seduce your wife! She's a girl too!

Instigation – You Make a Move

Instigation means to make something happen, so by advising you to instigate I'm saying you need to be active in your pursuit of women rather than passive. I've heard all the whining about how *"she doesn't initiate sex,"* but you will get far more sex by your instigation than by waiting for a woman to try something on you. Men tend to be the active pursuers seeking sex, while women tend to be the passive responders to sexual advances.

Instigation – Look Attractive

Looking attractive, a.k.a. Peacocking, is the purposeful wearing of highly attractive clothing, or clothing that displays a high social status and wealth. Essentially this is nothing more than a giant display of sexual availability and openness for interaction with the opposite sex.

If you wear clothing of sufficient value women will approach you and start conversations with you. If you wear crappy clothes, women will purposely avoid you.

The clothing you wear will: attract women, repel them, or simply be neutral to them. You don't have to crazily out-dress everyone around you and walk around like you're ready for the prom; you just have to dress better than all the other men in your social circle. All the women in your social circle will be acutely aware of the best dressed man they know.

The key here is remaining socially appropriate to your environment – dressing up in a Halloween pimp costume is pretty eye catching and the ladies *will talk*, but perhaps it's not the best thing to wear to the little league games you coach. So be socially appropriate, but also the best possible version of what is socially appropriate and tailoring the look to your personality and style.

Try and think of the whole package here: hair, teeth, skin, shoes, accessories, smell and clothes. Be the complete package. Don't start trying to look like a manscaped metrosexual; going in that direction starts looking increasingly like you are seeking to attract men. You can stay rugged if you like, just make sure that it is a calculated rugged.

Don't underestimate the power of one and just one focal item on your outfit. That can be a special hat, belt buckle, ring or necklace. One visually interesting item will draw the eye and can act as a conversation piece. If a woman is interested in you, she will often start a conversation with you about that piece.

And quite obviously all this purposeful effort at looking attractive goes much easier and better if you are becoming a fitter and leaner-looking clothes horse. I'd suggest not buying a whole raft of new clothes on day 1 of The MAP and then having to throw them all out on day 120 because you're thirty pounds lighter. The move where you unveil a whole new wardrobe is often the announcement that your Sex Rank is now up a point. *"Look honey, I'm not a 7 anymore I'm an 8. (Now let's go to bed.)"*

Instigation – Be Playfully Mean

The key to verbal interaction is keeping your banter light-hearted and playful, but also pushing the limits to see what you can get away with as well. You should be trying to playfully instigate her into engaging in further interaction with you.

Light teasing works very well. Don't be insulting or rude, but lightly tease her. This shows a lack of social fear and high confidence that women find attractive.

Look back over your early life at all the times when the naughty boys were a little bit mean to the girls and the girls just lapped it up, making a huge fuss over the boys that did that to them. If the girls were all in bikinis sunbathing, you can bet that the guy who sprayed them with a hose got a verbal telling off – but then was the one they all wanted to get with. Remember how girls would squeal at the boy chasing them with a spider?

If you ever push it just a little too far, you can always apologize and say *"I'm so sorry I did that, but there is a good explanation why I did that.... I'm an asshole."* Then you give a big naughty boy grin.

Instigation – Display High Value

It's also important to not allow yourself to be overly affected by the women you are talking to. Simply because you are talking to an attractive woman doesn't mean you should hang around her forever. It's possible to make greater progress with her by actually walking away from her than hanging around her. It's a Display of Low Value to hang around endlessly, so by walking away to do something else you can display that you are essentially used to attractive women.

Many husbands in love with their wives endlessly hang around them and unwittingly can display low value to them. It's best to be in motion somehow. By all means plant a kiss on her, but don't stick around too long after that, go do something. If she happens to follow you after you attempt to progress to your next task, take that as an excellent indicator of her interest in you and you can escalate the flirting further.

Isolation – Get Her Alone

Remember from the Body Agenda chapter the female sexual strategy of concealed ovulation? What that means is that women really do get horny and turned on, but they also don't usually like to broadcast to the world that they are horny and turned on. Almost all sex happens behind closed doors with just two people. If a woman is going to allow herself to become more intimate or sexual with you, you need to get her alone.

In a marriage this should of course be pretty easy; you just go to bed together at the end of the day. But for many wives that's not quite enough romance and emotional intimacy built up, so you do need to focus on getting her away from the kids and the rest of the family once in a while to rebuild the intimacy along the way.

Whether that's a date night, meeting for breakfast somewhere, visiting her at work for lunch every so often, or taking a half day off work to just have sex all afternoon, it doesn't really matter. The key is to isolate her from the herd and from her normal routine.

Isolation – Move to a Second Location

In dating the isolation play is pretty simple; you simply ask to relocate her and you to a second location away from her friends or other people. It doesn't have to be anywhere overtly sexual, just a second location. It could be another club, another restaurant, a place for coffee, a music store, your house or anywhere other than a gas station or emergency room.

Ideally you can frame the request to move to a second location as something that you are doing with or without her and offer her the chance to come along. *"Listen, I'm having a great time here, but I'm also getting really hungry. I know this great place to get steak down the road, want to come?"* Once you move your date to a second location, she can safely deny to her friends that she did anything with you. This allows her to be more openly sexual with you, because if no one else was there to see her do something, no one can question her alibi that nothing happened!

Even more isolated is actually being truly alone with you. A private date in a public restaurant doesn't count as truly alone, but being in your apartment with only you would count. Being totally alone with you puts her into a vulnerable position in relation to you; should you become aggressive towards her, she probably couldn't stop you. The female Body Agenda knows that being alone with a male may result in her sexual submission to him regardless of her consent, so she tends to avoid being alone with any male she does not want to give consent to. Males fear an aggressive male and have Approach Anxiety; females fear an aggressive male and have Isolation Anxiety. *(Do not misunderstand any of this as a positive spin on rape. Rape is beyond awful.)*

Coming at it from a sinister viewpoint, this principle of moving to a "second location" is exactly the same thing that serial killers use to murder their victims. No one gets sadistically killed in a supermarket parking lot, but if you get carjacked there and forced to drive to a second location, very bad things can happen once you get there. You'd usually be vastly better off crashing the car into a telephone pole than arriving at the second location "safely." The principle of moving to a second location is very clear – do *not* cooperate with going to a second location, unless you want what could happen there. Women will instinctively avoid being alone with men they don't want sex with. The word they will use to describe the situation of being alone with a man they don't want sex with is "creepy."

Simply being alone with you is telegraphing her very probable willingness to start progressing towards something sexual happening with you. She's not going to instantly throw off her clothes, but it's a very good indicator of her interest in you. Also something to watch for is women running an isolation play *on you*. Sometimes it is so subtle that you can completely miss it. A simple *"Would you like to go for a walk?"* at a party is a classic. What she probably means is *"Would you like to go somewhere and talk intimately/kiss/ make out?"*

There is an exception to this rule. She will be alone with males that have already proved to be sexual failures – by which I mean her

Orbiters – men who have agreed to "Let's just be friends." She sees those men as safely neutered because they can't even *talk* like they are a sexual threat, let alone actually do something. Furthermore, when you do have a woman alone with you and you fail to make a move on her, she will regard that as an acute sexual failure on your part. You may never get another opportunity with her again.

Isolation – Leverage Her Isolation Anxiety with Surprise

Moving to a second location works to make alone time more exciting to her, but that can be made even more exciting by adding the element of surprise and triggering momentary Isolation Anxiety. You might have gone somewhere together to do something, but the *surprise* little side trip on the way back, where you just turn the wheel of the car and take her somewhere, is exciting. It works because it's like a playful and safe version of her getting carjacked and taken somewhere against her will.

Even though your wife is with you and trusts you, she will experience a few seconds of Isolation Anxiety as you start taking her somewhere unexpected without asking. This triggers her Body Agenda to make an instant decision about either risking a physical fight with you that is likely hopeless or submitting to your intentions without resistance. Usually her Body Agenda takes the safe option and votes for submission, which frames you as dominant. Having created a dominant moment, that sparks a dopamine reaction in her and she will feel greater attraction to you and a little flush of excitement.

If you went to the mall to do Christmas shopping together, it's the *unannounced* detour on the way back to the secret pastry and coffee shop that engages her with you. Of course she'll just think it's romantic, exciting and non-boring, but that's just the dopamine doing its job.

Another way of doing this is starting at home and simply telling her to get in the car with you in ten minutes. Then just drive her to dinner out somewhere random. Don't tell her where you are driving to; just arrive. She might complain loudly the first couple of times, but that just means she's emotionally engaged with you.

Isolation – Text Her

She can't answer a phone call from you without broadcasting to nearby people that she is talking to you. So if you say anything cocky, funny and a little racy, she can't respond to it and her protection shields come up. But texting is done in secret apart from the incoming text sound. Even so, most women can keep a straight face as they text back the color of their underwear and/or how much they liked your semen on their breasts the night before. So texting is a natural isolation play.

Isolation – Keep Her Secrets

If you get a reputation of talking about who you have had sex with, you damage your ability to isolate. If every woman knows that having sex with you is going to be broadcast to her social group, she will likely never expose herself to sex with you unless you are of such astoundingly high sexual value that her value increases for having been chosen by you.

It's fine to broadcast that you are good with women and that they go home happy and satisfied, you should just refuse to name names.

Escalate – Touch Her

Someone you want to have sex with is going to be someone you touch a good deal. Obviously you aren't going to grab her boobs in public on a first date, but you are going to escalate the level of physical touch as quickly as you can without pissing her off.

Start with touches on her hands and arms, just incidental as you are talking to her. Hands on her shoulders and back are usually fine after that too. Going for things like arms around her waist, hand holding and kissing usually require some sort of isolation before she is agreeable to it. The dance floor is a twilight zone where such rules are suspended and nearly anything goes.

Once isolated from people she knows, you can go for the more intimate moves like the hand holding and so on. Once in private you can start going for boobs and trying to get clothes off her. Framing it all as your assumption that everything is coming off eventually anyway works best. Kiss and grope and break and do a little something else and back to kiss and grope and a little gentle tug on the clothing to be removed. *"Your blouse is in the way."*

Generally, you are better off trying to go a little too fast than a little too slow with physical escalation. She may get a little pissed off at you, but that is better than her being bored with you. Being pissed off just means she is emotionally engaged with you, which is generally a direct line to her vagina. If she does say stop though, you do back it up a bit.

Physical touch is vital to seduction because just touching a woman causes her body to release oxytocin, which causes her to feel more socially bonded to you and trust you. Going straight for the sex before enough touching makes most women resist you, but a good amount of touch can make her feel warm and fuzzy about you, so that when you ask for sex she complies, or even asks for it herself.

Escalate – Kiss Her

"Why don't we just kiss and find out how good this chemistry between us is?"

Kissing is one of the most potent steps in seduction. It creates gobs of intimacy, and male saliva actually contains testosterone that the woman absorbs, making her feel more sexually interested. This is why you hated kissing your aunts when you were little.

If you're married, you should make the time every single day to have an extended kiss with your wife. Kissing for at least ten seconds will cause an entire neurological and hormonal cascade inside not only her, but also you, creating sexual interest and bonding to each other. It can't be a few short pecks on the lips; I'm talking a proper kiss.

Escalate – Always Be Closing

Let's be serious here...you want to have sex with her, so you should be focused on that as an end goal. The goal is not a phone number, a date, a movie, a kiss, a marriage. The goal is her legs apart and crying out your name as you cum into her. So if that is the goal, it's okay to state that goal as an intention to her along the way. Women cannot stand a guy that flakes on them at the last minute and can't for whatever reason have sex with them.

You can proceed to that end point fairly quickly on a verbal level, touch on it and then withdraw to a safer topic or activity. That way she doesn't really have time to put up defensive shields to ward you off because you have already withdrawn from putting pressure on her for sex. But the thought of sex with you is still on her mind. *"You look so good in those shoes. Okay I admit it, I'm interested in sex with you, but I've really got to concentrate on this assignment right now. So if you could just walk yourself away from me about five feet I could get some work done."*

Escalate – Ignore Anything That Doesn't Help You Close

Frequently women will make little verbal defenses along the way as to why they can't or shouldn't have sex with you. For the most part the best plan is to simply ignore or deflect these defenses. Frequently these are nothing more than half-hearted attempts to derail your seduction. All women have a slutty aspect to their nature and usually actively want to be seduced. By focusing on her half-hearted complaints, you can halt progress towards the bedroom.

The classic dating defense line is *"I have a boyfriend."* Of course having a boyfriend is exactly the reason she is currently at the club without him at midnight, half naked, drink in one hand and grinding her ass into your crotch. So you can just ignore the boyfriend. Correct response, *"I don't care."*

The key here is to pay careful attention not so much to what she is *saying*, but to what she is *doing*. If she is saying *"We really shouldn't do this,"* but she is already topless and pulling her panties off, then you saying *"You're right, we shouldn't"* isn't really what she wants to hear. Correct response, *"I don't care."* If, on the other hand, there is clothing going back on or she is pushing you off her, that's a good sign of not wanting sex from you.

The thing to watch for is her giving a reason not to have sex, but not actually saying *"No." "I have to get up early in the morning,"* isn't a *"No."* The word *"No"* is a fairly clear directive and trying to proceed to sex after a *"No"* isn't good at all. Just don't do it.

Wives can pull out all sorts of last minute nonsense on husbands as well. It's late, I am tired, the children are awake, I have a headache, it's a Tuesday, the birds are flying south for the winter and on and on and on. Wives are a little different from a date in this area in that they are always around you and simply being in the same bed with you isn't an automatic signal indicating interest in sex. Often a wife giving a reason not to have sex is in fact saying a clear *"No."* She just doesn't want to feel like she had to say no to you, so she says she is tired or headachy instead. All that really means is that she doesn't want sex with you tonight. The long term solution is to increase your Sex Rank rather than winning an individual night's sex.

Escalate – Plan the Logistics of the Seduction

If you're going on a date and want sex with her, having no practical plan as to where you can have sex and how you will get there will always end up with you masturbating. If the idea is you meet at a club and then go back to your place, you need to have a plan as to how you will be transported back home. If you rode to the club on the train and the last train out is at 11:05pm, you are out of luck if you can't get her on the train with you at 11:05pm. You can call for a cab or something, but then you need to make sure you have cash on you for the cab. If you're down to $10 in your pocket, then you are out of luck as well.

If you get back to your apartment and the entire place looks like a large dinosaur had an unfortunate bowel movement in it, she's going to feel all the blood in her vagina move directly up into her brain. No sex for you.

Having a couple of set planned first few dates that you run on new women will make you more confident and relaxed on the dates. The first might be a simple meet for coffee and feel each other out date. The second might be a dinner date. The third date might be meeting at your place for dinner and then out to a movie date. The fourth date is desserts and porn night. Whatever your dating plan is, you can get better and better at it if you practice them as routines. If you're a real player you can run multiple women at once by running the dates carefully and planning ahead. Coffee with Tina at 4pm, dinner with Catherine at 6pm, and Helen for desserts and porn at 9pm. What could go wrong?

Likewise with a wife the same sort of thing still applies. Wives detest husbands who can't come up with a simple plan for an evening out once in a while. Most of them will assume that you as the male half of the couple will take the lead in this sort of thing. Don't take her to the same restaurant over and over for a night out. Yeah I know, *"But we love it here."* Just because she said she liked the first time she went in doesn't mean it does anything for her nine years later. Mix it up on her. Don't even tell her where you are taking her sometimes. A simple *"Okay time for dinner, be in the car in 15 minutes,"* will suffice.

Escalate – Plan the Sex

In heading to the bedroom you should have a rough plan as to how the sex is going to play out. Most women find that a passive,*"So what do you want to do?"* a huge turn off. Usually what they want to happen is for you to sweep them away in your torrid passion for them. You asking for permission and guidance is like switching her vagina off.

The way it works best is to simply announce some intentions or directives and see if she agrees with them. Simple directives like *"Get on top of me,"* *"Suck me,"* *"On your back and legs apart,"* or *"When you want me to cum inside you, say it,"* work very well. Stated intentions also work well too, *"I'm hot for you, so I want to just cum inside you right away. After that I'll work you over good as long as you want to orgasm. Then I'll have another one for myself. I think it will be more relaxed that way."*

Wives in particular can respond better to stating plans for a specific sex act, rather than an all-purpose request for sex. An all purpose request for sex could be anything and could take ages, but asking for a blowjob means a blowjob and takes five minutes of her time.

Also stating sexual intentions to a wife hours before bedtime can frame the bedtime routine better. *"I'm really horny today baby, tonight I need you,"* can get a *"Yes"* at 2pm and sex that night, whereas the exact same line delivered at bedtime can get a *"No."*

If you announce a plan and she asks for a different sex act that doesn't bother you, then by all means go ahead and do it. It's not meant to be set in stone. If she's horny for something then do it and make her happy and sexually satisfied. That way she'll be more likely to want to come back for more in the future.

Summary

So while *"Instigate, Isolate and Escalate"* is the basis for seducing a new woman, I also think you should run this on your wife as well. Note that this is not something that you do when you want sex; this is something that you do all the time. This sort of attitude and approach to women is a skill set that requires constant practice until it becomes second nature to you. The idea is that you constantly display sexual interest and receptivity and just present yourself as a sexy, fun guy to be with.

You may not be trying to get sex right this minute, but simply being who you are will mean that someone will respond to you sexually eventually. Once your wife senses you could pull a new woman without too much difficulty, her sexual interest in you will very likely take a large step upwards. It's attractive in and of itself, but also because it threatens losing you to another woman... or her best friend.

Chapter 9
Captain and First Officer

Women Sexually Respond to Dominant Men

Now I know that saying *"women sexually respond to dominant men,"* is so radical and politically incorrect, that many of you reading will struggle with it as a thought. So let's come at that from a slightly different angle first and say...

Men are taller than women.

If I just write *"men are taller than women"* and leave it at that, some feminist reader is going to want to hunt down my email address and point out that I am small-minded and offensive for saying so. Clearly there are some very tall women and simply stating that *"men are taller than women"* is sexist. My angry reader simply couldn't imagine living with such a bigot as myself, who believes that men are taller than women. After all, she is quite tall herself and knows a man that is of average height, who she is taller than. Where do I get such wrong ideas from?

Then should I happen to mention that I am quite tall and my wife Jennifer quite short... well then my angry reader could wonder if Jennifer is okay being trapped in a marriage with my offensive tallness. Frankly, it seems like I may be making her short on purpose. I might be despicable.

So anyway... the truth is just as we all know. There are some taller men and some shorter men, plus some taller women and some shorter women. There are two bell curves of height, one for men and one for women, and the male bell curve is clearly higher than the female one.

So another statement...

Women are attracted to taller men, especially to men taller than themselves.

This is again quite true. It's a fairly rare couple where the wife is taller than the husband. The overwhelming majority of couples have a taller husband than wife, far more so than random chance would suggest.

Circling back around to the more pointed statement...

Men are more naturally dominant than women in personal relationships.

If I just write *"men are naturally more dominant than women"* and leave it at that, some feminist reader is going to want to hunt down my email address and point out that I am small minded and offensive for saying so. Clearly there are some very dominant women and simply stating that *"men are more dominant than women"* is sexist. My angry reader simply couldn't imagine living with such a bigot as myself who believes that men are more dominant than women. After all, she is quite dominant herself and knows a man that is of moderate dominance that she is more dominant than. Where do I get such wrong ideas from?

Then should I happen to mention that I am quite dominant and my wife Jennifer quite submissive... well then my angry reader could wonder if Jennifer is okay being trapped in a marriage with my offensive dominance. Frankly, it seems like I may be making her submissive on purpose. I might be despicable.

So anyway... the truth is just as we all know. There are some dominant men and some submissive men, plus some dominant women and some submissive women. There are two bell curves of dominance and submission - one for men and one for women, but the male bell curve is clearly closer to the dominant end of the scale and the female one closer to the submissive.

So another statement...

Women are sexually attracted to dominant men, especially to men more dominant than themselves.

Keen observation of women's sexual attraction shows they clearly respond to those men who present themselves more forcefully and have a higher social status. Women like socially dominant men. Women are attracted to the professor and not the junior lecturer. Women are attracted to the doctor and not the lab tech. Women are attracted to the quarterback and not the kicker. Women are attracted to the CEO and not the pizza delivery guy. Women are attracted to the leading man and not the comic relief. I'm not saying that it's right or wrong that women react like this, just that they do.

Dominance and submission are not outlandish games that only happen in sex clubs with leather clad people whipping other scantily leather clad people. Dominance and submission are elements in every single social interaction. A bus driver for example is a low status job, but on their own bus the bus driver is in charge and is socially dominant in that arena. A doctor may give a nurse an order and the nurse is submissive to the doctor, but then the same nurse can clearly be dominant over their nurse's aides. Outside of work the same doctor can give the same nurse a directive and be laughed at for trying. A teacher is hopefully dominant over their classroom and the children behave submissively to the teacher's instruction. Outside of the school the teacher likely has minimal dominance over the same children. Hopefully at home the same children are submissive to their parents.

As clarification – if you read my acknowledgments page carefully, I said I was a nurse. So what happens when I as a male nurse come in contact with a female doctor and she gives me an order? The answer is pretty simple – I go do it. It's not a male/female thing; it's a social hierarchy thing.

If you are reading into the word "dominant" a mandate for violence or cruelty to someone submissive to you, then you are very purposefully misunderstanding my intent. Nor am I saying that all women should be in submission to all men, frankly there's no way to even organize that effectively even if I did think that was a good idea. I'm also not saying that men are superior to women, or that women are incapable of leadership.

To be sure, many women have suffered violence or cruelty and now respond highly negatively to men who act with a normal male zest towards a woman. Misunderstanding male social dominance as "thugs up, bitches down" leads to bad endgames for all concerned.

But for the last several decades, the overall impression given of men is that we are some kind of badly designed female. It's like men are Humans 1.0 and women are Humans 2.0. Like all that testosterone surging through our veins is, well.... *wrong.*

All I'm saying is that for most men, tending toward a dominant social interaction with a woman is a natural state of affairs and that most women sexually respond to men that are dominant. In a marriage, having the husband take on a leadership role tends to keep the wife sexually interested in him. This works for exactly the same reasons as women are more likely to have an affair with their boss at work, rather than with some guy they supervise.

Unlearning that Being Male and Dominant is Evil

This pattern of male dominance and female submission has a basis in Body Agenda because the female Body Agenda literally thinks *"if he can't handle me, he can't actually protect me from anything"*. Often a woman will tear her husband apart over quite minor things, seeking a reaction to correct her. If she doesn't get that correction she can become increasingly agitated with her man and progressively more extreme in efforts to force that reaction. The majority of drama queens are just seeking the king to finally show up and tell her to knock it off.

For myself I'm not a particularly aggressive Alpha Male type guy by nature. I do by nature totally rock on the Beta Male goodies. Much of the Alpha stuff I've learned along the way over the last decade and in the last few years in particular. One of the things I was very careful to do when Jennifer and I married was to strive for equality between us, and I was quite careful to not be domineering over her.

The result of those good intentions was that often we'd grind to a halt in a deadlock of mutual submission. *"What do you want to do?" "I don't know, anything is fine. What do you want to do?"* Just repeat that conversational cycle for about ten years and you get the picture. I've often wondered in the last couple of years how someone more forceful didn't just poach her from me early on. Clever tactics like being assertive toward her and doing something like asking her out on a well planned date would have had an appeal to her. Sometimes it's better to be lucky than good I guess.

About five years ago, I started getting grumpier with some of our mutual submission deadlocks and just started saying what I wanted. Jennifer lapped it up. This was initially very confusing as I thought and felt that acting like this was in fact offensive. So I expected a response of anger and annoyance at my being bossy, but to my surprise, it never came.

Since then, I've reprogrammed myself a great deal away from the idea that everything has to be perfectly equal and fair. I've come to realize that being submissive is something she actually gains an active enjoyment from. Some of that is social submission; some of it is sexual submission. It's only in the last year or two that I've found myself actively enjoying being dominant. I've given orders on and off for much longer, but felt quite weird about it at first, then felt neutral, but now can sometimes get physically turned on simply by requesting sexual submission.

Some of this is exceptionally simply everyday stuff. If we have four things that have to get done, Jennifer is great at defining the tasks, but if I step in and say, *"Well let's both go and do A and B together because they are close together, then you go do C and I'll double back to here and do D,"* she positively beams simply because I made the decision and set direction. Likewise, if she wants to go out to dinner, if I decide the place it makes her happy.

We often do grocery shopping together. After one of our recent trips, when we came out of the store and I said I wanted coffee, I got an *"Oh that sounds good"* and off we went. We went through McDonald's and got coffee and had a Filet-of-Fish each. I get a *"this was a fabulous idea"* from her. It sounds too easy – a ten minute, five dollar detour on the way home, but she's made happy by this.

At first all this confused me, but it was hard to argue with the obvious results. All I can say is that we did not cover this sort of positive female reaction in my Sociology of the Family course in college. Oh yeah, did I mention I have a degree in being non-dominant towards women? True story.

The Captain and First Officer Model

Jennifer is certainly not mindless. She's not sitting at my feet as I write with a leash and a collar. She doesn't just sit around and wait for direction. She's actually one of the most competent people I know. I'm not going to spell out what she does for work, but I can assure you she is extremely talented and a vital resource for her company. She's a smart lady.

I've come to understand our personal relationship as being a Captain and First Officer relationship. And yes I first thought of this as a Star Trek metaphor (I don't dress up for conventions, I just like the shows) though it's basically standard for commercial airliners and military chain of command. The Wikipedia summary of a First Officer is short and perfect...

"In commercial aviation, the first officer is the second pilot (sometimes referred to as the "co-pilot") of an aircraft. The first officer is second-in-command of the aircraft, to the captain who is the legal commander. In the event of incapacitation of the captain, the first officer will assume command of the aircraft.

Control of the aircraft is normally shared equally between the first officer and the captain, with one pilot normally designated the "Pilot Flying" (PF) and the other the "Pilot Not Flying" (PNF), or "Pilot Monitoring" (PM), for each flight. Even when the first officer is the flying pilot, however, the captain remains ultimately responsible for the aircraft, its passengers, and the crew. In typical day-to-day operations, the essential job tasks remain fairly equal."

I've always liked the dynamic on the Star Trek series between Captains and First Officers. It's quite apparent that the First Officer is always competent and skilled, and if anything happens to the Captain, they step into the role of being in command immediately. The Captains always listen because sometimes the First Officer has a better idea than their own. Picard endlessly seeking input from Riker, saying *"Options Number One?"* springs to mind.

Sometimes the First Officer actually overrules the Captain in a crisis and gives the crew an order. The Captain usually just trusts that the First Officer isn't doing this to make trouble and runs with it. But at the end of the day, the Captain is the Captain and the leadership comes from them and final responsibility for the ship lies with them. If it all goes to hell the Captain is last off the ship, usually with the dramatic effect of having to stay behind and push the red button *on yet one more* auto-destruct system that has a malfunction. (I don't think those things are safe.)

Wives want to be the First Officer

My realization is that most wives want the First Officer job. Not Crewman Third Class, but not Captain either. They want to have a say and be heard, they want to be trusted, they don't want to be micro managed on decisions they are capable of making themselves, they can happily step it up into *"having the bridge"* when their husbands aren't available. They just would rather be the second in command and follow someone else's leadership and general direction.

The challenge for the husband is to not go into marriage as a Redshirt waiting for the deathblow. The old joke being if Kirk, Spock and McCoy beam down to an alien planet with an unknown actor in a red Starfleet uniform, the guy in the red shirt is going to be killed in the first act. If that's what you expect from marriage, that's what you'll get.

Husbands shouldn't go into marriage and attempt to simply be a member of the crew. If the husband is lazy and declines to fulfill the Captain position, the wife will likely try and assume a First Officer role. But if she takes the First Officer role with an endlessly off duty Captain, that will make her the de facto Captain. That's going to piss her off. He can even do everything she wants and asks him to do, but by submitting to her perfectly, that can actually anger and disappoint her more and more. Most men find this extremely confusing.

Being the Captain Means Being More Responsible

With Jennifer and myself, we each have different areas that we specialize in and basically have complete control over. Sometimes I *"have the bridge"* and sometimes she does. We do talk together about the big decisions before us, but looking back over our marriage I can see that the majority of our direction and big decisions have ultimately been mine with Jennifer supporting me. I've not always been right. Sometimes I've been quite badly wrong. But even when I've been wrong, badly wrong, Jennifer somehow manages to stay supportive. I don't quite understand how she does that. I've come to be awed by that support. I don't fully understand it, but I am honored that it is there.

And like Uncle Ben says in "Spiderman", *"With great power, comes great responsibility."* As the husband, I believe I have a greater responsibility for the safety and well being of my wife and children than my wife has. Simply being in charge doesn't mean you get to have what you want all day every day at home. I very frequently try and make sure Jennifer gets what she wants and needs for herself.

So... Captain and First Officer. That's my theory for male dominance and female submission in marriage. Maybe not in yours, but in ours it seems to really work for both of us. There are hardly any of those mutual submission battles anymore. I just decide to do what I want more often, and I know what she likes quite well and a good portion of the time I decide we do that. Upon the rare occasions she complains, I might reach for the playful verbal nuke... *"Captains prerogative Number One."*

One thing to watch for is other women picking up on your dominant sexual vibe. It does not hurt at all to think of your wife as your Number One. After all, that is ultimately what she is to you.

How do you Know if Your Wife is Submissive?

You start asking reasonable requests of her and say thank you when she does them. If she does them and looks generally happier after the tasks, she's probably got a submissive streak in her. The key phrase there was *"reasonable requests."* You need to stop thinking of submissive as "groveling female." It's not. If she likes playing the help and support role... she's probably submissive.

If she does nice stuff for you without asking, she's probably submissive. Especially if she's trying to predict something you will need before you realize you need it, and just does it for you. If she offers to be constantly sexually available to you and she reads romance novels of any kind, it's a fair bet she's submissive as well.

You can also try some small moments of dominance on her and watch her reactions to it. *"We're going to the movies/dinner/out/whatever"* and just assume it's all going to happen. If she's acting more interested and attentive to you because of your dominant display, she's probably submissive. You don't have to turn into the boss of everything overnight and micromanaging anyone is tediously annoying to both parties. Just start setting the tone once in a while and watch and see how she reacts.

Where Do I Find a Submissive Wife?

I get asked this a lot... so here's the answer.

You're missing the point just a little. A very large number of women tend to desire an element of submission to their male sexual partner. So submissive women don't really hang out anywhere in particular, they're basically everywhere. If you want a rough guide, probably 4 out of every 5 women are going to enjoy submitting to the *right* guy.

The way you find your particular sweetheart is not by seeking a submissive woman. It's by being an assertive Alpha, and creating attraction that draws that sort of woman to you. Actually walking around asking women if they are submissive is going to creep 99% of women out on the spot. You have to carefully frame it as you *"like to make things happen"* or something like that. *"I'm not interested in being a bully, but I like to take the lead."*

Submission is not something you can take from a woman. It's something they give to you. So become the sort of man who entices them to give it. A submissive wife isn't a doormat or a bimbo. Well they can be I guess, just personally I'd tire of them very quickly. You should be hunting for First Officer material. Upon occasion you are really going to want her to be able to step up for you and your family.

Alpha Male of the Group

It's also important to understand that being a husband usually comes with a dual role of fatherhood. The close relative of the Alpha Male traits is being the Alpha Male of the Group (AMOG). In other words, leadership of your wife has also got to be leadership of the children as well. If a kid is running the show you aren't the AMOG, they are...which is really, really bad on so many levels.

If the kids are running around uncontrolled, you're screwing the whole thing up and look increasingly Beta at best and Omega at worst. You're responsible for the raising of the kids, *more responsible for them than your wife is.* As I've said before, you're the Captain and she's the First Officer. Oh sure, the mom can step up and kick ass and take names if need be, but for the really nasty stuff she feels like G.I. Jane when she'd probably rather be Barbie. Ideally a Barbie hooking up with a G.I. Joe. (We all knew Ken was nervous about G.I. Joe right?)

Family Discipline is Self-Discipline

You must maintain discipline over your children. Discipline sounds like a harsh word, but often it really isn't in practice as it's mostly just maintaining your own self control and not letting the situation get out of hand. You explain clearly things like:

"These are the limits, and these are the consequences of the limits being broken. This is me not enabling you to break the limits."

"I can easily not drive you in the car all day long."

"You made a huge scene when we left there, so I'm not taking you back for a week."

"You are screaming at me, so this conversation stops until you can express yourself appropriately."

"You are having a tantrum in public, so we are leaving public now. Yes I understand that we left a shopping cart full of food behind, we can make cheese sandwiches at home."

"Thank you for being good, let's get ice cream. You were both well behaved, thank you."

"There is no "X" until "Y" is completed."

When you discipline one kid, you actually discipline them all. If kid #1 gets punished for doing something, kid #2 is going to expect to be punished for it too. If kid #2 does it and gets away with it, kid #1 is going to be livid. The kids are a social unit and they expect discipline for one of them to apply to all of them, and if you don't, the bad behavior will intensify until you learn to. Likewise when you discipline your kids, you're in a sense disciplining your wife as well, and vice versa: *This is how we treat each other in this family. I'm not going to let anyone act badly in this family.*

Perhaps that explains the relative lack of testing behavior (we will come to this hot issue in an upcoming chapter) that Jennifer directs at me compared to the way most husbands express it. I've proved that I can handle bad behavior from the kids, not flinch and calmly and methodically address it. So getting bad behavior from Jennifer would net her the same result, so it's just easier being nice to each other. Though to be quite fair, Jennifer is the sweetest person I know and acting out isn't really an issue anyway – that's part of why I married her. It's actually hard imagining her being bratty to be honest.

Positive touch, kind words, humor, playfulness, and a firm "No" are all tools in the discipline tool chest as well. Playfully grabbing your wife and kissing her in front of the kids, or cuddling on the couch together, might make the kids groan in mock horror, but they do find it enormously comforting. *Mom and Dad love each other, which means they love me too.* Together you can set a tone for the whole family's interactions together.

But mostly the person you're disciplining is *you.*

Controlling the Kids

Back in the day we used a technique of letting our girls choose what they wanted to do. That sounds very permissive, except for the fact that we completely defined the choices offered to them. Seeing both offered options were acceptable to us, it didn't matter what they choose to do. A little kid isn't going to be aware of the manipulation going on and will feel a sense of empowerment from making the choice.

Sometimes the options offered were a choice between two good things; a walk in the mall and a pretzel… or… go to the park and get an ice cream.

Other times the options were far more behavioral; be mad and stay home… or… be a good girl and go to the park.

See how that works? I'm just not taking a misbehaving child into public. If she wanted to be a cranky shit weasel, we'd do that at home thanks very much. You'd be surprised how even a two-year-old can turn around a tantrum if they are missing out on swings and ice cream from the ice cream truck. I swear the ice cream truck had GPS tagged my kids as he never failed to show up when we were at the park.

We also purposely and somewhat randomly rewarded good behavior. *"You know what? You girls have been being so good, LET'S GO THROUGH THE CAR WASH!"*… They don't fall for that one anymore which is a real pity. Simple praise works wonders. *"Thank you girls for being good back there, I'm very proud of you."*

Upon a handful of occasions they really did have a complete public melt down. Daughter #1 had a tantrum in the supermarket and was removed by me to the car where we did *not* listen to the radio. Jennifer and daughter #2 finished the shopping. Daughter #1 had a second outburst a month later in the supermarket and we repeated the removal process. Daughter #2 went berserk in California Pizza Kitchen and I removed her from the restaurant as she sobbed openly on my chest. Outside the restaurant she was given a final choice to behave or sit in the car while Jennifer and Daughter #1 ate pizza. She pulled it together and we all had a pleasant meal.

About two-and-a-half years later Daughter #1 started acting out in Old Navy... and it's off to the car we go... she had this odd look of remembrance as off we went. *"No radio huh, dad."* Nope, no radio. She still hates Old Navy to this day.

There was also the night where we broke Daughter #1 of her demands to be entertained in the middle of the night when she was about one-and-a-half. She'd stand up in her crib and flip the light on and call us. I kid you not. The night we broke her of this, I checked on her, ensured she was in good health et al, and then left her in the crib No entertainment. That cued up about 90 minutes of her wailing and flipping the light on and off and generally screaming in outrage as Jennifer wept in my arms. Next night she slept right through. At least I think she did, I'm a heavy sleeper. But I slept through and that's all that really counts anyway. So job well done.

As I said earlier, when you discipline one kid, you're actually disciplining all of them. Daughter #1 got yanked from the store three times, daughter #2 tried it once and decided the rules also applied to her and toed the line from then on. The message was clear, bad behavior was not going to be tolerated in our family. In all five critical behavioral incidents, I was the parent that really laid down the intervention. There is very little that gets a wife wetter than watching her husband correctly discipline their children.

Act, Don't React

There's usually minimal need for raised voices and certainly no need for hitting in a family. Staying calm and clear and *acting* in the moments of crisis and family drama, rather than *reacting*, is a key skill to learn. This takes a long time for anyone to learn and I don't believe I'm perfect at it either. Sometimes you just have to say that your emotions are getting the best of you and you need to step out of the situation until you are calm.

Sometimes what you do in the heat of the moment is worse than the actual event that sets you off. When you come back to address whatever the drama is, your guide is *"What would a mentally together person do in this situation?"* Then do that, even if you're still feeling a little crazy about it all.

Sit at the Head of the Table

Possibly the simplest Alpha/Family Dominance move ever is to sit at the head of the table during dinner. It's a simple move, but it works by framing you as the leader of the family. Sitting at the head of the table = Alpha Male of the Group = Captain. Everyone else at the table is de facto stating their social deference to you wittingly or not. After a few months of stating deference to someone, it tends to become internalized.

I love it when Jennifer sits to my immediate right. She's close enough to touch from shoulder to waist and she can lean toward me. I've noticed that the last few times we've been out together we've been seated at wide tables and we're physically far away from each other, thus defeating the point of a romantic dinner. Our own dining room table is more intimate. I'd much rather sit together than opposite each other any day.

Plus how can you squeeze her thigh when you're sitting opposite her without looking completely awkward?

At Work?

Just underlining this point again – I'm outlining a husband and wife relationship rather than all men and all women. Acting like a Man-Bear-Pig at work isn't the idea at all. I work with a ton of women, I supervise some, I'm peers with some and I've *always* been supervised by women. Currently my job assignment is being part of a team of just two people and of that pairing she's the "Captain" and *I'm* the

"First Officer." First Officer isn't a demeaning role. *It's how we get things done as a team.*

I certainly don't pretend to be female or "blend in" by being silent. I used to be like that, but I've moved on from that well and truly. There's not much question in anyone's mind that I'm male at work and I play up that angle as an advantage as best I can.

But it would be just stupid trying to do a Ten Second Kiss on my boss, as try to pretend she should really submit to me. I'm not trying to have a sexual relationship with these women... I'm at work.

Chapter 10
Be a Nice Guy with a Hard Edge

The Betaization Trap

The basic trap with getting married is that you give up doing too much of the Alpha trait things and begin to do nothing but Beta trait things instead. The Beta stuff is all very good, don't misunderstand that. I've covered in the Beta chapter the importance of cooking, nest management and playing with the kids. That's all true and helpful, but I'm not turning this book into a cookbook or advice on laundry softeners because I think any adult can figure that stuff out for themselves. If you stop doing the Alpha and focus only on the Beta, you become Betaized.

Most husbands charge into the Betaization Trap like lemmings. After all, everyone in the world told them that marriage was about "settling down" and being obedient husbands. Being married is about teamwork and being helpful to one another. There's a house to run and babies to tend. She's asking him to do things for her and the kids, and she gets upset if he doesn't help out the way she wants him to. Everyone says that husbands should help out, but fast forward a few years and "the man" is getting chewed out because the vacuuming wasn't done right. Somewhere along the way he turns into her kitchen bitch/roommate. And you know if she's screaming at you about vacuuming, it's a bad sign of sexual disinterest. *"The house is a mess and my vagina is angry at you!"*

The Betaization Trap is that by trying to do everything possible to make her happy and being endlessly nice to her, you undo what created her initial attraction to you, so she falls out of love and loses sexual interest. Most men never understand this until it is too late and she gives him the *"I love you but I'm not in love with you"* speech, which also usually means she is already having sex with someone else.

By being endlessly nice you are displaying low value to her. By repeatedly doing what she wants you are broadcasting to her, *"I think my Sex Rank is lower than yours, so you're in charge of this relationship."* So if she's an 8, your catering to her constantly makes her think that you are a 6 or 7. If you married her as an 8 or 9, she was probably extremely hot for you sexually and followed your lead. Once married though, your behavior changed to cater to her, resulting in your nerfing your own Sex Rank; so she falls out of love with you.

The problem of Betaization is also caused in no small part by wives setting ridiculous tasks for their husbands... in order to test them.

Fitness Tests

Periodically women Fitness Test (a.k.a. Shit Test) men. This can be quite purposeful and conscious testing, or it can be unconscious testing that just springs up from seemingly nowhere. The simplest variant is when she suddenly just *feels* something negative and the man must *do* something to alter the way she *feels* to something more positive. *"Well I don't feel like you really care about me, why can't you bring me flowers once in a while?"* On one level it seems a reasonable request, but the language is one of manipulation. I feel a negative emotion (unloved) so you must complete a task (get me flowers) so I can feel a positive emotion (happy).

These tests start fairly small, but over time they can grow larger and more demanding. The obvious intervention here is for the man to jump up and comply with her request, and this may appease her at first. If the husband runs out and gets flowers for her, she is happy for a few minutes, but then it can intensify. *"I don't like that I have to ask you for flowers, why can't you just bring them to me without my asking for them?"*

Fitness Testing is the female equivalent of a sonar ping to determine social status. In general, those of lower social status defer to those of higher social status. Women are hypergamous in their sexual attraction, so they are seeking their mate to be higher social status than they are. So when the male suddenly jumps up and complies with her request and seeks to appease her, he is deferring to her and demonstrating lower social status relative to hers. While her minor inconvenience for the moment is taken care of, she becomes less happy with him because she finds him less attractive.

I first really ran into Fitness Tests with my first serious girlfriend Mary. It started off small, first she was late... and I tolerated it. Then she was nagging... and I listened. Then something about me wasn't quite right... and I changed it. Then she was really late... and I tolerated it more. Then we just had to go to this horrible dance club... and I dragged myself there. Then we could do this and not that... I said okay. She nagged on and on and on and it just seemed to endlessly build.

Being clueless, I stuck to my game plan of being nice and after three months of getting the mixed messages of physical affection and disrespect... I flipped out completely and dumped her. Then I was very sad for about 18 months getting over her. For those kind readers who periodically ask where was I twenty years ago with the info I have on the blog... well that's where I was twenty years ago. Dumping my girlfriend in frustration and just bawling about it. A Kodak Moment...

If I knew everything back then that I know now, Mary and I might still be together. I think there was real love there on both sides, it's just that she repeatedly tested me and I failed every time. In the end when I bumped back on her and stood my ground, I did it way too hard and destroyed the relationship. Probably all I really needed to do early on in the relationship was to semi-playfully swat her on her ass a couple times and tell her to stop being a brat; tease her a little. In the aftermath of the breakup she admitted she had been testing me *on purpose*, but was too hurt to try again for fear of my nuking the relationship again. We both did it wrong.

Fortunately, I've since learned to give a few playful swats on the ass and tease back a little. That's seriously about half the battle right there.

How Do You Pass a Fitness Test?

You just say *"No."* Then you don't give in to her intensifying reaction to the *"No."* It's really exactly the same sort of thing that happens with a kid crying for candy in the supermarket. When you say *"No."* to a kid crying for candy, the crying always gets louder and more emotional as they try to break your resolve. The solution is to just pay for your food and walk to the car; the kid has to follow.

Wives, of course, don't cry for candy, but they can dream up some near impossible tasks for husbands. Like asking for a $20,000 kitchen remodel when she hardly cooks anyway and they are already starting to struggle with credit card debt. When a husband says *"No"* to that, you can bet he's going to get hit with some sort of emotional outburst as she seeks to break his will and grant her a better kitchen to not cook in.

If he sticks to his guns she will probably be emotionally upset, but after her initial angry mood passes, she will be happier and more attracted to him. As the husband shows his dominant frame, she responds with increased attraction for him.

What is and is Not a Fitness Test

Most Fitness Tests your wife will toss at you come in a few standard variations that are seemingly easily spotted, but they also come very close to things that aren't Fitness Tests at all. The trouble is figuring out which is which. You can mess up just as fast by failing a Fitness Test as by bumping back on her on something that wasn't one in the first place. If she was trying to be genuinely nice and you tell her off, that's legitimately going to upset her.

Importantly, most times the woman isn't even aware of the testing nature of what she is doing, so there's no easy way to just ask her what's up either. If you happen to get tangled up with a woman that is consciously testing you and gaining some kind of pleasure from watching you squirm, it's about the worst red flag there is. Personally I'd avoid relationships with these women with such an enormous need for stimulation. If a woman actively wants to chew a man up she will find a way: divorce, alimony, child support, false rape, cuckolding, restraining orders, bank accounts pillaged... it can get pretty bad.

Some basic Fitness Test variations, coupled with things that aren't tests...

The Small Request Test – This is where she asks you to do something that she is perfectly capable of, simply so that she doesn't have to. These are often small tasks that barely require any effort, so you can unwittingly start performing them for her simply trying to be "polite", or "nice". But if you're starting to find yourself being her butler, then you've established that she is the dominant one in the relationship and you are Displaying Low Value. A tip off is if she is seated on something and instead of getting up to get something, she asks you to go get it and bring it to her.

The Small Request Non-Test – A request to perform a small task where you have natural advantages over her. For example Jennifer is very short and I am very tall, so when she asks me to put away something in the kitchen that goes away very high in the cabinets, it just makes sense that I do it. A couple times Jennifer has been injured by heavy items falling back down on her, so I actually get testy at her for not asking for help sometimes.

The I'm a Cute Girl Test – A request to comply with something simply because she has asked for it in a coy seductive manner and, being a boy, you are powerless before potential pussy. There's usually some sort of inflection of voice that tips this off. The request is an *unreasonable* one, such as getting out of an unwanted task, or getting something from you like a drink or money. It's best not to comply and find a way to get her to do it if she is perfectly capable.

The I'm a Cute Girl Non-Test – This is a reasonable request, but comes with a quite purposefully aware display of sexiness. She's purposely using the request as an excuse to be sexually playful with you and display her interest in you. The question/request is just a cover. Jennifer tends to have an almost comic approach with this and sometimes loads up a Small Request Non Test with a dose of sexual coyness just for fun. I'm cool with my wife rubbing her breasts on me asking me to put away kitchen items high up.

The I'm Getting Emotional About This Test – As soon as a woman finds out her tears is your Kryptonite you're in deep doo-doo. Don't respond to her drama and hysteria over minor things. Sometimes this is tied into her menstrual cycle, but typically the women that reach for this tool use it an awful lot. After a while the entire relationship can be based on her mood swings. She is unhappy about X so you must do something about X right now. Now she's unhappy about Y, why can't you fix Y? Z also displeases her. The more you cater to her, the worse it gets, until eventually she becomes the unhappiest woman in the world and you are near death from exhaustion.

The I'm Getting Emotional About This Non-Test – This is when something really does happen that isn't trivial or minor and she's upset. Everyone has a crappy day once in a while. As long as she's not making a lifestyle of it, you should be standing in, standing up, or standing with her during these moments. The key here is not to try and bail her out of a bad situation and solve her problem for her, but to be present and available to her to aid in solving it herself. Sometimes you just have to let them cry it out for a bit.

The Badly Inconveniencing You Request Test – This is where she asks you to do something that would cost her little of her time, but costs you a lot of yours. So *"Can you pick up the girls from school today"* when school is five minutes round trip from home on a work from home day for her, while you have to leave work early to get to the school on time. That's a big test. Just say *"No."*

The Badly Inconveniencing You Non-Test – This is when yes indeed this is going to screw your day, but if you don't help out she is going to be royally screwed. Today the kid is sick and someone has to stay home, but today she has that presentation thing and that meeting with her boss. So you save her with your best smile.

The Sexual Denial Test – You can't have any sex from me because... [insert statement of accusation of what you did or did not do]. This is just cruel and really eats away at the relationship. Personally I'd just reflect that verbally back to her and say that it's dirty tactics. The other version is simply saying she doesn't feel in a sexual mood, it's not you... just that she doesn't feel sexy or sexual anymore. At this point you start talking about visiting doctors and naturally running The MAP on her.

The Sexual Denial Non-Test – She is feeling acutely ill, or having her period, or cramping, or is just physically exhausted. Basically her body is not going to be terribly cooperative with the *"bouncy bouncy"* session today. As long as it resolves in a day or two, it's not testing behavior. If it starts going on and on and on... then it's doctor time.

The Not Responding To Your Calls Test – You're calling and texting her and she's basically blowing you off. Can't find my phone. I'm kinda busy. I'm dancing to my favorite song. I can't text with a drink in my hand. I'm just dancing. The whole Lady Gaga *"Telephone"* BS. Slap this down as soon as possible. It's very rude.

The Not Responding To Your Calls Non-Test – She's in a meeting. She's driving and there's a cop behind her. She's on a plane. She's at the school picking up the kids and there are 500 screaming brats in a gym and she didn't hear the phone ring. Once Jennifer accidentally blocked my cell phone number on her phone in the middle of a very positive and happy week in our marriage... I was very close to tearing her head off before we figured it out.

The Remodel The House Test – The house is actually fine and isn't broken. But she somehow needs something torn out and rebuilt with something more expensive. Doesn't add much value, if any.

The Fix The House Non-Test – Something in the house is broken. It's usually best to just fix it. Upgrade if it's a good idea and adds value to the house.

The Second Date Rule

A quick and dirty way of deciding if something is a Fitness Test is The Second Date Rule.

"If what she just did happened on the second date, would there have been a third date?"

If the answer is "No," then it's a Fitness Test.

Mostly it's all about knowing what is appropriate "playing as a team" and what is simply seeking to use you. It's your job to sort that out. It's okay to make a few mistakes along the way; you just can't get into a losing streak where she endlessly wins something over you.

Nice Guys Actively Strategize to be Taken Advantage Of

Let's play a game. Assume for a moment that a husband and a wife could choose one of two cards each day in a game that decides how their evening will go that day. One of the cards is marked "nice"; the other card is marked "mean". They each choose a card in secret and turn them over at the same time. The cards determine who does the chores and who relaxes.

Husband Nice, Wife Nice – Both husband and wife split the chores together. Home cooked meal together.

Husband Nice, Wife Mean – Wife too tired to do anything and has a headache. Husband has to do all the chores and make a quick dinner.

Husband Mean, Wife Nice – Husband watches TV all night and complains about Wife. Wife does all the chores and makes dinner.

Husband Mean, Wife Mean – No one does much of anything. Takeout is ordered.

Now it seems fairly clear that having both husband and wife be nice to each other is the ideal setup. Obviously, both being mean to each other is unpleasant too. But the options where one half plays the nice card and gets screwed for it while the other plays the mean card and wins a servant for a day can be.... well tempting, if only for once in a while.

Now imagine in a real relationship how this game is played over and over. I know it is oversimplifying things to say that a couple coming home from work each day decide to be either nice or mean to each other, but in general it's true. As even well below-average intelligence humans are extremely bright compared to other mammals, both husband and wife will learn the other's strategy very quickly.

The Nice Guy strategy is simple – *always* play the nice card. No matter what happens, whether the wife is nice or mean, he will just continue to play the nice card night after night. Very quickly the wife will learn that her husband is using the Nice Guy strategy and will always play the nice card. That allows her to very safely use a strategy called "Whatever I Feel Like" where she on her own whim can either choose to be nice and have a pleasant time with her husband, or simply choose to be mean and be waited on by him.

Over time the husband gets increasingly frustrated with this combination of strategies. He is being nice and she is not. He rationalizes that she *should* be nice back to him, but she isn't always or even terribly often, though she is sometimes. The obvious solution to an impartial observer is to tell the Nice Guy to stop being so nice. Unfortunately the Nice Guy nearly always refuses this advice until it is too late.

Why Nice Guys are Addicted to the Wrong Strategy

The question is, *"Why are Nice Guys so fixated on the wrong strategy when everyone else can see that it is failing them?"* Even the Nice Guys can say they understand it's the wrong strategy, but they persist in it anyway. An easy answer is that Nice Guys are simply psychically damaged from some sort of childhood trauma and can't break free of the early programming. Though that may indeed be true, that helps us little as an actual tool for change. The way I believe it is best understood as an adult is that the Nice Guy gets hooked into a behavioral response pattern to being given a *random* reward.

Imagine a lab rat in a cage that has a lever on one wall. If every time the lever is pushed a food pellet is given, the rat will only push the lever when it wants a food pellet. The rest of the time it will ignore the lever. If the lever does nothing, the rat will play with it, figure out it's useless and then ignore it. However if the lever *randomly* drops a food pellet into the cage, the rat will spend a lot of effort working the lever to ensure it has a supply of food pellets. It's the same basic principle that addicts people to gambling on the one armed bandit slot machines. You may pull the lever nine times and get nothing, but the tenth time might be a winner, or maybe not until the 100th pull.

It's *random* and creates a large dopamine response when it finally works.

Sex already triggers a big dopamine response as a reward mechanism, so a *randomized* sexual reward is a double whammy and creates an utterly massive dopamine response. If a Nice Guy is in a low sex marriage, when he finally gets sex it creates the same sort of hormonal response as winning a good sized jackpot off a slot machine; it's an intense and addictive high.

For the Nice Guy, the problem isn't that he *never* gets what he wants; the problem is he *sometimes* gets what he wants. It's not that she never has sex with him, but that she drip feeds it to him.

Rather than understanding that the Nice Guy strategy is a losing strategy, he mistakenly believes that it is in fact a winning strategy. Rather than altering the strategy *he resolves to be even nicer to her*. The thought process is that nice does affect her and that by being even nicer, she will reward him more frequently (i.e. "be in the mood"). After all, he thinks to himself... on the nights that she did have sex with him he was being nice, so nice must have an effect, so therefore... increase the nice! It's the same dopamine driven approach as someone buying not just one lottery ticket, but dozens in the belief that more chances to win are better. Or like the rat in the cage hammering on the lever that drops food pellets at random.

Ultimately though, his Nice Guy strategy has a negative effect on her sexual interest level in him. He's always going to be nice, so she can do whatever she wants. She can drip feed him sex once every two to four weeks for years on end. If she carefully manages his frustration level so he doesn't flee the relationship, she can avoid a great deal of the more mundane tasks of everyday life and have a guy handing over his paycheck to her to boot.

Very importantly, more than likely this is all done completely subconsciously on her part and stems from her overall sexual disinterest in him. She's also, far more likely than not, quite unhappy in her marriage.

The "Tit for Tat" Solution

The "nice" or "mean" game I described earlier is essentially an iterated version of the classic game "Prisoners Dilemma". In Prisoners Dilemma, two criminals have to make a decision between "plea bargain" and "stick to the lie". If one plea bargains and the other sticks to the lie, one gets a much reduced sentence and the other goes to jail for a very long time. If both plea bargain they both go to jail for a moderate time. If both stick to the lie they both stay out of jail.

In an iterated game of Prisoners Dilemma, the game is played over multiple rounds and the memory of previous choices of the opponent is known and can affect the future rounds of play. This game has been extensively studied and the winning solution to iterated Prisoners Dilemma turns out to be a very simple "Tit for Tat" strategy.

In a Tit for Tat strategy, the default plan is to be nice to the opponent, but if the opponent is ever mean, the Tit for Tat will play the mean card right back at the opponent until they decide to play the nice card again. Once playing the nice card, Tat for Tit will resume being nice. It is utterly simple and utterly effective. Summarizing some key points of the Tit for Tat strategy, there are four key values in a Tit for Tat strategy. (I have altered some language below to reflect my emphasis on it as an interpersonal strategy, otherwise please consider it sourced from the excellent Wikipedia page on Prisoners Dilemma.)

Peaceful – The most important condition is that the strategy must be peaceful, that is, it will not defect before its opponent does and is "optimistic". From purely selfish reasons a peaceful strategy won't cheat on an opponent because the best chance for getting the highest scores is possible that way.

Retaliating – However, the successful strategy must not be a blind optimist. It must sometimes retaliate. An example of a non-retaliating strategy is the Nice Guy strategy, which is a very bad choice, as "nasty" strategies will ruthlessly exploit such players.

Forgiving – Successful strategies must also be forgiving. Though players will retaliate, they will once again fall back to peaceful cooperation if the opponent will also cooperate. This stops getting mired in long runs of revenge and counter-revenge and will maximize points.

Non-envious – The last quality is being non-envious and not striving to score more than the opponent. In trying to score more points than an opponent, you are forced into trying attempts to "win" by being non-peaceful. By being non-envious you accept that while you can get a high score in Prisoner's Dilemma, the best you can do is *tie* your opponents score. You can't actually "win" without giving up the peaceful element.

Be a Nice Guy with a Hard Edge

Coming back to understanding marriage – if you see your wife trying to sucker you into a Fitness Test, you just have to see that test as her as playing a "mean" card at you. So you just retaliate against it and are "mean" back at her by declining to meet her Fitness Test demands. Once she backs down and behaves better, you resume being nice to her. It's all that simple.

If you have been locked into the Nice Guy routine for several years and are having a non-existent sex life, there's no point trying to ask the wife to be nicer and offer up sex more often. Like I've said many times, talk is near pointless in changing behavior while action is a much faster route and often the only tactic that works anyway.

The solution to not being taken advantage of is simple self assertion. Say *"No"* and tell her to do her own crap for a change. If you were only going to get sex once this month for a hundred hours of domestic service, you may as well just take the month off and see what happens.

Chapter 11
Behavior Modification 101

Everything is a Behavior

Behavior modification always sounds scary, like there are going to be guys in white lab coats giving rats electric shocks and making notes on clipboards. In reality though, behavior modification is always happening. Every time you have a social interaction with someone, both you and the other person are performing some sort of "behavior". If you get on a bus and pay the bus driver and take a seat on the bus, you are behaving like a bus passenger. The bus driver is behaving like a bus driver.

Every time you interact with someone, you are establishing a routine as to how future interactions with that person will go. If I meet you and bump you out of my way rudely and you don't do anything about it, the next time we meet you're probably going to get out of my way automatically. We would have both trained each other as to how we would interact in the future.

Because husbands and wives interact with each other constantly, they create deep patterns of interaction with one another. I'm sure you've experienced occasions where you and your wife have held a conversation, that reads like a script of the last six times you had the same conversation. Breaking out of those patterns of interaction requires some extra effort and thought.

The key remains the same though – you can't usually change her behavior simply by asking for it. You can change your own behavior and that can spark a change her behavior. The two core behavior changes to make are to be sure that you reward her positive behavior and that you do not reward her negative behavior.

Reward Positive Behavior

One thing you must do is to positively reward the sexual (or other) behavior you seek from your wife. This sounds simple, but it's very possible to totally screw the whole thing up accidentally if you are not being somewhat mindful of this basic point.

Here's an example...

Mike has long complained that Cindy never initiates sex. Cindy says she wants sex and is happy to have sex when Mike suggests it, but *"just doesn't think of it"*. Every so often the issue comes up and is rehashed and no progress is made. Occasionally Mike freezes Cindy out and waits for her to get horny and initiate, but after a couple of weeks he folds and initiates anyway. Cindy knows Mike is angry after these freeze-out periods and she cries either during or right after the sex that breaks the freeze.

During a Saturday afternoon when their son is at a friend's house, Cindy gets the thought in her head to actually have sex with Mike. Happy and proud of herself, she seeks him out and makes an attempt to remove his belt and unbuckle his pants. Mike is taken somewhat unaware of her intention and asks, *"What are you doing?"* while bringing his arms up defensively. When she explains she was trying to start sex, he tells her, *"Not now."* Cindy is badly hurt by this. Seven months later when Mike complains she never initiates sex, Cindy explodes on Mike and the D word is mentioned in her ranting.

It's not rocket science to figure out that Mike really blew it when she came on to him. So here's the deal: if you're asking for something special sexually, and you get it, make sure you accept it and acknowledge that you got it. Otherwise you can make things much worse.

That said, the best positive reward is not usually your spoken praise – that can sound awfully stilted and can draw attention to the fact that you are actively trying to positively reward her. The best reward you can hand out to your wife in bed is your obvious enjoyment of what she is doing with you. You don't have to turn into a screamer, but you certainly should at least turn into a moaner and groaner. Try a heartfelt *"mmmmmm"* or two. *"That's so good", "I want this to last forever", "You're amazing."*

When she is acting sexy the way you want, don't withdraw from her. Lean into it and let her know you're turned on and follow through on the impulse. The correct way to frame it is not that you like that she is doing what you have asked, but that she is inherently sexy and you are turned on by her. The difference between *"Oh baby you are so compliant to my direction"* and *"oh baby you make me so hard I'm gonna blow it if you don't stop"* is important. You want her to feel sexy and if she doesn't have the self-image of being a sexy woman (if only with you), you very much want that to develop.

The right time to follow up with "verbalized praise" is the next day. Remember during the act itself, you were hopefully so into the moment of her that you could hardly think. The next day it's okay to think. Text her something like *"You were amazing last night", "I can't stop thinking about you",* or *"Okay I give up. Where did you learn XYZ? I'm hard again thinking about it."*

Don't Reward Negative Behavior

In terms of negatively rewarding sexual behavior you don't want, (i.e. not getting any) the best response is for you to not react in an overtly negative way toward her. Don't become angry, frustrated, insulting, bad tempered, grumpy, sullen or otherwise freeze her out. All that drama will just underline that she has power over you to affect you by denying you sex. By having an emotional reaction about not getting sex, you are making it clear to her that she has enormous leverage over you by giving or not giving you sex. If you're running The MAP and getting better at interacting with and attracting other women, her endlessly denying you sex should become less and less of a lever to use against you anyway.

If she declines sex and you have a temper tantrum, not only is it childish, but you turn her into someone that can make you have a tantrum. The best approach is simply to minimize attention to what you don't want and to continue on with your day. It is highly counter-intuitive, but nearly any form of attention is a positive reward, even if the attention given is negative in nature. This effect is easily seen in badly behaved children, who do so for the express purpose of gaining their parents attention.

Again, be careful not to frame it as *"Please pay attention to the way I am minimizing attention to what I didn't want to see"*, but simply that if you weren't going to do XYZ with her, you were just going to go ahead and do ABC. If she wants to tag along with ABC she can, but you intend to do it regardless. It's just a natural consequence of her not wanting to be with you.

So if she declines sex, it's no big deal to you. Maybe you'll just go to sleep, maybe you'll ask her to cuddle with you as you masturbate, maybe you'll just stay up and play computer games, or watch a little porn and masturbate. On a case by case basis, it's all no biggie.

Over the long term though, constant denial does very much become a hot issue and outside the bedroom it should be something that is mentioned once in a while. Again, work hard to not frame it in anger or that she is trying to do something wrong; frustration and disappointment is a better angle. Long term though, (as in over months and years) you gain the most leverage by self-improvement rather than complaint.

What you do is vastly more important than what you say. It's one thing to be in a low sex marriage, complaining about it, arguing why you need more sex, how you are frustrated by it and slamming a few doors. It's entirely another matter to be in a low sex marriage and say, *"You understand this is something I need, right?"* and just start pumping iron, dressing better and going to get your teeth whitened. When push comes to shove on constant denial you can go out to a strip club, or meet a female friend as a serious announcement of intent. Though as covered in The Timeline chapter, that sort of thing starts forcing the marriage towards an ultimatum.

And for goodness sake... if she ever comes looking for you wearing lingerie... *that's her initiating sex dumbass!* You have to give her sex right then. No excuses. Make it good for her too.

Catch Her Being Good

A great move for any team leader is to recognize when someone is contributing to the team. I really recommend paying active attention to your wife and thanking her for the times when she does do things that benefit you and your family. It's an old tactic in dealing with children to try and "catch them when they are being good". It's no less effective on adults.

When your wife does something good, especially something good for you, say *"Thank you."* She may be holding out on you sexually simply because she has started to resent your lack of appreciation for the good she has done. Fitness Tests thrive in the fertile ground of lack of appreciation.

I realize this doesn't sound very Alpha Male and sounds very supplicating, but it actually is a somewhat dominant display. You are not asking for something or for permission, you are thanking her for acts of service you have already received. You need to reward the behavior you are looking for by at least acknowledging that it occurred. Failing to do so is actually a subtle punishment of good behavior and will result in it declining in frequency.

If you punish good behavior, you are ultimately starting to force her into thinking about engaging in bad behavior, if only in an attempt to get you to pay attention to her. Often this is why women test their men. Sometimes a Fitness Test is just a play for attention.

If by constantly ignoring her you are setting the stage to be Fitness Tested, it really doesn't matter whether you pass the test or not, you're basically screwing her over either way. She's getting punished for being good and for being bad. Who wants to put up with that for too long? Her best option is to simply leave the relationship.

So try saying, *"Thank you."* It's not that hard and much cheaper than a divorce. It shouldn't be every single time she is good either, just mix it up and be a little *random* with the praise as it's more effective that way. (Remember how randomness hooks Nice Guys into repeating their behaviors?)

Highly Problematic Behavior

Sometimes a basically fine wife has one particular area of being utterly obnoxious. One classic example is lateness, as in not just a little bit late, but seriously offensively late. It's one thing to be a few minutes late, but trying to find a seat in a movie theater 15 minutes into a movie for the sixth time is just aggravating. The solution is to own whatever half of the equation is really your problem and leave the rest of it as hers to solve.

In the case of lateness to a movie, there are two people that are late; she is late and you are late. When it comes down to it, her being late doesn't really bother you as much as your lateness. What is really annoying you, is that you are letting her control you and make you late. The solution is simple, you get to the movie on time, and she gets there late, but you don't wait on her like a chump.

One option is a sudden surprise where you just leave and she discovers that you are gone and so is your car. She's messing with her hair and finally finishes and walks into the living room 35 minutes behind schedule and the house is empty, apart from your note saying *"Meet me there; I'll save you a seat."* There's a lot of shock value in this technique, but I worry that it's too harsh. She may well comply in the future, but it's going to cost attraction points.

I would give her a warning shot about the lateness and frame it as *"I am late and that's not acceptable to me"*. Make no mention of her getting ready routine. If she complains or argues, just be a broken record *"I am late and that is not acceptable to me."* Use a firm tone of voice and maintain eye contact.

If you're late for a second event together, give her a second warning shot that *"I have already addressed this once before; I won't address this again with you. If you are late again, I will leave you behind and you will find your own way there."* If she wants to debate that, just tell her there's nothing more to talk about, you're just informing her what you will do.

For a third event of potential lateness, you just leave without her. Don't even tell her that you're leaving, just go. If she gets into a pattern of ignoring of fair warnings in the future, you should skip the second warning and jump to the consequence.

Of course you have to expect a counter attack if you do this. People rarely give up bad behavior without a fight! Leaving her behind may turn into the unforgivable sin and she may well scream at you. In that moment you have to realize that her behavior is rude and she is blaming you for not supporting her rudeness. Also she may well arrive forty minutes late and mad as a snake and start ripping you up verbally in public for leaving her behind. That's a whole other level of socially inappropriate behavior toward you.

Perhaps in those moments where she transforms into a venomous screechtard, you'll realize exactly what you married – and want to have a serious think about things and the direction of your life. If she is a wife perhaps you might suggest *"Maybe we consider taking some space from each other for a while to think about things"*. I'd just dump a girlfriend for chewing me up in public on the spot.

The way to deal with highly problematic behavior is to figure out what part of the behavior you are responding to and how you are supporting the behavior. Once you identify that, you change your own behavior so that it no longer supports the highly problematic behavior.

This works for a great many things. In a family with an alcoholic husband for example, the wife often spends a great deal of time hiding bottles, cleaning up vomit, sneaking the kids around him, calling his work and covering for his absences, lying to everyone in both families as to how it's not really that bad and so on. There's usually a whole range of caretaking and supporting things she does for "his problem". He'd probably not be able to be an alcoholic without her supporting the problem. If she stops all her special assistance and lets him flounder, he's going to be forced to take care of himself. He's going to be very angry at her in the short term though.

It's the same with kids who miss the school bus constantly and get a ride to school from mom; there's no consequence for missing the bus. But if they were loaded into a taxi to get to school and had the fare taken from their allowance, then you would be very likely to see them on time waiting for the bus each day.

Or in the case of oversleeping... *"Mom! Why didn't you wake me up?"* Correct answer: *"Because you have an alarm clock?"*

Natural Consequences

One thing to remember in dealing with highly negative behavior is that it is easy to get into a situation where you cope with the negative behavior and then complain to the other person that you had to cope with it. All that does is empower them to continue doing the behavior, because you have supported them doing it and you also have rewarded them with your attention. It may be negative attention, but it's attention all the same, so it's really a reward.

The solution is usually to not support the negative behavior and just allow the natural consequences to occur. This way you aren't actually punishing the other person, you just aren't saving them from their own bad behavior. Also you aren't wasting your own time and effort, or rewarding them with extra attention.

Let me give an example. Say your wife is terrible at getting up in the morning and oversleeps for work unless you wake her up every morning. Also you complain to her that you have to wake her up and you have arguments about you having to wake her up all the time. She blames you for being late to work if you don't wake her up.

The solution is not to wake her up and just let the natural consequence of being late to work kick in – getting written up at work etc. She'll probably be angry at you the first time you don't wake her up, but you just say that it's not your job to wake her up and walk away from the conversation. Adults get up and go to work. What's not to know? Very likely it will only take a single instance of this to alter her behavior and magically she will set an alarm and get to work on time the next day.

Should she parley this into getting fired, that's probably an enormously bad sign of things to come. But should she go that route, I would simply cut off her disposable spending – not having money to spend being a natural consequence of not having a job. If you have to, you can always set up a personal account and have your paycheck go in there and not into a joint account.

Plus one would expect a wife without a job would be actively looking for one, or keeping house like a stay at home mom. That would be a natural consequence of not having a job as well. Of course if she can't keep house, or keep a job, or some reasonable combination thereof...

...it would seem to be a natural consequence that she would not be able to keep a husband either.

The Golden Rule of Sex Rank.
Never force an ultimatum on your wife if she is hotter than you.

Chapter 12
Don't be a Chump

Seriously, Don't be a Chump

One classic thing you can do wrong with women is being a chump. You're a chump when you do something for a woman, hoping to eventually get to have sex with her. The woman, on the other hand knows exactly why you are helping her, but has no intention of ever having sex with you. You may look, but you may not touch. If you masturbate later thinking about the looking and the not touching, she does not want to know about it. You are just a friend and chump be thy name.

Just to be clear – if her request was a reasonable one and something that you would do for anyone, it's not being a chump to comply. But it is being a chump when she holds out sexual "cheese" and you run like a rat through her maze to get it and when you get to the end... there's no "cheese."

Whether you are single or married, some women will seek to use their attractiveness to influence you into assisting them in some way. Attraction is normal and uncontrollable and you can hardly blame attractive women for using what they've got to get what they want. The lead in is usually the same thing as the "I'm a Cute Girl Fitness Test"; *"Oh I need a man to do this thing I need help with"*. For best effect this line is delivered while pushing her breasts together and doing the reverse hand clasp and shoulder roll.

If the woman trying this is twenty-two years old and stunning, and you're a fifty-three year old man with only one medical issue, you are going to feel an enormous primal need to go help her. And by *"help her"* I mean *"have vigorous sex, like your wife of twenty-nine years can only vaguely remember."* If you go and help her though, you will get nothing for your efforts. To be sure she might say *"Thank you"* or whatever, but let's be honest, your motivation was sex and you didn't get the pay off. You're a chump.

Wives can do the same thing to husbands. If she sexually entices you to go do something for her, then you go do it and you get nothing, then you're a chump. Wives know exactly what they are doing when they do this. To add insult to injury, by agreeing to marry you, she was already promising you a sex life. So in this case, she was negotiating further with you on something she had already agreed to give you and then she didn't give it to you anyway. You're a double-chump.

The solution to all of this is pretty simple. Payment in advance or properly assured, or she can do it her own damn self. This way you can save yourself time and just skip to the end where you don't have sex with her.

Of course if you evaluate the hotness of the girl and the difficulty of the task fairly, not everything results in vaginal sex being the trade. In the interests of fairness, sometimes a flash of naked boobs, a long kiss, handing over her panties, watching her get herself to orgasm or a blowjob is the socially appropriate exchange. There's no point being unreasonable...

Shrek, Donkey and the Princess Fiona Plan

I still struggle with the biological impulse to rush to an unattached attractive woman and help her out. Seeing I'm married, this could get me in all sorts of trouble and is best simply avoided. Either I waste my time and effort and don't get offered sex, or I waste my time and effort and turn down sex. Either way I waste my time and effort and don't have sex, so it's very annoying. I hate the way it's drilled into my DNA that I should help attractive women. It really does take mental effort to force myself to say *"Good luck with that,"* and walk away.

As a result, I developed a little game that I play that helps me stay in control. If you're single or looking to screen women, you can play it slightly differently.

What I do is frame myself as Shrek and then come up with a predetermined list of things I would do for a "Donkey" and a second list for things that I would do for a "Princess Fiona". As it stands, only my wife has Princess Fiona status and the rest of my female friends are Donkeys.

Jennifer holds up her end of the Princess Fiona Plan very well, so I am happy to help her out when she needs it. She helps me out too, so it's all good. But basically if I rescue a princess, I bang a princess, and we're clear on that. If I'm in my driveway digging us out of a blizzard, she's inside trimming pubic hair in preparation for the returning hero. It's all good.

In comparison to that, I have a horny lonely female friend who posted a recent Facebook status update requesting help to dig her out after the recent heavy snow. In years past I would have blundered over there like a fool, dug her out, wasted two hours of my day and come home tired. Jennifer would have probably been proud of me for helping out a friend.

But my friend is a Donkey so I just ignored the status update. Actually to tell the truth I actively had to resist messaging her, *"I'll help you with your white stuff, if you help me with some of my white stuff"* and a smiley face. Of course if I had gone over there and actually shoveled her out, Jennifer would have just assumed I had sex with her anyway because she knows about the Donkey and Princess Fiona thing. So thanks to the plan, I get points with Jennifer for being a jerk to other women. It's freaking genius.

Shrek, Donkey and Princess Fiona for Screening Women

If you're single, you can use this game to screen women. Assuming they know of the films, you just ask, *"If I was Shrek, would you be Donkey or Princess Fiona?"*

Pretty much as soon as you ask that, she knows exactly the question you are really asking; *"Are you ready to have sex/seriously romantically interested?"*

If the answer is *"Princess Fiona"*, then you follow up with, *"Well you know that Shrek and Fiona totally have sex right?"* This will be fine because she is quite interested in you. You should get a positive laugh reaction from that. Continue gaming her, this one is in the bag.

If the answer is *"Donkey"*, then you follow up with, *"Oh great, I need a beast of burden"* and then you ask her to perform whatever trivial task you can think of...nothing insulting, just small. Most women will want to resist calling themselves the non-princess option, so it really is a fairly clear not ready/not interested signal from them.

The beauty of this is you can keep it going for months into the future as kind of a small running gag. A Princess Fiona will get one kind of treatment from you and a Donkey will get another. You just stop wasting much time on the Donkeys and you spend time and effort on the Princess Fionas. You don't have to treat Donkeys badly, you just keep them friend boxed and don't get suckered into their attempts to chump you into doing something for them.

So this...

Hot Girl Out Of Reach: *"Can you come over and help me move all these heavy boxes in my basement?"*
Chump: *"I'll be right over!"*
(Chump moves all the heavy boxes for two hours.)
Hot Girl Out Of Reach: *"Thanks! You're a great friend."*
Chump: *"How about a kiss?"*
Hot Girl Out Of Reach: *"Ewwww that would be like kissing my brother."*
(Chump goes home and masturbates.)

Turns into...

Donkey: *"Can you come over and help me move all these heavy boxes in my basement?"*
Shrek: *"Well I'd love to, but that sort of thing is really on the Princess Fiona plan."*
Donkey: *"But these boxes are so heavy and I really need your help".*
Shrek: *"Well you really need your man to help you... hang on hang on... were you just asking me to be your man?"*

Then you try and close for a date of some kind, before attempting the task she is looking for.

Also having got a Princess Fiona...

Princess Fiona: *"Can you come over and help me move all these heavy boxes in my basement?"*
Shrek: *"Sure I'll come over you in the basement."*
Princess Fiona: *"Shrek!"*
Shrek: *"(heh heh heh) I'll take that as a later baby... so what boxes?"*

If you really want to have fun with it...

Shrek: *"Hey Donkey I need your help. I want to take Princess Fiona somewhere really nice for dinner, what's your favorite place that's romantic?"*
Donkey: *"Well if it's romantic I love the Enchanted Grotto."*
Shrek: *"Of course! The Enchanted Grotto! You're such a good friend."*
Donkey: (thinks... *"Crap I should have said Princess Fiona when he asked. I want to eat in the Enchanted Grotto too; maybe I could be a Cinderella on the side...")*

The key to all this is that you are framing yourself as the emotional pivot and they have to make a choice about you, not you about them. That's a very Alpha frame of reference. They can't reject you this way; they can only choose to be one of two outcomes in relation to you and you don't care which. This is exactly the same thing I used to do with my daughters when they were little...

...*"Do you want to be mad and stay home, or do you want to clean your room and come to the park?"*

And to a grown woman of interest...

...*"Do you want to handle your own crap, or do you want me to be around to help out and lay you like tile?"*

Also if you're framing yourself as Shrek, you don't have to bother much with pretending you're Prince Charming.

Chapter 13
<u>Sexual Judo</u>

Your Wife has a Sex Drive

This may come as a surprise to some of you, but your wife has a sex drive. Oh to be sure you may not be seeing much evidence of it, but trust me, it's there. As long as there's not some kind of medical or childhood sexual abuse issue blocking her sex drive, she likely has a good sex drive. I get as many emails from women bewailing their husbands' low sex drive as I do from men. Women love sex. They are just awfully good at hiding it sometimes.

If you have a lower Sex Rank than her though, much of her sex drive is going to look like it's just drying up on you. She's just not going to feel "in the mood" and can be as confused by this as you are. But it is very important to understand that while she is less sexually responsive to *you*, her sex drive will continue on fairly unchanged. She might masturbate a lot when you aren't around, or she might not. But when a sexier man than you comes within her frame of reference, she might become very interested in him very quickly.

Husbands discovering affairs are hurt at the deceit of the affair, but are also often utterly shocked at the depth of her sexual response to her lover. The same husband who angrily complains that *"She just lies there and never does anything!"* can barely comprehend the hidden camera evidence of her squealing and bouncing on top of some guy. *"She said blowjobs were disgusting!"* But there she is, head bobbing up and down and moaning. It's a cruel stab in the chest to suddenly understand what she meant was *"Giving blowjobs to you is disgusting."*

Take a long look at your darling bride for a moment. Unless there's something medically or psychiatrically wrong with her, *she likes sex.* Think about that for a moment. She actually likes sex. She wants it. It's in her DNA to like sex. She's the product of millions of years of evolutionary sexual selection where the people who screwed around the best got to pass their genes to the next generation tens of thousands of times over. Your wife is from a long line of sluts.

Protection Shields

Because women don't want to have sex with men they aren't attracted to, they block his advances with their shields. Everything they say or do to avoid sex with you is part of their shielding. All that stuff that women say in bars like *"I have a boyfriend"*, *"My friends need me"*, *"I have to go"*, *"I'm just getting over a break up"*, are part of their protection shields. In married women you get exactly the same thing, they just use different content: *"I have a headache"*, *"Not now"*, *"I'm so tired"*, *"I need to answer this email tonight"*, *"Let's do this tomorrow"*.

Wives can also try and physically avoid you and do things like: going to bed either very early or very late, wearing horrible underwear, wearing full-length pajamas and having personal hygiene routines that you can't interrupt (how do you have sex with someone wearing a facial mask to bed?). Also there's the old-fashioned brush off when you touch her. Every time you try and pressure her for the sex she doesn't really want, her shields come up. Often the harder you push her, the stronger her shields get.

Once you understand her natural sluttiness, you can start to see that there's no point trying to pressure her to have sex with you. It's not like you are trying to make a non sexual woman act sexually. She *is* a sexual woman already. The only thing that putting pressure on her when she's not sexually attracted to you will do is make her act defensively towards you and put up her shields. By actually reducing the pressure on her to initiate sex, blow you, wear the lingerie, or whatever, she's got no reason to get her shields up.

Sexual Judo

When you stop pushing on her, all that's left motivating her sexual behavior is her own sex drive. Once you start displaying attractiveness, she will be compelled by her own sex drive to start paying you attention. She should start coming on to you. It's a sort of Sexual Judo where you use her own strength against her. She's not going to shield herself from doing something with you that she wants to do.

Of course in The MAP chapter I said that she would either respond or she wouldn't and that still holds true. If she does, then great, but if not, well then you keep going with The MAP and worst comes to worst, you find someone new. Either way you have a sex life.

Her Orgasm is Not Your Responsibility

It's a classic Nice Guy trap to think that you are somehow responsible for your wife's orgasm. Assuming she doesn't have a medical issue, if she doesn't orgasm it doesn't mean that you are a bad lover; it means *she's* a bad lover.

The wife's orgasms are up to her. It doesn't mean she has to masturbate after being pumped and dumped on her side of the bed by an oaf of a husband night after night, it means that she can't just lie there while you expect to magically divine and perform what it takes to get her off.

It used to be common that a woman lied to a man and faked an orgasm to let him think he was a wonderful lover, or simply to have the beast stop doing whatever the hell he was trying to do on top of her. But by faking it, all that happens is she ensures that she doesn't get the sex she wants. The whole scene in the Diner in the movie *"When Harry Met Sally"*, where Meg Ryan fakes a screaming orgasm isn't classic comedy, it's epic fail. Her character was groaning and moaning *"I'm really skilled at getting myself bad sex that I don't like"*. When a woman fakes an orgasm, it's the woman that doesn't get the orgasm. It doesn't really affect the man's orgasm, in fact he's probably happily blowing her vagina full of semen and thinking he can take a nap.

If she wants an orgasm, she needs to take responsibility for it and say what works and what doesn't and co-create that with you. If she doesn't want an orgasm on a particular night, you shouldn't feel the need to give her one. If she wants three, then work together for that. If she just wants you to have your fun with her and not try for an orgasm herself, then just go for it. If you don't take advantage of those opportunities when she offers them, you are on some level sexually rejecting her. Seriously think about that...

She: *"Here's my warm, wet, willing vagina. Have some fun."*

He: *"But I don't feel comfortable about that unless I get you off too. Tomorrow?"*

She: *"Fine."*

He: *(thinks... "Why doesn't she want to have sex with me?")*

So if she doesn't care about having an orgasm on any given night, you don't care either.

How She Orgasms Best is Up to Her

Not many women orgasm through intercourse alone. The *"Hite Report"* stats suggest that only 30% of women have a vaginal orgasm in their entire sex lives. So find out from her how she likes to get there the best. Maybe it's fingers, maybe it's tongue, maybe it's something in her ass while something else is working on her clitoris. Maybe spanking gets her hot, or hair pulling. Maybe this position works and that position doesn't. She needs to talk and say what makes her hot and orgasm and then you can do your part to help get her there.

Don't be embarrassed to have her own fingers working on her clitoris when you are inside her. As far as vaginal orgasm is concerned, the clitoris is in a really bad location considering how your penis basically misses it entirely. Orgasms with your penis inside her will likely make her very loud. Maybe not quite as loud as Meg Ryan, but then she won't be badly overacting when she has an actual orgasm will she?

Allow Her to Not Orgasm

By *definition*, half of all married sex is below average...

Some nights are going to be crazy hot lustful poundings. Others are going to be a little more sedate and relaxed. So rather than fighting hard to make every single night of sex a Hollywood production, why not embrace the fact that not every night is going to risk fractures from curled toes or shredded bedding. If you're only having sex one or two times a week and each attempt is *"hardcore sexing you up baby"*, she might be declining you another one or two nights a week because she isn't in the mood for the full on experience. You might be triggering her protection shields again.

She may be willing for something more low key. A little lubricant and a few minutes of her time may very well be more acceptable to her than another hour long attempt at intercourse. She might just be worried that when you ask for sex you're hoping for the thing with the jumper cables and the butter again.

So while it is counter-intuitive, try... *"Would you like some below average sex tonight?"* as a line once in a while. Remember to smile like a kid caught with his hand in the cookie jar attempting to use cute as a defusing tactic. Follow-up line... *"You know you almost want it."*

She just might like the husbandly version of a pump and dump once in a while. Remember when I said she came from a long line of sluts? Well based on their actions it seems clear that sluts love being pumped and dumped, so a couple times a week of just using your wife's body with her consent is going to meet her slut needs.

Sometimes women get off on the emotional closeness from the sex in and of itself. The quest for her to have three orgasms and a fourth squirting orgasm might be more about your fantasy needs of being a pro stick than her actual desires on any given day. Ideally you want to work toward having sex as being some sort of default setting where she has to make an active decision not to have sex, rather than an active decision to have sex. Also getting more semen inside her vagina is going to mildly increase her sex drive as well. There is testosterone in your semen that gets absorbed through the vaginal walls, so regular vaginal sex can turn a lower sex drive woman into a much higher sex drive woman. Take everything you can get.

Only About 30% of What You Try Works in Bed

Most women are bad in bed, as are most men. One of the great things about being married is you have enough time to make a few mistakes and do some trial and error and correct things. Sometimes you just have a conversation about what is working or not working in the relationship and most particularly in the bedroom.

Jennifer and I have always had a good sexual relationship, but it's really been a series of long plateaus followed by leaps upwards in understanding. Especially in the bedroom it can take years to learn each other's buttons and hot spots.

Sometimes you even change physiologically over the years as well. I remember that back in my twenties my balls were too sensitive to touch during sex and I'd just tense up from it. Everything about touching them just resulted in a sensation of weird discomfort. At some point around age 30 they started feeling deliciously good from being played with. We had to talk about that seeing as I had made it previously and quite expressly clear to Jennifer... in a couple of, ah... "short sharp directives", that she wasn't to trifle with my sugar-lumps.

"I thought you hated that."

"I thought I did too, it's just different now somehow."

"Well ok, I can do that."

/tweaks balls

"(Contented sigh)"

So talk and try new things – only about 30% of the things we have tried have really worked for us, but we have tried an awful lot of things. Sex is a team sport unless it's masturbation. This is how you both get good with each other. I'm by no means a bad lay myself. But I do Jennifer much better than I would somebody I was having a first time with.

Accept that most women are bad in bed... at first. But as long as they are into you and willing to learn, the sky is the limit. You just have to set that intention into your marriage.

Playing Pussy Hero 4 Isn't Fun Anymore

Much of what I talk about involves staying in careful control of yourself; paying attention to what you are doing, why you are doing it, how you are doing it, being mindful and having a plan. Overall this is a good practice but taken too far can make you a little less playful and animated than you could be.

There's hardly enough time in one day to: work, work out, work on the house, work on a hobby, work on the kids' homework with them and work her over really good at the end of the day. All work and no play made Jack a dull boy, even if it's all supposedly Sex Rank building stuff. Don't forget to relax a little and have fun once in a while.

In the bedroom there's a lot that can turn into work as well. Am I touching her just right? Is she going to orgasm? I'm doing this, then this, then that. I'm holding back on cumming because she's not done yet. How do I look? She's wearing something frilly to bed so now I gotta make sure this goes really well. We did it her on top the last two times and so I should be on top of her because she likes that but I'm so tired tonight.

A few rounds of mental gymnastics like that and you end up being very controlled and emotionally absent during sex. The old Woody Allen joke is that he thought of entire games of baseball when making love to delay cumming too quickly. I think modern guys tend to be so hyper focused on the mechanics of what they are doing that they can lose the enjoyment of sex. I'm kissing like that, a little hair pulling like that, a little spank like that, kiss the boobs like that, doing the sexy move to the clit like that... after a while it's kind like playing Pussy Hero 4 on the Wii. Just mash the A Button until the meter fills up, and then it's BBAB then DOWN UP DOWN really quickly to do the Ultimate Finishing Move. You're welcome baby.

Of course this is all just great for the wife, she gets a great orgasm, but you're turning into her favorite vibrator...which isn't any fun for you anymore. All this work to get good sex and you aren't even enjoying it.

Lose Control with Her

The solution is simple, you just let yourself lose control.

Imagine for a moment that she was so unbelievably sexy; you couldn't control yourself with her.

How would you have sex with her then?

How would you have sex with her if you no longer cared about anything other than what you felt and what you wanted to feel?

How would you have sex with her if you could no longer think and your body was totally in control of your actions for a few minutes?

How would you have sex with her if the only thing that mattered was getting semen into her vagina?

Then once your body is finished with her body, you drift back to proper consciousness.

She may or may not orgasm from that. Frankly it doesn't matter. She'll feel sexy and desired though. And don't blow it by apologizing either. Try these phrases...

"Wow that was intense."
"That was amazing, how did you do that to me?"
"I think my balls might hurt a little."
"Can we not do that more than twice a week please."
"Holy crap that was just half a tab of Viagra."
"We're gonna stay married together forever right?"
"What year is it?"
"I'm starting to like you I think."
"This was consensual right?"

I'm not saying you do this every time, that's going to get a little old after a while. But once in a while it's going to make her feel sexy and desirable, which in turn is going to prime her pump for more sex in the future. Also you're going to like it.

Make Some Noise When You Orgasm

For the most part I tend to work fairly hard on being in control with Jennifer and making sure she orgasms (if she wants it, which is most times), but then there is usually a vague crossing over to this out of control sense. Usually it's the last five to thirty seconds before I orgasm. There is a small element of acting to make it happen, but also a larger element of just going with it as well.

And when you cum into her, don't just hold your breath and ejaculate. Make some noise of some sort and thrust hard as you pour into her. Be like tiger. RAWR!

Draw Attention to Her Sexual Interest

Also it doesn't hurt to make her aware that you know she has some slut in her genetic makeup. It's okay to lightly tease her when she expresses sexual interest in something. If you pick up on her sexual interest, you can always frame it that you are responding to her sexual interest in you.

And don't misunderstand this chapter to mean that you shouldn't ask her for sex or try and initiate sex. You're still going to do all that, you're just not going to try and pressure her into sex with you. In fact, taking away the offer of sex can sometimes instantly make her drop her shields and start to pursue you. You ask and if she says "No", you go about your day.

Chapter 14
Variety is the Spice of Wife

Girls Like Bad Boys Because Girls Want to be Bad Too

In the last chapter I suggested you don't *push* on your wife for sex because it makes her defensive and she puts up shields. In this chapter we're going to take her inner sluttiness and use it to *pull* her sexual interest. Somewhere inside your wife is a slutty girl that wants to get out, so to meet her inner slut you need to offer her things that appeal to it.

This is extremely counter-intuitive as she may be denying you or having low levels of regular sex, so offering spankings, handcuffs, rough sex, blindfolded blowjobs etc seem like they wouldn't work. They might not work, but you won't know until you try. I wouldn't go for this stuff straight away if you think your Sex Rank is lower than hers, but if you're pulling level or ahead of her, you may very well be surprised at how eager for some of it she is. You simply willing to be "dirty" is an Alpha Male thing in and of itself and can pull some additional interest on you.

In fact, if she's interested in any of the more kinky stuff, she will very likely seek it out and find it easily enough; the Internet is the Wal-Mart of kink. If you don't make *you* an option for exploring that aspect of herself with, she might simply explore things by herself, which ultimately means another person will be involved. When your wife is exploring her personal kink with another man behind your back, you're in a bad place. I know of several cases where wives have developed an intense relationship with an online dominant playing BDSM games via chat. One case had the husband quite excited by his wife's new sexual interest and activity in the bedroom – until he found out she was performing sex acts on him at the direction of her online "master". Emotional affairs can be no less serious than physical ones.

When you are marrying a sexually inexperienced "good girl," you need to be particularly open to the possibility of change. Ten years into a marriage a thirty-four year old is going to feel far more confident than the twenty-four year old she was. If you scrunch her into the "good girl" mantle forevermore, she may start seeing you as the *jailer* of her sexuality. If she decides to plot some little escapes, you'll be the last to know.

Half the reason women like the Bad Boys so much is that they get to play the role of Bad Girl.

How to Get Her to Dress Sexier

This is easy. *You* dress more sexily.

I'll pad out this section with my usual rhetoric about women calibrating themselves to their man, but I think you guys should be getting this by now. The only person in your relationship you can really control is you.

If your wife is a 7 and badly dressed, your begging/pleading/demanding that she turn into an 8 is nothing but hot air at best and a Display of Low Value at worst. The solution is that you turn yourself from a 7 to an 8 and she'll probably calibrate herself to an 8 shortly afterward.

Your mere *talk* to encourage her to dress better is a waste of effort compared to your just pulling your own look together. Trust me on this, no woman wants to be tagging along after her man while he's Peacocking some threads and she looks like she's shopping at Goodwill. She's automatically going to up her game to keep pace with him. She knows in the pit of her stomach that if she doesn't step it up, some other woman will take notice of the incongruence between the couple and possibly start moving in on her man. Or Mr. Peacock will take notice and accidentally meet someone for some completely harmless coffee sometime.

There's usually a bit of a lag between upping your Sex Rank and her doing the same, but if you keep at it long enough she will likely respond. Women tend to disbelieve their husbands are actually improving themselves at first. And like I've said before, if you keep upping your Sex Rank and she doesn't respond, you're in a better place to attract someone new into your life.

When your wife shows off some skin, stare and get caught at it. She's trying to pull male attention when she shows off her legs or boobs. Why shouldn't she get that attention from you?

How to Get Her to Wear Lingerie

It's easy. *You* wear lingerie.

Oh relax, I didn't say you have to get yourself up into a lace teddy and fishnets. What you should do is get yourself some nice silk boxer shorts and wear them to bed. Have her experience the enjoyment of feeling them on you and playing with you in them. Flirt a little, tease her, play with her. Let her experience the moment of thrill when you finally take them off and your cock pops free. After that you can start suggesting that she tries wearing some for herself.

Go online shopping for lingerie together. There are plenty of stores online to choose from. You can sift through hundreds of items and pull out eight to ten things that you might like, then she can look through those and choose the ones she likes best.

Do bear in mind that 95% of all lingerie only looks good on lingerie models and professional transvestites. Most real women have nothing but an acute sense of embarrassment when trying to wear something the size of a Post-It note spread over their entire body. So if she tells you that something is going to look bad on her, it's pointless to buy it as it's going to make her feel less sexy when she wears it.

Lingerie is a *play* item, so you can make a lot more progress in *playing* with her while she's wearing a fun sleep shirt and a silky thong than with just about anything else. If it makes her feel stupid and fat, her shields will come way up.

How to Get Her to Use Sex Toys

Wait for it, wait for it...

This is easy. *You* buy some sex toys for you.

Go find a sex toy that you want used on you and bring it home and try it out together. Perhaps a small butt plug (try a SMALL butt plug before you get anything larger. Just trust me on this, I'm okay, but *damn* that hurt) or a cock ring. Perhaps you could try a masturbation sleeve, or handcuffs or a blindfold...all intended for use on you.

After you've tried a couple of things out on you and you've *played* with them together, she's more likely to be open to having something *played* with on her. Don't reach for a 12-inch angry dildo as a starting point either; find something she's comfortable with and more likely to enjoy.

Jennifer and I used to watch *"Sex and the City"* on HBO back in the day. One episode had a plot line about Miranda getting hooked on a vibrator called "The Rabbit." So naturally we got one of those as her first vibe.

How to Get Your Wife to Watch Porn with You

Okay, you got me on this one - you're already watching porn aren't you.

Porn is a contentious issue. Many people view it as immoral and against their religious beliefs. If that's you, then I generally advise you not to break your own moral code.

However even without a moral or religious issue with porn, most wives have some general concerns about porn use. Such as:

1. Allowing you to watch porn is going to open the door to something she really doesn't want, like your being a total porn-dog and ignoring her or being less into her.

2. Watching porn is just going to be awkward, embarrassing or just offensive.

3. You thinking less of her for watching it; the good girl image can die hard.

4. She may actually be worried that she will like it.

My personal view of porn is that *"It isn't a problem, until it is a problem."* Often things that are really fun and enjoyable become much less so and even destructive if abused. Take bacon for example - bacon is the most wonderful food in all of human history and probably will never be displaced from that status. Bacon is crunchy and tasty and fatty and delicious. A salad with bacon is just a game of hide-and-seek the bacon.

I could eat pounds of bacon all day, though and therein lies the problem. My heart would eventually stop from the extra hundreds of pounds of body weight gained from my bacon consumption. One possible solution is to just ban bacon, but who wants to live in a world without bacon? Well maybe pigs do, but that's not the point.

So anyway, I eat bacon, just not lots of it. Despite the fact that I avoid my doctor and cholesterol lab work, I'm fairly sure that for me, bacon is not a problem. All things in moderation being the key.

So to me, a few viewings of porn a month isn't really a problem. Especially if there is still enough weekly sex happening that both spouses are happy with their sex lives. If it was a case of the husband sneaking multiple episodes of heavy porn viewing a week and then not being able to have sex with the wife, then that's a problem. If you got fired for watching porn at work, that's a problem. If your children are all hungry and crying because you were meant to be watching them and you just watched porn instead, that's a problem. If you start making a pot of oatmeal and sneak away for a minute to watch some porn and you discover an hour later that you are trying to smelt oatmeal, then that's a problem.

For some people watching porn actually aids in their sustaining a monogamous relationship. There is a strong natural inclination to both create a primary relationship, but also an impulse to try and sneak something extra on the side with no strings attached.

Particularly the male Body Agenda fuels this impulse as a few minutes of fun can result in an extra offspring. So an erotic video can actually go some distance to meeting that built-in need for variety and excitement. I'm not saying that if the porn gets banned from your house that you'll end up automatically cheating, but I do think it can play a moderating influence on that promiscuous impulse.

The trouble is that so much porn is just bad. And by bad, I mean pathetically awful. Modern adult stores are overwhelming in the supply of titles that somehow all look nearly the same. Personally when I get surrounded by 1000 DVD titles with a picture of tits and a vagina on the front cover, I start shutting down from the over-choice. There's bad acting and then there's the stilted dialogue and faux orgasmic wailing of porn. Sometimes porn is just better with the sound off. And then there's the Internet, which is like the interstate system of porn. Got a particular kink? The Internet can hook you up with so much of it that you'll be sorry you asked.

Sometimes less is more. Rather than reach for *"Anal Gang Bang Cumwhores 23"* as the starting point, you can tone it down to something explicit but also sex ed in tone. About a decade ago Jennifer and I watched *"The Better Sex Video Series"* together. Being sex crazed, I'm not sure I personally learned terribly much new, but it had good production values and was helpful at opening up things between us. Plus Jennifer was basically drenched in readiness for me after watching them, so I'm pretty sure she liked it.

Make watching porn together more of a romantic time together. Slip into your silk boxers and cuddle up together on the couch with a glass of wine and watch some explicit sex ed. It's a great idea to fondle each other while you watch too. Plan ahead and have a washable something spread on the couch under you both; avoid the *"where are the body fluids going to fly?"* logistical cockblock.

Actually as I recall when we watched the first video in *"The Better Sex Series"* together, I hauled the whole mattress off the bed and dragged it to the living room in front of the TV. But then I am the master of subtlety aren't I.

Over time you can start stepping it up to something more racy and explicit if she likes it. Baby steps are the way to go.

The Question to ask About Porn

When I watch porn, is the sex with my wife getting better or worse?

Use Porn, Don't Abuse Porn

My general advice is very simple - your wife comes before porn. I don't care how much I watch, but if I do watch, I don't masturbate to orgasm unless Jennifer has passed on sex for the night and I can't fall asleep which is fairly rare. Most couples get into problems when the porn becomes a tool for one of them to meet their needs for sexual release without their partner being involved. If the husband orgasms without his wife, he can't then immediately have sex with her, even if he wanted to; he's all done for the day.

What moderate porn use can do however, is create a sexual charge for one or both of the couple, which then can be used as fuel for more intense sex together. Most women are not going to have a problem with their man watching a moderate amount of porn, getting sexually wound up and then unleashing that pent up need as a great flood inside her vagina.

The wives gaining a sexual charge from watching porn together is exactly what most husbands want to happen. He wants her all wound up and taking that pent up desire out on him!

What She Means by Saying "I'm Bored"

I do think dressing sexy, lingerie, sex toys and a little porn can greatly improve both her and your sex drive and desire for each other. Monogamy is not always easy and in some ways – if you remember the Body Agenda chapter – is somewhat unnatural. The problem with monogamy isn't that it doesn't work, but that it does work and is so successful. All that monogamy promises is a happy family, nice home, steady jobs, and well behaved kids...just with the same old pussy and penis forever and ever. It can get a little boring at times, thus the need to purposely enrich your sexual environment together.

You need to pay particular attention to her when she says *"I'm bored."* On the surface that doesn't really get many guys' attention because it doesn't sound critical. She's not yelling or screaming, she's just bored... so it's easy to ignore her saying it.

However, you have to remember that most women have a submissive element to their personality in relation to their love interest, meaning they actually can get stimulation from being submissive to a man. The word "stimulation" is carefully chosen, it's not so much pleasure or enjoyment as the right sort of thing to activate their sexual interest. What she's really saying when she says *"I'm bored"* is *"I'm not getting my submissive itch scratched. I'm just sitting around waiting for you to make something happen so I can react sexually to you."*

Or put more crudely, *"I'm bored"* = *"I need a dominant male fix."* You should take this phrase as a clear warning sign that you need to take some immediate action, or risk bad things happening.

The first and most common way to get that need met is by trying to force the issue by creating a Fitness Test for you to bump back on her. She's being not so much a "bitch", just under-stimulated and is trying to create stimulation. When you pass the test and act dominantly towards her, she's getting her submissive itch scratched which is what she wants.

It's very rare that a woman knows herself well enough, to realize on a conscious level that she's feeling the need to be submissive. It's also an additional step to be able to express that verbally and still be pleased when her husband dominates her on cue. Most women find that having to say they need to be dominated *just ruins it* when he complies; *he's just supposed to know and do it.* The phrase *"I'm bored"* is about as far as women go with hinting before they start feeling like they are the one running the game, rather than the game being run on them.

The other way a wife can get her dominant male fix is pretty simple; she can find another man to excite her. Most wives will still love their husbands, they're simply... well, boring. She probably didn't even mean to go looking for another guy, but one thing can lead to another quickly as soon as the dopamine pathways are getting all lit up inside her head. It's so exciting. Pretty soon she's addicted to the flirty texts, emails and phone calls. You sure as hell want to interrupt that before she decides meet him and do something physical.

You can probably say to yourself, *"Oh really? But we have this, and that, and I give her everything she could ever want and we don't fight or anything. Things are great."* No they aren't great; she's bored. I'll finish with a line that isn't exactly 100% guaranteed to happen, but it rhymes so it will stick in your head and you'll remember it better when you hear her say *"I'm bored"* to you....

If you're boring, she's whoring.

As an aside, if your wife knows that you know about this section of the book, if she say's *"I'm bored,"* she's usually doing it quite purposely to instigate gaining your attention and/or seeking to initiate sex. But she can do it without directly saying that is what she wants to happen. Once you realize it's a big playful submissive hint, it can be quite fun to take your cue and un-bore her.

Be Unpredictable With Sex

Never have sex in the same position more than twice in a row. This is a rule.

It's boring to keep doing the same thing night after night, which means in time she will think you are boring. And while there is not a "three doggy-styles and you're out" rule, you're digging yourself a hole. Years might roll by and she'll be just as faithful as can be, but women are sexy creatures and if you serve up the same wilted salad, eventually she may take an interest in another chef's celery sticks for a little variety. Heck, the goldfish probably has more toys in his bowl than most wives see in their bedroom. Mating in captivity equals sad pandas.

Here's the deal...stop asking her for sex. *"Are we having sex tonight?"* *"Do you want sex tonight?"* *"Are you in the mood for something?"* These are yes/no questions. If she says *"No"*, you'll get nothing...

...again. Now your job is to lie there with a rock hard throbbing cock and not touch her. Die quietly.

If she says *"Yes"*, she's either mentally agreeing to the same old stuff (which is boring), or is having a flashback about the time some high school chump asked her on date and when she asked him *"A date where?"* he just said, *"I don't know, just a date."* Which is to say a date to nowhere.

What you should do is go to bed with a plan. Set your own mental agenda for how sex will play out tonight. It doesn't have to be anything over the top. Maybe tonight is missionary. Tomorrow is doggy. The next night is her on top. After that she's on top again, but this time when she wants you to come, she has to pull herself off you, lie on her back and ask for it rough and fast.

A man without a plan is not a man. So instead of asking for sex, just announce your plan to her. *"Tonight I want to go down on you first, then kiss my way up your body and slowly grind in you until you tell me to come."* See how much stronger, how Alpha that is compared to, *"Are we doing it?" (Oh please say yes, please, please, please.... awwwwwwwww).*

You should announce your plan before you go to bed. Say it as you nuzzle her from behind in the bathroom as she brushes her teeth before bed. Lay a deep kiss on her in the hallway in passing between dinner and the kids' homework and whisper it in her ear. Text her the plan at lunchtime. As you lay together slick and cuddling in the afterglow, casually mention your plans for the next night. If you do that last one, make sure it's with a playful cheeky smile.

If she has a plan of her own, then no problem, you can roll with it. Maybe she's so turned on she just breaks your plan halfway through and heads towards orgasm #2. Dude, roll with that. The point of your having a plan is to trigger her sex drive by getting her excited about what is going to happen.

If she says "No", then so be it, but at least she's got a clear idea of how good "Yes" is going to be. It helps to make the idea of having sex the default setting in the bedtime routine. Instead of deciding to have sex, she has to make a decision not to have sex. It's a subtle but important difference.

Try a Rough Sex Experiment

If you haven't tried having rough/very firm/hard sex with your wife, try a little experiment.

The next time you have sex, without particularly asking permission or announcing your intention, just pound her harder than usual. You can get her off first by fingers or tongue as the curtain raiser, but once it's P in V time, climb on top of her and go hard at it. Don't worry about whether or not she'll like it or if she'll orgasm, don't worry about how perfect your orgasm will be this time either. All you're testing out is how she responds to getting vigorously screwed. You can work on the finer points later.

If you're worried about really injuring her, relax a little. Vaginas are pretty solid things as they are designed to have eight pound babies get pushed out of there. Unless you have some sort of porn stunt-cock, it's very unlikely that you could really injure her if you have enough lubrication and wetness. Your cock would break before her vagina does, so give going rough a trial.

If she likes it, a good sign is her being unusually cuddly after sex. Another thing to look for is *what is she like the next day?* Happier? Doting on you? Smiling at you more? She cooked you a favorite meal? She may not even realize she liked it as much as she did.

Several years back I started trying rough sex on Jennifer. The first few times I tried really pounding Jennifer hard, I was nervous about it and honestly expected a negative reaction. I was a Nice Guy and she was a good girl and it all just seemed out of character for us both. I only starting thinking about doing it based on reading things saying women liked it. So as awkward as that first attempt felt, I tried it anyway. To my surprise, my sweet, shy, naïve, polite, quiet wife lapped it up like the head cheerleader. Plus instead of our usual post coital routine of me snuggling into her, she snuggled into me every time I tried it. Not once or twice... every time. The next day she would be all giggly and a little silly with me. Huh... who knew?

So even though I was surprised by her reaction and I felt uncomfortable doing it, I'm not stupid. I quickly learned she did in fact like it and added it to the regular sexual menu. Over time I grew less worried by it and started really enjoying her reaction to it. Eventually it grew into becoming something I actively enjoy as well. It's not the whole menu by any means, but it's a reasonably frequent choice for us.

Give rough sex a trial run if you haven't already. Your wife may just like it. And if you haven't talked about a safeword, consider "Ow!" to be the safeword for now.

Breaking Down the Sexually Shy Wife

Some wives are just sexually shy; I know because I married one. With a really slutty girl you can simply Alpha up and demand something sexual and you'll get it. But taking that same approach with a sexually shy wife will probably backfire on you. If you become too assertive too fast, it may become too stimulating and simply drive her deeper into her anxiety. Ironically, the behavior that can unpick her locks is actually adding Beta comfort building. The comfort building decreases her anxiety so she can fully relax enough to start enjoying it more easily.

Here's an example... I've had some recent email from a blog reader with a very shy wife when it comes to sex. My advice to him was to try the Sexy Move in the shower routine (described later in the book); when she's showering he climbs in with her and playfully washes her back, asks her to wash his back, some playful little sexual teasing and then he asks her to step out of the shower so he could finish his shower. This is intended as a playful Alpha invasion of her space in the shower as enjoyable attention. In fact the entire point of the routine is that you turn her on a bit, but then you don't have sex with her, it's all a little bit of a tease toying with her. To which he replied:

"Very good stuff. I loved the shower pass post. She locks the door to shower, so I think I'm going to get a stick at the ready to pick the lock...probably in a couple weeks when she's ovulating."

To which I said, *"Oh hang on a moment, she's more anxious than I thought!"* If very shy wife has the door locked to the shower and it's likely she does it on purpose to keep her husband out. So if he pops the lock and marches into the bathroom with a hard on, she will probably experience this like a normal wife would experience a SWAT team entering the bathroom. She's going to scream in terror, try and cover herself with a hand bra and fall over in the shower crying. Not as sexy as intended.

A better approach is to let her know the overall plan and get her to agree to it. Yes this takes away the element of surprise, but that's the point. Then you break down the process into a number of smaller steps. The first step would be to have her shower with the door unlocked. That's it. Maybe do that for a week or so. Then the next step is to have him come into the bathroom while she showers. They can have a conversation in there...he can brush his teeth or something. Do that for maybe a week. Then the next step is opening the shower door while he's in the bathroom, a week of that. Then maybe he can get in with her and wash her back.

Is this long and tedious? It sure is. But it also might work a lot better than popping the lock and rocking the cock at her. It does take a slow steady pressure to continue to advance through the steps. Each step comes with a degree of discomfort that needs to be passed through. The Alpha doesn't let her off the hook for developing her sexual confidence and stretching her limits, while the Beta praises and soothes. You must have both tools in the toolbox.

As each step is made she needs praise and positive attention. As long as progress is being made in the direction you want, you just stick with the process. You're not going to go from a very shy wife to a well trained slutty wife in a single day, or a week, or maybe even a year. But you can make constant progress toward that goal. It's all vastly easier to have her consent and understanding to purposely stretch her limits together, but you can make some progress with rewarding the behavior you wish to see - it's just going to be much slower.

At the beginning of our relationship, Jennifer was extremely shy and sexually naïve from her sheltered upbringing. By "naïve", I mean utterly clueless, as in the first time I fingered her to orgasm before we were married, she didn't even know what had happened to her. I had to explain what an orgasm was and how it happened. Talk about finding a way to Display High Value.

We've always had a lot of sex, but early on it was fairly bad sex compared to now... though I was so excited to be getting laid I thought it was awesome. The first month of vaginal sex together she lay there stiff as a board and soundless. I considered adding a strobe light to the bedroom to make it look like she was moving. Each time did get a little better though and I gently pushed back her boundaries. I didn't force her, just wore her down with expressions of enjoyment, pleasure for her, praise and thanking.

Getting Jennifer to give me a blowjob took months of work. It started off with one little kiss on the tip of my penis as a starting point for a handjob. I let her know I liked it. She kissed me a little longer the next time. I let her know I liked that. Then she took the tip – just the tip – into her mouth... and so on and so on. Eventually, blowjobs were on the menu as something she tolerated and could do. Now giving them makes her wet and horny; I can *gently* push her head down on me further and tug on her hair when she gives them and that turns her on even more.

Even now, we are still learning things together. Now Jennifer relishes doing sexy things that once made her nervous. Now she does things that I could never have imagined her doing in the beginning of our marriage, *including some things I could never have even imagined either of us being into* when we married. There was an understanding between us that we were going to push her boundaries together. She was comfortable in her discomfort. Now, apart from her persistent fear of the thing with the jumper cables and the butter, she's positively slutty with me in the manner of my choosing. What's not to love about that?

It's an old joke between us that I've corrupted her and am *"a very bad man."* I always say that's why she likes me so much. She always nuzzles into me after I say that. Even sheltered good-girls have an inner slut that likes to come out and play.

Chapter 15
Ovulation Game

Women Aren't Random

To many men, women are frighteningly random creatures. One day she seems perfectly fine, then suddenly mad, then horny, then sad. It's confusing to find something that worked with her on one day totally backfires on a different day. The problem usually comes from not anticipating the effect of her menstrual cycle. Once you understand her cycle, a great deal of her behavior will start to make sense and you can start to predict and plan for her general mood, months in advance.

I work with a lot of women and if I pay attention, I can start telling where they are in their cycles based on the variation in mood and appearance over time. The ones on birth control are easy because my wife is on it too, so I just think of them as a week ahead, a week behind, or opposite my wife's cycle. I track Jennifer's cycle in my day planner, so I'm trying to not sound creepy about this, I just can't help but notice where they all are in their cycles too. It's probably best if you just consider it a very minor superpower.

Birth control pills stop ovulation, so the effect of their cycle is less dramatic, but there is still a variation in their mood and interest. Ovulation is a subtle effect, one week she starts just rocking a slightly sexed up version of herself - it's a slightly lower cut top, the extra sheen on the lipstick, the earrings they like. Her ovulation means she thinks, *"I spent an extra ten minutes on my appearance today just because I wanted to"*. Then the next week she's a little snippy and easily annoyed. The week after that she's *"headachy"*... because usually she isn't going to broadcast she is cramping up because she's on her menses. The week after that she's back to "normal" and then the cycle repeats. It's really not rocket science to figure out where a woman is in her cycle if you have frequent contact with her and pay her basic attention.

I suppose I could use this information for evil, but I only use it to influence my decision matrix; *"Let's do lunch"* versus *"Giving you some space"* versus *"You okay? I have some Motrin if you need it"* versus *"Let's really push and get this project done."* It just makes it smoother and easier to get along. I don't have an Excel spreadsheet of this stuff or anything creepy like that (that would make for an awkward meeting in Human Resources), like I say – I just notice it.

I once had a female co-worker drive ten miles out of her way to bring me a bagel because I said I was hungry. Lower cut top, chatty as all get out, full hair takedown and redo in front of me, playful swats on my arm. Okay... I really can't tell a lie on this one.... *I really like this sort of treatment.* The very next week I tried to finesse a repeat bagel delivery and was given a curt, *"Find your own damn lunch!"* The first time she was ovulating, the second time she had PMS. See how that works?

Women have a predictable cycle of generalized mood and interest, but most men never bother to learn it and just think women are random. If you play hard Alpha on a woman with PMS it usually backfires, while if you play soft Beta on an ovulating woman that usually backfires. If your wife is ovulating, playfully chasing her, escalating to a tickle fight and trying to pull her pants off might work a treat. Trying the same thing on her when she's starting to PMS... probably not so much. The same thing in the middle of her having her period is going to be... *funky.*

So you can see that learning both Alpha and Beta approaches to a woman is a key skill in marriage.

Menstrual Cycle 101

Perhaps if your sex ed teacher had explained you could more easily score when she was ovulating, you would have paid more attention in class. In case you drifted off, he's the breakdown for the typical woman. (Some women have very long menstrual cycles and the day count will be off for them.)

The first day of a woman's menses marks the first day of their cycle. So "day 1" of her cycle is the first day that she starts bleeding on her period. Menses can last 3-7 days. Most women aren't feeling all that sexy during their period and honestly, who can blame them? My advice is to use this time productively and get some of the items on the "to do" list completed. Make sure you have items like handjobs and coming all over her breasts on the list. (Notice how much better you feel about yourself when you get things done. It's energizing!)

After her menses stops, she moves into her essentially most normal phase of the month. She's not bleeding, she's not wildly horny, and she's not PMSing. After this comes the ovulation phase.

Ovulation can happen at any point from day 7 through 16, though it typically hits on day 13, 14 or 15. From the time her menses stops, her sex drive will be active, but around ovulation itself she is going to feel a surge in sexual interest. This is when she is most likely to experience orgasms, want multiple orgasms, be the wettest, cheat on you and generally seek raw dog Alpha Male pounding. This is the time when you grabbing a handful of hair and bossing her in the bedroom is will likely get a positive response. *This is when you try your rough sex experiment on her.*

The days surrounding ovulation are when she is most likely to suddenly decide she wants to *"go to a club, just to dance"*... this is why so much of the Alpha Male-oriented game works for pickup artists. It doesn't really work on women in general, but it does work on ovulating women in specific.

After ovulation, her sexual interest tends to drop. Around day 21 of her cycle the infamous mood swings and drama from PMS can start up. A sudden burst of temper or irritation can flag her as being on this part of her cycle. Her physically uncomfortable and bloated feelings generally continue until menstruation itself starts. Trying to pulling her hair and boss her about in the bedroom will likely prove counterproductive. Leg shaving behavior decreases this week. These are great times to proactively up your Beta Male skill game. These are good nights to offer to cook, do that extra errand and offer backrubs.

It's a fine line to walk...*do* cater to her because she isn't feeling the greatest, but don't cater to temper tantrums - those need to be addressed, or they will get worse and worse over the years. Men aren't allowed to use hormones as a defense for bad behavior, *"Sorry your honor, the testosterone made me do it."* Neither should women be allowed to excuse bad behavior for their hormonal surges.

As an aside, if you're out in the dating market, PMS is a reason why you shouldn't wait 3-4 days to call a girl back. If you really click in the club when she's near her ovulation sexual activation, the longer you wait to call her, the further you move from her ovulation and the closer you get to her PMS. Maybe this is why she didn't seem very excited to get your call.

Generally speaking, all the sexual attempts for the smart husband during the month should be all-purpose mutual satisfaction, but around ovulation it is very important to make her feel desired. This is when the "why don't you just rip my clothes off and take me" gene kicks in. You should always assume that an ovulating woman is going to act like a total slut.

Track Your Wife's Menstrual Cycle

Since Jennifer is on birth control pills, her cycle is very stable and I can predict it as far into the future as my current day planner goes. Her day 1 always hits on a Tuesday and knowing that makes it all a piece of cake to map out her cycle. I use colored highlighters and mark her menses, ovulation and PMS for months in advance. Days 1-3 (Tue-Thurs) as her period marked in pink, Days 13-17 (Mon-Fri) her ovulation and being "sunny" marked in yellow and Day 20-22 (Mon-Wed) as PMS emotions and feeling "blue" as... well blue. As it is with this system, I generally know my wife's cycle better than she does. No one has ever asked me about the highlighter marks in my day planner either, so it's really pretty private.

This all may sound like overkill, but a couple of times now I've saved a weeklong vacation from being ruined by knowing months in advance that she would be on her period the week we planned to go. We just went the next week and had a much better time of it. We haven't wasted babysitting for Date Nights either. I also used to get quite frustrated when I got all worked up during the day thinking about getting home to her, only to discover the invincible underwear on in bed. I don't mind the blowjobs, but if I've been worked up all day for pussy, I get frustrated.

Learning a New Woman's Cycle

Now for the guys meeting new women...

...if you can discover when your target is having either her PMS spike or her menstrual flow, she has also by default told you when her ovulation is. You just need to do a little math. Ovulation basically comes two weeks after her menses starts

Week 1 Menses   (Day 1 = Menses Starts)
Week 2 Normal
Week 3 Ovulation   (Day 13-15 *usually!*)
Week 4 PMS

The days that you particularly push for dates and breaking out of the Friendzone with a woman are when she is ovulating.

Women that are on birth control packs usually start menses on a Tuesday, though they seem to have reduced effects of horniness from the ovulation effect, mostly because the birth control pills stop ovulation from happening. They still have a cycle of mood on birth control pills, it's just not as dramatic.

Bear in mind though that not every woman is on birth control pills and some women have very erratic cycles, or cycles longer than 28 days. There's an element of educated guesswork involved.

How to Tell if a Woman is Ovulating

Of course everyone wants to know how to look at a woman and just know if she is ovulating. The trick is that it may take some time to do it, but once you have it down, you usually have it down pat with that particular woman forever.

The key point to remember is that ovulation lasts only a few days, usually not more than two and that it is the highest point of sexual interest for a woman. Even quite low sex drive women can perk up and mew for sexual attention during ovulation. It's when a woman is most likely to cheat on a partner, they are more likely to orgasm and in plain simple terms when they like sex the roughest.

Remembering back to the Body Agenda chapter, unlike most primates a human female has a concealed ovulation. This forced her The Time Before Writing mate to pay constant attention to her, otherwise he could just bang the female two days a month and then go drinking with his buddies the other 26 days. Or maybe just work on his cave paintings which the female thinks will never sell.

The women are usually just as tricked as the men are by her ovulation being concealed. They don't wake up in the morning thinking *"Oh wow, I'm ovulating, I'm going to need the Come Fuck Me heels and a Brazilian wax"*, they just wake up and think, *"I want to wear the red dress today, I feel great"*. This is why women struggling to have a baby wander around taking their temperature half the month waiting for the sudden increase in body heat signaling it's time to make the donuts. Most women don't know either.

So what you're looking for is a number of small subtle changes in her appearance and personality away from her normal baselines appearance and mood towards the sexy. Women just stick to their basic appearance, but up the effort slightly. It's not a move from "demure angel" to "raging slut." It's a move from *"I look like a Sex Rank 7"*, to *"I dressed nice and did my make up to max out my Sex Rank to an 8 today."*

Usually it's easier to peg her grumpy week from PMS and her not feeling as great weeks when she's having her menses. Once you have those down just watch for the day when she just seems perky and smiling. Then you'll notice a few extra little touches of her making herself look sexier. It's more time on her hair, it's the big dangly earrings, the top that is a little lower than usual, she touches you on the arm when talking. Suddenly you'll just see it. So make a move.

A Gentleman is Always Ready

If you are still in the dating market, it's important to always be ready for sex. You should always have condoms easily accessible somewhere and a little bottle of lube may not hurt either. If you're with a woman and you're making progress with her and sex gets put on the table, it can come off the table if you have no condom.

Importantly, the seemingly random Single Night Lays almost always happen with a woman that is ovulating. So if she says "Yes" to sex and then changes to a "No" after you reveal no condom, then you are missing the opportunity that her ovulation gave you. Asking for sex four days later as she starts heading into PMS will get you nothing.

The other problem is, she might not care about the condom and because she's ovulating, you'd be quite possibly having a one night stand with your new baby's mama. Women won't usually be conscious of their own ovulation and when she is ovulating, it's the time she's most likely to dispense with the need to use a condom as well. (The Body Agenda votes to her to get her pregnant.)

Have More Than One Woman

This is really a dating/player thing, but here we go. Always have more than one woman that you are dating. If you get hooked into just one woman, your entire sex life will be dominated by her availability and mood. If she only offers sex when she is ovulating and a few more times a month, you're only going to have sex four to five times a month.

If you get a case of Oneitis (covered more in the next chapter) on a single girl, you're going to be very nervous and anxious around her and that will likely decrease her interest in you and cause your seductions to fail. The most likely time to get first sex from a woman is around her ovulation. If you wait two weeks until she ovulates and you mess it up, you've probably got another month to wait until your next shot at it, which means you don't get laid for six weeks total.

The solution then is to have more than one woman you are dating and always feel like you have a couple of back up women to fall back on. If you have three girlfriends, if one leaves you, it's not nearly as dramatic as when you're only girlfriend breaks up with you. If number three falls off the radar, you just call up girl number four from your cell phone address book. Always be making new friends and flirting with women. Players get laid all the time because women like having sex with players when they are ovulating. It's just a numbers game to tap them when they are ovulating.

If you have multiple women you are playing with, you're going to have far more sex as you hit multiple ovulation periods. If you really want to play a numbers game, you can approach a great many women let them know that *if they ever are in the mood, you can be discreet.* (The mood being ovulation, but the women won't realize that.) Then when they do ovulate, the mood strikes and *they can call you.*

Always track the first time a woman had sex with you. Make sure you call her and try and date her every twenty-eight days after that. There's a reasonable shot you're landing a date on her ovulation day over and over. If she sounds grumpy (PMS!) when you call, contact her again in three weeks.

Also women are pretty aware of the guys that are really getting laid. The more women you sleep with, the greater the Preselection effect and the more attractive and sexually dependable you seem. When ovulation hits them, they really don't have much interest in a Nice Guy; they want a womanizing asshole.

When She Initiates Sex

Because women are sexually responsive to men, most wives hardly ever "initiate sex". If you're a husband, you just need to get over this and understand that it's basically your job to initiate sex. She isn't really making a statement of dislike about you by not asking for sex, anymore than the TV does by not turning itself on and asking if you want to watch it.

You have to get up off the couch and push the buttons. You not initiating sex regularly is a bad sexual signal to her. Get-her-done!

However the times when she does come to you and ask for sex, you have to understand that she isn't really initiating sex; she is already sexually responding to you and it's very likely because she is ovulating. If you then turn her down for sex, it's a huge red flag to her Body Agenda that you aren't really a man that can get it done.

So if she ever initiates sex with you, you must take her up on that or risk her declining sexual interest in you. You have some leeway on this for wives as you have an established relationship, but turning down offered sex on a date typically ends things permanently with that woman, as she will always see you as sexually weak. From a Body Agenda point of view, there's no reason for a woman to risk getting pregnant to a man that can't have sex on command and without qualms. Passing on sexual hesitancy to her baby risks the child also being a sexual failure.

Declining sex to any woman who offers it usually results in their utter disgust with you. In comparison to men, women are sexually spoiled by the ease in which they can find a sexual partner; being turned down for sex is a shock to their sense of self-worth. So the typical reaction is to become offended by the man that turns them down, and that deep disgust can be permanent.

The exception to that rule is when the man is able to frame his declining of sex as not turning down something of value, but that having sex with her would in fact be a waste of an ejaculation. When a man is clearly having sex with better options than her, the frustration of not getting what she wants because the Preselection effect is so strong, primes her to find him enormously attractive.

Obviously don't actually say to a woman *"You're a waste of an ejaculation."* That might make things... awkward. Just make it reasonably clear you're having regular sex with women more attractive than she is.

Chapter 16
Timeline For Using The MAP

Start With Your Weak Areas First

If you add up everything that you *could* be doing to improve yourself, it's an impossible list of things to do. I've suggested that you: get in shape, make more money, play with the kids, be more dominant with her, flirt with her, flirt with other women, dress better, do more around the house, pass her fitness tests, fix up the house, and on and on and on. Unless you have a small army of clones, it's going to be impossible for you to do it all at once.

Your greatest gains are going to come from working on your weak areas first. If you're already making $100,000 a year, then you making $110,000 a year probably isn't going to get the same positive result as someone going from $20,000 a year to $30,000 a year. If you're already in great physical shape, an extra hour a day working out might make little difference to your wife. But for a badly out of shape guy an hour a day of working out could make a huge difference. If you're a stay at home dad, more time playing with the kids won't have the same benefit that it will have for those that work outside of the home.

The solution in a broad sense is to keep in shape, add Alpha if you're too Beta and add Beta if you're too Alpha.

The Goal

The goal for most husbands is to be in a relationship with a woman who is sexually interested in him and to have an enjoyable sex life with her. That is, after all, the reason most men marry in the first place. Ideally the woman who responds to your changes is your wife, but it's always important to accept that she may not respond to you doing The MAP. Ultimately the willingness to move on and leave her if you have to is what makes The MAP powerful as a strategy.

What follows is a timeline that can be used to estimate how things should play out as you do The MAP. Keep in mind that you don't have to play things through all the way to the end point where divorce happens. If you get halfway through and she starts responding to your changes and your sex life gets back on track, you've reached your goal and don't have to force the issue further. All you have to do is keep doing what you're doing and enjoy it! The general goal is to find the sweet spot of your Sex Rank being a little higher than hers (similar to Phase Three detailed below) and stay there until one of you dies of old age.

Phase One – When You Have a Lower Sex Rank than She Does

The first phase assumes that your Sex Rank is lower than your wife's. Just be honest here, is she hotter than you? If she is, then you're starting out here and working your way up from the bottom.

The first and most critical thing to do at this point is to start an exercise routine. Physical fitness primes the Alpha pump on so many levels that you simply can't ignore physical fitness and body appearance. There's nothing I can teach you that can bypass the need to be as physically attractive as you can be. If you're badly out of shape, Phase One might take a very long time indeed and you should assume that you're in Phase One until such time as you are within 5-10% of your ideal body weight. Work on building lean muscle mass rather than pure cardio and weight loss.

Also during Phase One you're going to start educating yourself more and more on what's coming in later phases and reading around those topics. If there are obvious mistakes that you're making with your wife, you're going to try and address them as best you can.

In Phase One, because you have a lower Sex Rank, she likely still has control of the relationship and control over the bedroom. You can of course ask for sex, but don't be overly concerned or surprised if she is still turning you down.

It's also up to you to tell her, or not tell her, what you're up to. Just be aware that telling her doesn't impress her one bit, only action can do that. I think you have less chance of saying the wrong thing if you say nothing though. You'll know you're making progress when she asks you what you're up to.

Phase Two – When You Have an Equal Sex Rank

At some point, you will improve yourself enough to where your Sex Rank is equal to your wife's. Once you reach this point you should start to notice some changes in her behavior toward a more positive relationship. It's also possible that she can act more threatened by the changes and attempt to sabotage your progress. An example of this would be if you just lost 50 pounds and she was supportive all the way with your weight loss, but now suddenly she's shopping and bringing home all of the junk foods that you have a weakness for. She may not be consciously aware she is doing it either – her Rationalization Hamster was the one that suggested she should buy you donuts, because you love them so much and you've been working so hard.

If you're in Phase Two just keep doing all the good things that got you there and try to add a new area to work on as well. Maybe you're learning to cook, starting on fixing up the house or taking a class to learn something useful. Whatever it is, you just add it into your routine and continue to self-improve.

You also continue your physical fitness routine towards your target. Fitness never goes away as a need. Start practicing flirting with your wife and other women, just don't expect wildly excited reactions to it and keep it light and fun.

When you ask for sex, you should request a particular sex act rather than asking her if she wants sex. You should be framing the conversation as your sexual interest being valid, rather than directly giving her an opportunity to just say no. Again, it's no biggie if she doesn't agree to have sex. If she declines, you just move on with your day and keep self-improving.

Phase Three – When Your Sex Rank is Higher than Hers

Phase Three can be triggered with a noticeable switch in upgrading your clothing. Once you pretty much hit your physical fitness/weight /appearance target, it makes sense to do a planned wardrobe improvement to show yourself off. Generally your clothing should be the best quality garments you can afford, appropriate to your location. Don't wear a suit to the Laundromat unless you run it or own it, wearing track pants to the gym is fine, but not to your in-laws for Sunday lunch. Once you switch up your clothing, female heads will start turning in your direction more readily and women will enjoy your flirting. Some previously disinterested women will become interested in you. The clothing upgrade is a bold statement of your wanting to attract female attention.

Once women start showing you more attention (that can be as simple as basic flirting and smiles) the Preselection Effect will also start kicking in and will push your Sex Rank up even further.

Once you reach this phase there is a reasonable expectation that your wife will start being sexually interested in you, far more than she was in Phases One and Two. You being more attractive and dressing to attract other women *and actually succeeding at it* will strongly engage your wife's attention. On one hand she is going to be more attracted to you herself, but on the other hand she can feel threatened by your increased attractiveness and seek to compensate for it by increasing her own attractiveness.

Usually a wife will seek to compensate and start working out and looking better. She can dress better and she can provide a more intense and fun sexual experience for you as well. All these things will increase her Sex Rank.

With your higher Sex Rank you will start to find all the Alpha approaches toward her will be far more effective than in Phase Two. You will start finding just making a simple statement that you want sex, becoming effective in gaining her compliance. She might even start initiating sex. Outside the bedroom too you will find her more easy going with you and more likely to follow your direction. Being in an endless Phase Three where your wife gives you all the sex you want is ultimately the goal of running The MAP.

Of course she still may not respond to you even though you have a higher Sex Rank. You'll know this by her continuing to refuse sex and the increased intensity in her fitness testing of you. You just stay the course and continue running The MAP on her. At this point I very much suggest you do not do anything further than flirt with other women.

If she is not responding, Phase Three can last as long as you want, though I suggest you let it run for about two or three months before moving into Phase Four. If you go too quickly into Phase Four, you may not have given her enough time to mentally process the difference and adjust to things. If you wait too long, you're sending the message that you really are very reluctant to force the issue and lose her, which she will interpret as you being weak and assume it's because she has a higher Sex Rank than you.

If you think that you are in Phase Three and you are still having a badly inadequate sex life, if you don't push to Phase Four within a few months... you are actually still locked in Phase One. Which means all your work has been for nothing and she is still in charge of your lack of sex.

Phase Four – Stating Your Intentions Clearly

This is a very short phase and shouldn't last any longer than a week at the very most. Phase Four is where you make it clear that the situation is intolerable and that *her choices of behavior are forcing you into an unwanted position*, where you have to start seriously considering the possibility of having to leave the relationship.

Phase Four is a direct statement of your needs that are not being met in the relationship and framing it as a problem that you can't work any further on. After all, by this point you've made serious gains in your Sex Rank and that has taken a great deal of effort. The lack of sex and companionship in the relationship is now something that only she can give a solution for. The threat of you leaving is implied rather than directly threatened as something that could happen immediately. You are literally saying, *"Staying in this relationship as it is now is clearly an unreasonable expectation you have of me."*

You want her to fully understand the problem that you are experiencing in being with her. Possibly something to review with her is the matrix of how sexless marriages play out as covered in Chapter Eight. Explain that she has defrauded you of a reasonable expectation of marriage and that she has forced this issue on you. Explain that you have not had sex with anyone else and that there is not a secondary relationship in the background and that your hope and intent is to return to a sexual marriage with her, but she has to actively choose that option herself; you can't force that choice, she has to want it.

Otherwise she forces you toward choosing one of the only remaining options for resolution, either you seeking extramarital sex or leaving to find someone new. Neither of which you find ideal.

Also be clear that you aren't going to be impressed by merely her *talking* about restarting a sexual relationship, she does have to start showing signs of action towards that goal. You shouldn't have an expectation of an immediate sexual frenzy, but you should have an expectation that she would regard this as the low point and start turning things around. Consistent positive progress is the key; she can't just cry, have sex with you once, promise she'll change and then resume as before as if nothing changed.

Anything more than a week of no results and you move into Phase Five.

Phase Five – Give Up On Her

Phase Five means that you did not get a clear response from her that she would improve and that you are putting plans in place to move on without her. At this point you've essentially given up on asking her for sex, knowing that you already have a clear "no" answer.

Your moves now can either be open or in secret, though being open probably has the best chance of success at turning your wife around.

You just pursue other avenues for your own enjoyment as if your wife was a non-factor. You do things like openly enjoying porn, strip clubs, surfing dating websites, building friendships with other women and just going out and having fun without her. Staying low key and private is also perfectly acceptable too.

Another possibility is that you can run up the skull and crossbones flag and set your Facebook relationship status to *"It's complicated."* This is Facebook code for *"My relationship sucks, I don't know why I'm in it."* One would expect that to send a minor shockwave through your social network, which could play to your advantage as friends and family may seek to positively influence your wife towards fixing the problem.

Also during Phase Five you start getting all your ducks in a row for your ultimate exit from the relationship. Organize the money to your best advantage, including opening a personal account and seek legal advice for how things will play out. Make copies of all important records and keep them in a safe place. Remove any items of special personal interest that you worry may be ruined or lost and keep them in a safe location. Now is also not the time to have firearms in the house either. A spare set of car keys may be amazingly helpful should she hurl them somewhere in a fit of rage. At this point you're trying to salvage what you can from the wreckage of being married to someone who doesn't love you.

Phase Five lasts as long as you want, but has a natural stopping point by moving to Phase Six.

Phase Six – The Ultimatum

Phase Six is a simple choice for your wife to choose between Option A or Option B.

Option A contains whatever demands you have that she must meet in order for you to stay in the marriage. These demands can be marriage counseling, sex together, her starting medication for depression, her finding work or whatever the issues are that fuel the critical problems in the marriage. These need to be clear obvious actions rather than vague conditions, i.e. *"sex twice a week"* rather than *"have sex together"*, *"Attend marriage counseling together on Tuesdays at 6pm for the next eight weeks,"* at a specific counselor, rather than *"get marriage counseling."*

The Option A demands should not be silly or trivial. Just focus on the critical issues that are driving you out of the marriage. If there is anything that you can set up or book in advance for your Option A demands, you should do so. Write out your demands for her in a clear concise letter that is no more than a single page...the more you talk, the less powerful it becomes.

Option B is the divorce/separation paperwork. This should be the actual paperwork and prefilled by you as much as you can. For some women this is where the light finally comes on that you really are serious about all this. There's something about reading it all in black and white that cuts through denial and magical thinking.

If she wants time to think then you give it to her, but you should also separate yourself from her as much as possible too. If there is a way you can be out of the house for a few days and have no contact with her, then that would be ideal. This is meant to be a little taste of the reality of divorce and life without you. Note that you shouldn't "move out" as once that happens you tend to set a precedent that she is in possession of the house and that you are not; this could come back to haunt you later on in the proceedings.

The difference between Phase Four and Phase Six is that in Phase Four you simply stated your needs that she needed to meet to continue the relationship; you appealed to her ability to change her own behavior. In Phase Six, you ignore that completely and force the issue, making her immediate compliance a direct requirement for you staying with her.

Another tactic that may work is to contact her family and closest friends and tell them what is going on and request their assistance in trying to influence her towards choosing Option A. This is probably best done as a short letter, or email, where you explain what has happened up to this point and explain that she has a choice to make. Say that you want to save the marriage but also say that you aren't willing to tolerate what is currently happening either. Most people close to her will still be sympathetic to your case if you have been denied sex constantly and yet not cheated on her. For your in-laws, you should also thank them for anything that they have done for you over the years and express sadness that if divorce happens, the relationship with them will change as well.

By you exposing the real reason for leaving her and your willingness to make it work with reasonable demands, it severely hampers her ability to spin you as the bad guy in the relationship. You were the good guy that got screwed over, yet you honorably and gracefully withdrew from the relationship. You took your vows seriously and respected not just your own marriage, but marriage as a concept. You do this because of what you want to achieve in Phase Seven.

Phase Seven – Your New Life... and Maybe New Wife

The divorce itself can take as long as the lawyers drag it out in court, but Phase Seven starts as soon as she opts for Option B. To be sure, you're going to be very sad that your marriage ended, but there's now a world of better opportunities for you out there. Having made a clean and clear break from your marriage, you are better placed to find a new love and start something new, or maybe just play the field for a bit. It's up to you.

I do want to warn you that divorcing your wife, for another woman *in particular*, doesn't usually work very well. If you've actually been having an affair all the way through Phases Three through Six and moving to Phase Seven means you're directly moving in with your girlfriend, you have to know that the statistics are pretty awful for these relationships surviving. Only roughly 3% of all affairs turn into marriages for the affair partners and even then the marriages have much higher failure rates. It's hard to trust each other when you both know that you're willing to cheat.

I am not naïve enough to think that people don't use an affair partner as leverage to escape a marriage, but the very real likelihood is that your affair partner is going to be a "transitional person" rather than a success story. Women who have affairs with married men tend to not be terribly stable, because being involved with a married man requires poor judgment on her part. It's quite possible that you end up with both an ex-wife and a crazy ex-girlfriend as well. Matters may be quite worse for having an affair. Plus by making an honorable break from your marriage and not being involved with someone, you're much better set up emotionally to forge a new relationship.

So in one sense The MAP may very well fail and your marriage end. If this happens I am sorry for your loss, but you know that by this point you tried everything possible to have the marriage that you expected to have on your wedding day. On the other hand, you exit your marriage physically fit, confident, attractive to women and with your conscience clear. So in that sense The MAP has done all that it promised it could do. In the end, you cannot choose your wife's behavior; you can only influence it with your own.

Part Three

The Sexy Moves

Chapter 17
<u>Kissing</u>

Kissing Makes Her Horny

Kissing is a vital relationship skill. It's sensual, it's comforting, it's caring, it's love and the gateway to lust. Male saliva also contains testosterone that her body absorbs and it makes her horny. So do take the time to kiss her, if only for your own self-interest.

The Ten Second Kiss

The Ten Second Kiss is a foundational move.

It's easy to get in the friendly roommate rut and stop being passionate lovers. The friendly roommate road just leads to bad sex at best, but more likely affairs and divorce. The Ten Second Kiss brings back that feeling of romance and passion. Ten seconds is actually quite a long time to kiss someone, especially if your intimacy has been cut down to 0.1 second pecks in passing. Peck, peck, peck. It's like you're eight years old and trying to evade the ugly aunt who tastes like cigarettes, *"Come kiss your auntie! MUAH!"*

Okay... maybe that's just my childhood trauma talking, but the principle holds. All those kisses that amount to a peck in passing do nothing to light the fires, for either of you.

If the routine is new to her, just walk up to her and say... *"It's being so long since we kissed. I mean really, really kissed. I want to kiss for ten seconds, but I do have one rule..."*

She's pretty much forced to ask, *"What's that?"*

Then you say, and it's very important you do this with a cocky smile, keeping it light and fun as possible, *"You have to pretend to like it."*

She should laugh and say *"Okay"* or something similar. Then you hold her and lean in for the kiss. When you go in for the kiss, only go 90% of the way in and hold position, making her come the final 10% of the distance to you. This forces her to actively engage with you (she is kissing you), rather that it being something she is passively allowing to happen to her (you are kissing her). We're creating emotional engagement here. It's also a highly confident approach, which most women find very sexy. It means you aren't scared of her not responding to you. This is a fairly Alpha Male move as the underlying message is *"I know you will respond to me."*

Then hold the kiss, for all ten seconds. If she breaks it off early, lightly tell her off, *"That wasn't ten seconds, come back here and do it right."* Then repeat it until you get a full ten seconds. This again is Alpha Male goodness in that you are asserting yourself and not letting her evade you. Don't go in trying to cop a feel either, *you're kissing her.* If you're hard for her, press against her, letting her know that she is affecting you. You're not trying to convert this kiss into sex right now. If you try and do that she may try and defend against it because she may not want sex just that second. By just kissing, there's nothing she needs to defend against, so her guard will come down and she will let you "in" emotionally.

What you will find is that somewhere around the six second mark, her shields come down and she will become quite passionate about the interaction. All those 0.1 second "peck" kisses are simply social in nature. The romantic biological hormonal kick-in from kissing doesn't happen until at least five seconds, so that's why you've got to hold the kiss. Feel free to keep the kiss going on as long as you both want. Also, you will find the long deep kiss will not only trigger passionate interest in her, but also in you. It is very difficult to stay emotionally neutral about a member of the opposite sex when you kiss like this.

The beauty of the Ten Second Kiss is that it works every time. You can do this once a day and it will connect you both again. Don't automatically try and turn this into an attempt to close for sex. Kiss her like this, make some small talk, and move on with your day. The goal is to connect you both emotionally. Once she's emotionally connected to you, your wife will be far more interested in sex.

Locking-In Her Kiss

After you have the Ten Second Kiss down pat, here's an additional step to make things more interesting.

When you kiss, if she has jeans with front pockets, simply slide a finger or two into them and gently pull her into you as you kiss. It kind of locks her into you and is controlling and dominant, but with a minimum of force. Plus you're literally starting to get your hands in her pants.

When the kiss breaks, let her breathe for a second and then pull her back to you and kiss a few seconds more. Just say *"I'm not done with you"* in a light playful tone as you pull her in and kiss her some more.

If she's recently lost a little weight, you can mix this up a tad and just slide your hand down the back of her pants (which will be fitting a little looser) and under the panties and cup her ass. Then you compliment her... eyes.

Another kissing move is to tell her to put her arms around your neck or even placing them there yourself. It's telling her what to do (Alpha) and makes her breasts lift up and rub against your chest better. Personally, I like that feeling.

How to Make Her Stop Talking

Sometimes women need to talk about their day. It usually pays to listen and let her decompress. Don't try to problem solve her day for her unless she explicitly asks for help with something. Just listen, pay attention, nod and smile at the good bits. Usually what she wants most is your attention, so treat it like a small stage production and clap for the good bits and boo the villains. Once she's decompressed a little, she is usually far more receptive to you for the rest of the evening.

Of course, sometimes she does just go on and on and on, and having started listening properly, it can become difficult to get yourself out of the conversation without looking like you're flaking on her. Faking a seizure usually gets you out of a couple conversations a month, but beyond that you start looking more and more like a liability to her.

The solution is simple. You simply close the distance between you, pull her into you, and then kiss her intensely until she loses her entire train of thought. If she wanted your attention... well she's getting it.

The Cleavage Pull to Kiss Move

Need something else to try? When you go in for a kiss, rather than your diving in towards her, smile playfully and reach out to her and gently hook a finger or two into the front of her shirt/cleavage. Gently pull her towards you for the kiss. Don't rip the front of her shirt open or anything silly, just reel her in for the smooch.

Kiss Her Neck

One of the weak spots on the human body is the neck. If someone has you by the throat it's immediately bad, likewise a blow to the back of your exposed neck is life-threatening.

Dozens of cultures have some combination of bowing and hats off (think "armored helmets off" as the early ancestor of "hats off") by the social inferior to the social superior. It's a social submission signal to expose yourself to physical weakness. Likewise in the animal kingdom there are readily observable submission signals where the weaker literally bows their head to the stronger. The message is clear: *"Okay I get it, you're in charge here and I'm better off aligning myself to you rather than trying to compete with you"*. Humans are much the same. In a stand-off building towards a potential fist fight between two guys, the first guy that drops his head to the other loses the stand-off. The social signal of submission avoids the physical fight happening.

So actually reaching out and touching someone else's neck is a potent statement. Touching the *front* of the neck crosses the line into naked hostility and most people will automatically physically fight to defend their airway by any means necessary. I'm more talking about touching the *back* of the neck. Anyone who touches the back of your neck is announcing very clearly that they are expecting your submission to them.

All of which is why women love their necks being kissed. Especially those *sneak up behind them and wrap your arms around them and gently nuzzle on their neck* moves. You get bonus points for doing this when you kind of trap them up against the kitchen counter when they are making you a sandwich. Kissing the back of her neck is a powerful statement of physical dominance and sexual intent; she is wired to respond to that with attraction.

Another move to do is a very light hold on the back of her neck when you are kissing or making love. Note I said *very light hold* and not *crush her windpipe* or *shake her by the neck like a rag doll.* The entire point is that you're signaling dominance with a social signal, rather than having to go through the violence of an actual physical confrontation.

Anyway... neck kissing... maybe some ladies out there just discovered they are more wired for submission than they first thought....

The Other Place You Can Kiss

I mentioned at the start of the chapter that male saliva contains testosterone. So when you kiss her, you actually give her testosterone and that turns her on.

So if you give her oral sex... all that testosterone from your saliva can be just as easily absorbed through the walls of her vagina.

Something to think about perhaps?

Chapter 18
Just Bust a Move

Ask for Nothing and You Shall Receive it in Abundance...

Upon occasion guys are just incredibly clueless about a woman being interested in them. I'm not really a dating writer but I got this email from a guy trapped in the Friendzone:

"Hi! I have a problem regarding the friend zone. I have this girl who I am really falling in love with... we've known each other for about a year, and have had the same best friends whom we hang out with a lot for the last 6 months. She and I have many little things only we joke about, flirting etc... And especially the last month. But I cannot figure out if she is interested, or just being a friend. And because we are so close, and have the same friends, it would be embarrassing to ask her out or something if she wouldn't go.

We never do anything alone though, it is just with our friends. The last time we were out, we danced kind of sexy, and if this had been any other girl, we would have been making out a long time ago. But since I'm falling in love with her, I don't dare to go for the kiss, in case I blow it. I even slept in her bed that night. (There were 5 other friends sleeping in the living room next door though). Nothing happened."

"Should I ask her out, try to get her alone? How? For dinner, for a drink? What?"

Dude... everybody knows that you're totally into this girl. You know. Your friends know. She knows. It's no secret to *anyone*. She's just waiting for you to make your move. Your friends all cleared out and slept in the living room and left you and her alone in the same bed and nothing happened????

All you have to do is bust a move and do something. If she's into you she'll jump at the chance to do something with you. Just decide on a place to have a date, call her up and tell her when and where the date will be. But tell her she should only come if she's willing to make out on the date. Then tell her that she has a choice for the first date as to whether or not she wears her good underwear or her bad underwear, but that any future dates would require the good underwear. This would mean that is clearly in everyone's best interest that the make out session be quite in depth to see if the chemistry you think she has for you is really there. Then get off the phone.

You can just as easily stumble into a Friendzone relationship with your wife by a simple lack of activity. The solution is to become more active and just bust a move or two on her. Most women respond to the advances of men, so ultimately the person that traps you in the Friendzone is you.

Play With Women All the Time

You may only be trying to sleep with your wife, but all women can enjoy a playful interaction with you. You don't have to get into heavy flirting and secret lunches to do this, just keep it playful with the women you meet. Most men learning Game say that not only does their wife react better to them, so do all the women they meet and work with.

There's a marked difference to walk through your front door knowing that you had four or five women earlier that day laughing and smiling at you. Somehow that is all internalized and your wife will pick up on your being confident and happy. She'll like it.

Practice Asking Women Out

One of the skills you can learn is asking women out to lunch or coffee. It's fairly harmless and good practice; just don't let yourself be hooked into someone emotionally. The trick is to avoid getting locked into thinking about what they think about you, because then you turn into a creepy guy because you have a mental delay in trying to process the simple task of saying, *"Hey I'm going to lunch, want to* come?" Considering that most women do in fact like to eat lunch, I'm pretty much assuming the creepiness factor is the issue here.

In talking to women and getting to them to go for lunch or coffee there are three basic elements to your verbal interaction:

The False Time Constraint – *"I can't stay for long though, I have a meeting/report due/call/thing I have to do in 30 minutes"*. That means you aren't going to stay locked in laser beam focus on them for an unknown length of time. Plus it means that you are an active guy and busy, which means you have value.

Playfully Deny Interest In Them – *"Now if we have lunch, you have to promise not to hit on me"*. Or my favorite, *"I'm trying to cut down to two girlfriends... and my wife."*

Don't Offer To Pay For Lunch – That kicks in the ASD (Anti Slut Defense) where she feels leverage being used against her to buy sexual favors. Even if she agrees to let you pay she'll be scanning the menu for something that says "handjob" rather than something she actually wants to eat. You won't get that handjob either. (Incidentally for the women reading, chicken Caesar salad is the default handjob menu choice, lobster means you have to go all the way. Everyone knows by now that sushi = oral sex and baby back ribs means you are a nasty, nasty girl and I'm embarrassed to be so aroused by you.)

That's the basics for getting your foot in the door. Don't be needy or creepy.

Ask as a Man Going His Own Way

Jennifer and I both work for the same company and on our rare days of both of us being at the main office, I do the standard Man Going His Own Way (MGHOW) invitation for coffee together. *"I'm going for coffee, want to come?"* Then either way she answers, I go get coffee. It's not *"Would you like to go get coffee?"* because then she has to make a decision to leave or not, whereas the MGHOW invitation is making her make a decision on whether or not to be left behind. If you start turning your body away and start moving to the door, you're taking away something and people tend to latch on to things being taken away from them. So usually she comes with me, but it's no big deal if she doesn't; it's just coffee.

This simple request tactic works great on nearly anyone, male or female. But when asking for people to tag along with you, do watch out for the fitness test that can follow up this request to go for coffee. This happens when you ask her to come with you and she declines, but then she asks you to bring coffee back for her. If you bring coffee back for her, you're running her errands for her, which means she's the dominant one in the relationship. Simply say *"No thanks, I'm going to get coffee to relax not to run errands."* If she calls you an asshole for doing that, just smile and say thank you for the compliment.

Of course I would bring coffee back for Jennifer, but then she's getting the Princess Fiona treatment. Everyone else is a Donkey though, so they can be their own beast of burden.

Don't Care What Women Think of You, Just Mess With Them a Bit

The more you care about what women think of you as a romantic partner, the less they think of you as a romantic partner.

For the most part the key to Gaming females of all ages is a mixture of being unafraid of them in an "I notice you but I'm not affected by you" way, and staying light and playful. Gentle teasing is like catnip as well. Not harsh put-downs, just a light ruffle drawing attention to their weaknesses. They love a little mild naughtiness too. It's mostly just a male way of flirting.

The more you start to do it and practice it, the more natural it becomes and the easier it gets. Eventually it just becomes second nature. As an aside for the work related examples below, my wife works at the same place I do and is all purpose loved by everyone and frankly is hotter than everyone else as well. The chance of anyone really getting the wrong idea is very, very low. That being said, I don't go as far as sexual comments with anyone other than Jennifer.

Some examples:

Female Co-worker to maintenance guy doing a complete bathroom remodel: *"Well look at this kitchen, we need a new kitchen."*
Guy: *"What's wrong with the kitchen???"*
Female Co-worker: starts rant of all kitchen weaknesses.
Me: *"Wow look how easily she just slips into wife mode."*
She laughs and rant ends.

Jennifer by text: *"Daughter #1 is at xxxx house until 6pm and daughter #2 is at xxxxx house until 5pm."*
Me: *"Get naked. OMW!!!!"*
Jennifer: *"lmao yes sir!"*
Me: *"Oh... hang on, Brazil is about to play. Sorry :-D"*

Next day...
Me by text: *"Lingerie top of your choice. Stockings. Me on top. You loud. That is all."*
Jennifer: *"Gotcha :-D that is all."*

Favorite Female Co-worker (FFCW) asks for feedback on her new job assignment.... I reply via email with seven good points and slip in "feed me baked goods". (I totally trust she won't react badly)
Email Reply: *"yada yada yada and I will not be feeding you baked goods, but I might make cupcakes for the next staff meeting."*
Me later text: *"LOL I forgot about the baked goods line."*
FFCW: *"Hahaa."*

5th Grade Field Trip at Boston Science Museum chaperoning three girls. I'm hungry and need a snack and decide to spring for snacks for all three as well. They have all been very well behaved all day...
Me: *"Ok girls you can choose a snack or a drink from this display."*
Daughter #2: *"Yay!"*
Friend #1 looking: *"Ohhh, hmmm..."*
Friend #2 looking: *"Ummm maybe I'll have... no..."*
Daughter #2: *"I don't know what I want."*
Friend #1: *"Me neither, but I am hungry."*
Friend #2 picks up item, returns it to shelf, and repeats.
Daughter #2: *"maybe some fruit."*
Friend #1: *"well that looks good, what are you having?"*
Friend #2: *"I can't decide between the apple and the Peanut Butter Cups."*

Repeat this conversation twice more...
Me: *"SNACKS UP ON THE COUNTER TO PAY OR MISS OUT IN...TEN NINE EIGHT SEVEN SIX FIVE FOUR THREE TWO ONE ZERO."*
All three decide and grab on the "one" and we go pay for the snacks.

Me: *"Come here."* patting sofa between my legs.
Jennifer comes over and we cuddle with her back to me on my chest and chat and snuggle. After a few minutes it becomes apparent that this is one of those slightly awkward positions that are nice for closeness but not 100% comfortable long term.
Me: *"You're just tolerating this like a good* girlfriend *aren't you?"*
I get the faux arm slap thing from my wife of sixteen years.

FFCW: *"What do you think of ABC?"*
Me: *"Blah blah blah ABC is good."*
FFCW: *"Yeah but I was also thinking maybe the exact opposite of ABC as well."*
Me: *"Well blah blah that could work as well."*
FFCW: *"Well blah blah blah reading between the lines I'm trying to find a way to get you to commit to a position so I can disagree with you on this trivial point blah blah blah."*
Me falling to knees dramatically and faux pleading: *"I don't know how to please you.... what do you want me to say?"*
FFCW: laughs.
Two minutes later...
FFCW: *"So what kind of cupcakes do you want?"*
Me: *"Lemon Poppy."*

They were delicious too.

"Bedtime is the Make Sexy Time, Yes?"

The transition from the living room into the bedroom at bedtime is a key moment in the day. You should own that moment and frame yourself as dominant. I have several moves I use here and I mix them up from night to night.

We typically go to bed around 11pm and I have a clever technique of noticing it's 11pm and then stating *"It's bedtime."* There's hardly a hint of overt dominance with this one, but being the one that is announcing bedtime for both of us frames me as dominant in the relationship.

Adding a stronger twist of dominance is the old "use the married name" thing where I address her as *"Mrs. Kay"*. So that is a stronger frame in that it implies in a direct sense that she has marital duties to perform. Yet it's formal enough that it can be used at family gatherings for exactly the same purpose.

You can do the Ten Second Kiss routine, followed by extended hand as a compliance test. Basically you just hold your hand out to her until she takes it. Then you lead her to the bedroom.

Just text her a booty call. Even sitting in the same room it's funny.

Go over confidently goofy, the Borat approach is great, *"Is now 11 o'clock and is the make sexy time. Very nice!"*

If she walks in front of you lightly spank her butt.

"Cum to bed baby." (Think Austin Powers inflection here)

Tell her to go put something on from the lingerie department.

Just announce the way sex is going to happen. *"Here's my plan. First I'm going to finger you to an orgasm, then you're going to be reverse cowgirl on me for about five minutes, then I'm putting you on your back and finishing on top hard and rough."*

Just don't care what she thinks.

Find Some Stolen Time Together

This comes back to the *"Instigate, Isolate and Escalate"* chapter ideas. The instigation part is that sense of playful engaging interaction with her. Whether that's banter, teasing, deep and meaningful talking, humor or whatever, you're trying to start something with her beyond asking her, *"So what's for dinner?"*

The escalation part is the "always be closing" approach of physical touch, sexual touch and let's go to the bedroom. I'm not saying every time you touch you are forcing the issue towards naked sexy time *now*; you're setting the intent that there *will be* a naked sexy time and it's going to be good. If she wants sex, you can follow through on that. Instigation and escalation are fairly easily done in a marriage. You can always talk and play together, and no one gets offended if a married couple plays a little grab-ass and kisses each other. But the harder one to get done is isolation if you have a couple little cockblocks roaming your house asking for things to eat and an allowance.

What we do is try and find sneaky ways of alone time together. Our kids are old enough to be home alone for a while so Jennifer and I often do grocery shopping together. That seems dull I know, but we're together without the kids and just get to hang out like old times. Plus we can plan the meals we're cooking together during the week. I get to do the heavy lifting and stuff like that. We both like it.

Also shopping only really takes about an hour and we're usually gone for about an hour and a half. There's a Panera bakery next to the grocery store and we have coffee and a medium fancy snack/lunch of some sort together. We talk. The kids have no clue that we actually escaped them and had fun.

Chapter 19
Man About the House

Work the L-Spot

You're probably wondering where the L-Spot is and if I just made it up. I can assure you that it is real, it does exist, and if you can stimulate it correctly, your woman will look at you like she has never looked at you before. Once you start tapping the L-Spot just right, she will want it forever. She will probably NOT tell her friends about your doing this as she couldn't trust them not to go behind her back to you. It's just that powerful.

As a warning though, once you start working this area, you can't decide later on that you're going to stop working it. Once she gets L-Spot action, she is always going to remember that she was getting it. You can't stop-start-stop-start on this. You want to drive her crazy *for* you, not *at* you. It's all or nothing, so be advised.

The L-Spot is so reliable you can probably just spring it on her without warning and watch her face light up with surprise and delight. It is somewhat stimulating though, so I really recommend making the bedroom area as low key and low-stimulation as possible. You don't want to have her get over-stimulated and suddenly shut down on you halfway through.

To make the bedroom low-stimulation, do some quick decluttering and make sure everything is clean. Strip the bedding off the bed and wash it, and do the same for all of your clothes that are lying around as well. If you've got an en suite bathroom, then you can wash the bath towels and mats as well. If you have white towels (which go with everything by the way), you can wash them separately with a little bleach and that will whiten them a little more, plus kill all the germs in the washing machine. I very much suggest for her clothes though, you just find her hamper and toss anything of hers that is unwashed in there and stash the hamper off to one side. All women have precise washing techniques and it's probably best to not mess with that. Then just remake the bed, fold the clothes, hang the towels up.

Congratulations! You just did the laundry... a.k.a. the L-Spot.

I might have tricked you a little there... but stick with me and I'll explain why this is a vital sexy move. Do not knock this until you have tried it.

If you've actually not been helping out with the laundry at all, try and get this whole routine down while she is out of the house. Just get it done and play it cool. Don't follow her like a freaking toddler that just pooped in the right place all by himself. Just be cool. It's no big deal.

Okay maybe hover a little bit. Watching her face is half the fun! I can guarantee you will get a positive reaction from her for this.

The point of this move is that it is a Beta Male trait and is one of many nest management tasks that you can do. This isn't going to make her pulse jack up, her nipples hard and her panties wet, but it is going to build comfort, relax her and reduce her stress. You're going to perform Alpha Trait moves to *"turn her on"*; this is to make sure you aren't *"turning her off"*.

If she thinks she is being abandoned by you to do all the nest management by herself and she is overwhelmed, her Body Agenda will ensure that no more babies arrive to add to her workload by cutting her sex drive off. No sex drive = no sex = no more babies = workload stays tolerable = current babies get enough care. It's vital to understand that this is a hardwired response in her. She will not have a conscious control over this; she will simply look at you one day and realize that while she loves you, she is not in love with you.

When you first moved in together, maybe her doing your laundry made her feel giddy and silly... for about the first three weeks. After that... *not so much*. By the time the kids are here, the laundry starts to pile up in a battle that doesn't end until they can fend for themselves. I don't care how the domestic chores get divided up in your house, but I can assure you that if she is doing *your* laundry she feels like your mother. And your mother never wore lingerie for you, licked up every last drop of you, or arched her back while pulling you deep into her... at least I really hope your mother didn't do that.

Doing the laundry is not really a male or female skill; it's just a basic life skill. So go grab a pile of laundry, shove it in the washer, push a button, transfer it to the dryer, push another button, and fold the clothes and Bam! You just worked the L-Spot. You know she's going to love it.

Fix the Broken Stuff in the House

A man's use of tools has been sexy since The Time Before Writing...

...once upon a time, back in The Time Before Writing there were two males squaring off over a female. The older larger Alpha Male was Sal and the younger, smaller male was Throgg. The female knew that Sal was going to beat the smaller Throgg and like it or not she would be mated with Sal. Then something very unusual happened. *Throgg invented Pickup.*

In a smooth, fluid motion Throgg picked up a four-foot long solid piece of wood from the ground and pounded Sal like a rented punching bag until he learned to exhibit Approach Anxiety. Armed with his club, Throgg felt confident and sexy and he naturally got the girl. Brains plus some brawn beat pure brawn.

Throgg became famous and taught classes to aspiring males about his amazing Pickup technique. Pretty soon if a male didn't know about Pickup, they didn't have a chance with the ladies. All the females started paying more attention to the males who could hold a club. After awhile a female who wanted to get laid would just tell all her friends she was going out clubbing.

After a few hundred generations of sexual selection for males good with clubs, everyone was starting to get good with clubs. Cool stuff like axes, knives, hammers, spears, bows and slings had been invented too. It turns out that the males who were good with one tool usually turned out to be pretty good with all of them. They could fight and build a better home as well. The females loved the newer, predator-safe villages and homes the tool-using men could create. In fact after a while all the females started insisting on well-built homes to keep critters and predators away from crying babies in the middle of the night.

So that's why today, a man's use of tools is so sexy. When your wife asks you to repair something around the house... it's a requirement programmed into her DNA where she's driven to live in a nest safe for children to be born into. She's going to see it as your job to repair the nest. Failing to do basic repair work and general nest maintenance is going to flip her sexual attraction switches for you off.

I'm not saying you have to be able to build a house from scratch, but a minimal level of ability with basic tools and home repair tasks will make your wife feel safe and comfortable. So while skill with tools was the original Alpha Male skill, in modern terms it's really a Beta Male Trait.

That being said, do know the difference between a bathroom remodel that you can't afford – that's a fitness test – and making sure the things in your home are functional and safe. Just make a list and start fixing. Unleash your inner Throgg.

Be a Tool Man

As an aside, if you remember the sitcom *"Home Improvement,"* try doing a few "Tim The Tool Man Taylor" grunts as you do the repair and present your finished repair job to your wife. It's always funny and sets up an expectation that you deserve a little extra attention for your efforts. Plus, if you actually botch the repair job, you have an automatic lead into humorous *"oh no"* grunting and a second attempt at the repair.

You can also ham up your repair work with a little Alpha cocky and funny instigation as well. The use of nearly every word associated with repairs lends itself to purposely comically bad pickup lines.

"Is there anything else that needs to be nailed?"
"Mind if I work on your plumbing?"
"This tool is strong and quite hard."
"My technique is just to pound it hard."
"I'm looking for the perfect screw."
"If anything else is dripping, I'll take a look at that too."
"If you stand any closer baby, you'll need protection."

"I can't stop and have sex now, doing you is seventh on the list and I'm only at number five."
"I'm done with the sink. So how long until your husband is back....?"

Feed the Family Something Special

I tend to get up earlier than Jennifer on the weekend. By which I mean her lazy fine ass stays in the bed as long as humanly possible. Actually it sounds a little like a fitness test, but it's really not. She needs her sleep and there's nothing she really needs to be doing early on a Saturday anyway. Let's face it, she does her Wonder Woman routine all week and I *wear her out* as well. She really doesn't need me screeching like a newborn on the weekend mornings.

So usually I time a breakfast or coffee run for about when she is getting up. Sometimes it's fancy stuff, but usually not...just a good cup of coffee and something to eat. It's both predictable and a little random. Chicks dig that.

Just like a man bringing back fresh meat in The Time Before Writing, I've gone out successfully hunted fresh, er... deli meat and bagels. Admittedly bagels are only dangerously aggressive on rare occasions, so a *little* of the warrior flair is lost, but it's quite symbolic anyway. She gets her sleep and I get to do a very comfort building little ritual for us. Jennifer is a generally upbeat person, but this really does make her feel good and it sets the mood for the rest of the day.

Also no one bugs me for a couple of hours on Saturday mornings.

Get Her to Cut Your Hair

One of my favorite nights is Sunday night, because Jennifer cuts my hair then. Admittedly there's not a lot of it left, but rather than do some stupid comb-over, we just buzz it all off very short each week. She was nervous about it at first, but it's basically impossible to screw it up. Clippers, my head, *neeeerrrrooooowwww....*

I suspect it's so nice because it's some sort of primate grooming hold over from well before even The Time Before Writing. Maybe it's just nice to be pampered, touched and cared for by your wife. Maybe it's because from when I was fourteen to seventeen I had a young, cute and very busty hairdresser who used to take a very long time to cut my hair and always ended up somehow rubbing her boobs on my shoulders and upper back. Seriously, I have no clue.

Jennifer on the other hand, gets to indulge in that favorite female fantasy of making her man over to look better. Maybe it's some sort of primate grooming thing on her end too. Plus she gets to tend to the magnificence of me. (I don't believe it's possible to be too confident).

When you ask her to cut your hair for you, I suggest you frame it this way...

"Honey, there's something I want to do and I really want to be able to do it with you. But if you don't want to do it, I'll understand and still love you, just understand that I've decided I'll have to see someone else and have her do it for me. I do love you and I'm not looking for a relationship with anyone else or anything like that. I'll probably just find someone willing to be paid to do it and not get involved."

Remember to be smiling a very naughty boy smile as you do this. Be playful, not serious in tone. If you think you're going to blow it, at least hold the clippers in your hand or be in the store looking at the box or something as a defense prop. Then you spring that you are, in fact, looking for a haircut rather than some sort of kinky sex act.

The closing line is... *"I mean I could do it myself, but it's just not the same".*

Ask for Her Special Dish

Let's face it, most of us are not professional chefs and we turn out quite edible food, but on average it's all quite mundane. Your wife, however, will usually have a small handful of things that she's really good at making, but she only makes them for special occasions.

So just ask for it anyway. And then you eat it. Slowly and sitting with her. Once done eating you say, *"I don't really understand why, but when you make this, I just get this wonderful feeling inside that we're a family."*

You should get some sort of positive reaction from that one as it tugs on her heartstrings. So enjoy the moment of warm fuzziness and cuddle and kiss. Once that starts to settle down a little say in your best I'm a naughty boy voice, *"It also makes me a little horny."*

Jennifer's special dish is sausage rolls. They are basically sausage wrapped in pastry in a long roll, cut into two to three inch long pieces and baked. Sausage rolls are a traditional party staple in New Zealand and it's one of the very few things that I get homesick for. Jennifer was originally stressed out by making them, as bad sausage rolls are a divorceable offense in New Zealand. Her first few batches were a difficult time for us.

Clean the Kitchen

Cleaning up a kitchen is easy. Just clean all the counters off and wipe them down. Pick up and put away the dishes and cups and plates and crap that are out everywhere. Having a kitchen sink full of dirty dishes just makes it unusable and energy draining. If a date walks into your house and sees dirty dishes in your sink, she's adjusting your Sex Rank down in her mind to accommodate having to be your future maid if things progress; your wife feels the same way.

To be honest, Jennifer does more clean-up work in the kitchen than I do. But I do make a special effort on nights that Jennifer is out working late to tidy up the kitchen and clean it all away before she gets home. As she drives home on those nights I'd prefer her to dream about starting to sink into my arms, rather than her arms in my sink.

Chapter 20
Playful Sex

The Shower Move

Let her get in the shower first and have her shower as normal. Then time your approach to when she would be just about ready to get out. If you're not sure, go a little earlier rather than later. If she's already out of the shower, you're basically screwed as you can't really ask her to get back into the shower without looking like you failed the timing.

Then you get into the shower with her. This is a fairly obnoxious/ strong/Alpha move in that you are clearly invading her personal space, but you're her husband so you shouldn't have too much of an issue breaking her down.

Have a line ready to disarm her if she seems a little shocked at the invasion. Almost the sillier it is the better. You are trying to convey playful fun rather than a dangerous scuffle in the shower seeking penetration. Big goofy grin, light tone. Suggestions:

"Pardon me, I didn't know this shower was occupied."
"The hotel sent me up to you, but I'll need some ID."
"You seem familiar, have we met?"
"Shhhhh, don't tell my wife I'm in here with you."
"Shower Boy" (say it in the same tone as "Room Service")
"Reporting for duty."
"I'm a building inspector. I need to check the structure in the shower; this will only take a minute madam."

Then just tell her you're going to wash her back. Have a nice facial scrub soap of some sort, and use it to wash her back. You can get these from any supermarket for a few bucks, and she probably already has something like this in the shower anyway. Use a nice big squeeze of it. Take your time. Make it a sensual experience for her. Everyone loves having their back scrubbed, it feels great. Just scrub her back down.

Once done she'll need to turn around and rinse off. Then you unload...

"Wow nice rack, are those real?" Remember to use your naughty boy grin and playful tone. The words don't actually matter all that much really. You can probably recite the Pledge of Allegiance and make headway if you keep the grin going and the right tone.

Then say it's your turn, which comes to the delicate passing maneuver where you swap ends of the shower. You don't have to full on grope, but do obviously enjoy any and all incidental contact as you brush past each other. *Oh yeah.*

Then she scrubs you down. You rinse off and it's time to end the routine. If she's obviously wanting sex right here and now, well go ahead. But otherwise she's probably going to be wondering if you're going to try something on her. Kiss for a bit then gently order her out so you can have your shower. That just might mess with her head a little... in a good way.

Finish your shower, and continue on with your day. After a morning start like this, you can probably run rampant with flirting with her and physical touch all day. Remember – light, playful, fun, and a little I'm being a naughty boy thrown in as well. She'll be primed for bedtime. *You're welcome.*

The Neapolitan

Everyone has a favorite sexual position, mine is not so much a single position but a three step combination I've taken to calling The Neapolitan after the triple flavored strawberry vanilla chocolate ice cream. As an aside we tend to get Jennifer off as often as she likes (typically once but that's her choice) before going into this routine. If she wants another one along the way she can, but she doesn't usually. I find the three different stimulations make my orgasm excellent at the end. It also sets up a very intense finish that would probably injure her if we attempted that all the way through. Giving her the control to call readiness for that makes it less likely to really do some kind of damage, but still get the full thrill ride ending.

Strawberry is a blowjob. See I knew you'd like it. The difference is that there's no particular effort to get me towards an orgasm. It's just enjoyable sucking for as long as she likes, doing it however she likes. This lack of goal seeking actually seems to make things nicer quite often (sometimes I have to tap out!) and gives her complete control to enjoy what is happening, which generally turns her on. When she's ready we go to vanilla and she kisses her way up my body and climbs on.

Vanilla is woman on top a.k.a. "Cowgirl." I can last forever in this position unless I'm purposely forcing the issue toward orgasm for me. So once again we're in a position of not really forcing the issue towards completion. This is relaxed and intimate. There's kissing, some mild spanks, breast fondling and sucking. Like I say, I can do this all night no problem and she likes it, but eventually she wants it to come to the big finish and when she wants it she climbs off and lies on her back.

Chocolate is the Missionary Position which is her favorite. Up until this point she has pretty much been in control of the pace... but no more. I don't care about anything beyond how good it feels for me in this stage and she's basically pinned helplessly under me while I finish hard, fast and rough. She's usually not so much sore from it the next day, but shall we say... *still aware of it.*

If she complains of pain or discomfort in the immediate aftermath, I tell her *"you're welcome"*. She seems to like that answer.

Ask for a Massage with a Good Lotion

A while back I played with the idea of turning into a massage therapist and attended an open house at a massage school. I didn't actually apply, but I did shop in the little school store and basically stumbled upon the most fantastic lotion for ~~handjobs~~ massages.

The best lotion we have found is Biotone Advanced Therapy Massage Cream. It comes in either an 8-ounce pump thingy or a gallon bottle. You can find it at Amazon.com, but is cheaper from the manufacturer. We usually get a gallon every couple of years and refill a smaller bottle and it never seems to go bad.

We often ensure that I get lots of ~~handjobs~~ massages when Jennifer is in that time of the month when she likes giving ~~handjobs~~ massages. Sometimes I lie on my back and I get a lovely ~~handjob~~ massage, sometimes with her on top of me and sometimes she lies on her back with me over the top of her and I get a nice ~~handjob~~ massage that way. Though honestly that way is a little messy and the ~~cumshot~~ lotion goes everywhere, but it's non greasy and cleans up well.

Also as a side benefit, it's good for handjobs. So it's win-win.

Trim Your Nails

It's a simple little thing to do, but makes everything go so much smoother in bed together. Just trim your nails.

NO sharp edges.

NO dirty fingernails.

NO tiny little sticky up bits.

NO nail polish unless you're a drag queen.

You don't want to be heading to bed doing your Wolverine impression in the nail department. Typically if she wants her lady bits scraped, she wants the full deal with medical insurance, trained professionals and that specially chilled KY Jelly being involved.

Your wife probably has an emery board stashed away in the bathroom somewhere, just file everything nice and smooth and wash your hands. Oh.... emery board... um.... it's like a little strip of 600 grit sandpaper. Filing = sanding. See it's really a male task after all, there's nothing metrosexual about having properly sanded smooth nails.

If push comes to shove you can use actual sand paper. I tend to recommend not using a belt sander though. (That's for toenails.)

Drink Pineapple Juice

Generally if you eat a lot of crap then your semen is going to smell and taste worse. Generally better food and liquid tends towards better smell and taste. I've heard many good things about pineapple juice changing the flavor positively. Personally I'm not wildly excited about pineapple as a flavor, so I did try that myself once but strayed from it. I quite like orange juice cut with seltzer water 50/50.

That being said, I have hit upon a much quicker and easier use of pineapple juice to improve wifely complaints of the taste of blowjobs. Once you come in her mouth, just immediately offer her a small cup of pineapple juice.

You're welcome baby, you're welcome.

Put a Pillow under Her Butt

The Missionary Position is as vanilla as it gets, but vanilla is an actual flavor rather than the absence of flavor. Most women quite like the feeling of their man on top of them. It's a naturally dominant position for him. In fact, her obviously liking the Missionary Position is probably a good indicator that she gets enjoyment from being submissive in general.

If you want to change it up a little though, try a pillow under her butt and see how that feels. It can very much alter the tilt of her pelvis and change the sensation for you both. Look around the bedroom... you probably already have a pillow or two.

Return the Favor

Only about 30% of what you try in bed will actually work for you both. You may get a hot sex tip from a friend that just raves about it, but for you it's just simply awkward or dull.

As an example Jennifer and I sometimes do a rear entry position where I lie on my back and she lies on her back on top of me. It works for us because she's petite and I'm far larger and solid. If I was medium sized and she was too, I'd probably just be too crushed under her to enjoy it. As it is, my enjoyment of that particular position ends roughly a tenth of a second after I orgasm; my Body Agenda suggests quite firmly that I get a hundred twenty or so pounds of panting wife off me so I can breathe again.

Likewise we can look at pictures of face to face sex where the woman has her legs thrown up over the man's shoulders and it looks sexy and hot. However we have tried this and Jennifer simply does not bend that way. Not even close, her legs would fall off like a used Barbie doll if we tried that.

So you mess around together and keep trying stuff until you find what works. However, sometimes your partner likes something and you don't. It's not so much of a dislike of anything, just not a turn on, so the idea of doing it to your partner may never occur to you.

Personally I don't care very much for biting. When I was a teenager I had a nine year old cousin bite me on the forearm...and I mean really sink his chompers into my arm and just *bite* me. I don't even know why he bit me... it was very random. As a result I have basically written him off as a human being and never bothered with him again. That's how not into biting I am.

Anyway over the last few months I'd noticed Jennifer giving me a couple little nips on the neck during playtime. In general I appreciated the passion, but got nothing from them as a turn on. In fact I think I told her to knock it off during a longer session where I racked up several little nips. Do not want.

One night as an experiment I gave her a little nip... and she did this whole clutch/moan/writhe and sigh routine. So I think she might have liked it. I repeated the experiment a few times, and post playtime recap reveals one or two little nips are good for her, three or more is a distraction so please stop. This is no problem because biting her isn't much of a turn on for me, but I don't mind doing it to turn her on.

So sometimes what your partner does to you is actually what they want to be done to them and turns them on. In any case it's worth trying it out and seeing if you found something new in the 30% of things that work.

If not... um... I suggest you don't break the skin first time around....

Make the Bed Squeak

One very simple tactic to make her think she's being completely pounded into a pool of her own juices is to find the right rhythm of thrusting that makes the bed squeak. We have a pretty sturdy king size wooden framed thing that took an awful lot of effort to get into the house and put together. It's really solid. However when I'm on top of Jennifer there is a just right level of my movement I can do to make it start oscillating just a little and the whole thing starts making a five decibels above discreet squeaking noise. It's kind of the same principle that high winds can rip a badly designed bridge apart by getting it slowly wobbling more and more. (See, this is why you should have paid more attention in physics class.)

It's really not anything hugely rough that's going on, it's firm to be sure, but it's not even as rough as it could be. It's about 87.3% of maximum roughness. It just *sounds* like she's getting pounded by the Lord of Cock. If you were standing outside our bedroom door you'd be touching yourself.

Bonus points if you can bang the headboard against the wall. That's like hotel sex. Women love hotel sex. Half the reason women have affairs is just to be in a hotel I think. They will say it's because it's romantic... "romantic" being the girl-talk word for "costs money".

Pro Tip – Some beds can be made squeakier by the use of a screwdriver and the loosening of a few screws. No one ever got divorced because they broke the bed by having sex. However, I am not buying you a new bed.

Warning – Make sure the banging sound is not her head against the headboard. Women detest that.

Cum On Her Breasts

I've not been a huge fan of sex during menstruation. I'm not particularly grossed out by it, just that I find blood to be somewhat irritating on my penis during sex and Jennifer isn't usually all that excited by it either. So by mutual agreement we tend heavily to avoid intercourse during her menses.

Which just opens the door to different fun...

One of my favorite things is Jennifer lying on her back giving me a handjob while I'm on all fours over of her. That way I cum all over her breasts. It's a physically intense way to orgasm for me, more so than my orgasm from regular intercourse, it's just that I usually prefer being inside her. However for nights when Jennifer isn't up for a regular pounding this is a fabulous Plan B.

At first I just liked the strength of my orgasm and physical sensation, but over time I've started getting increasing enjoyment just from the position of dominance and her enjoyment at me cuming hard on her. She quite likes this position as well...both for its own sake and because it's an easy five minutes of fun to get a contented husband.

The Jedi Mind Trick: Make Having Sex the Default Assumption

You want to influence your wife towards a mindset where instead of deciding *for* an unknown sexual romp, she has to think about deciding *against* a known sexual romp.

That's a complicated concept, so let me expand that a little – we are all creatures of habit and overwhelmed with choices in our daily life. Nine times out of ten when faced with a decision, most people will just go with the flow and do what everyone else is doing, or revert back to a pre-planned default choice so they don't have to think.

When most people go into a McDonalds or Starbucks they order the same exact thing every time. They don't think for more than a tenth of a second, just front up to the counter and order their default choice. Sometimes your default choice is so well known, the counter staff doesn't even let you have a choice anymore, they just see you come through the door and they start making your default choice for you. Here's your medium low-fat cappuccino with a dusting of cinnamon and a swizzle stick ma'am... just the way you like it.

So when you're asking her for sex, if she's deciding whether or not to say *"Yes,"* then the default choice is more of a *"No."* When you're telling her what the intended sex is going to be, she's deciding whether or not to say *"No"* and the default choice is more of a *"Yes."* Most times she'll just go along with the default choice of having what you said the intended sex was going to be.

Putting this another way – imagine how she is going to react differently to you asking, *"What's for dinner?"* and you saying, *"I'm in the mood for pasta tonight, can we have pasta for dinner?"* The first question is going to annoy her because it's forcing her into having to think about *yet one more thing* today and come to a decision about it. The second question is going to relax her, because you just held out the big red easy button to her about dinner. There's a very good chance that she will just go along with your idea of pasta for dinner, because you made it the default choice. The frame of having pasta for dinner might be so strong, that if she discovers there's no pasta to cook, she might just nip out and buy some to cook for dinner. The default choice is that powerful sometimes.

For Jennifer and myself, our normal bedtime routine involves closing our bedroom door almost all the way and propping it with a pillow. We have a very friendly cat that would endlessly scratch at the door if we closed it fully and that might wake the children. Also Jennifer has that Mom radar thing, where she needs to hear the children not making any noise, or she can't relax enough to orgasm. Jennifer doesn't want us to wake the children, so the door needs to be almost shut. But the cat would just push the door all the way open, so the pillow propping the door stops the cat doing that. Okay that sounds horribly complicated...

...the point is most nights I don't even ask for sex anymore. I just come out of the bathroom from brushing my teeth and Jennifer has the door already propped semi-closed with a pillow. So I know I'm getting some sort of sex, simply because having sex is the default setting. Usually on nights she really doesn't want anything she tells me *"Not tonight, I'm using PTO"* (Pussy Time Off) and she does so early in the evening. We don't have a firm calling out sick policy in place; we try to keep things informal between us.

If you work this angle long enough, you can make having some sort of sex every night the permanent default choice. What? You think we're better than Pavlov's dogs? Ding ding time for food = drool... night night time for bed = vagina tingle... Damn straight it's a Jedi Mind Trick.

Sweeten the Deal

So... assuming you made a clear statement of intent... *"Tonight I want to go down on you first, then kiss my way up your body and slow fuck you until you beg me to come"* ... and she declines your offer. What next?

You sweeten the deal.

You dispense with her initial *"No"* and simply restate the initial offer and add something more to it. *"Ok... well how about before I go down on you, kiss up your body and slow fuck you, I put you on your hands and knees and spank you for a little while?"* It's really important to keep this both light and playful in tone, with a naughty boy devilish smile as you do this, and hold eye contact. Absolutely do not mumble and look down on the word *"spanking."*

If she is not used to such negotiations from you this should really get her attention. She should become emotionally engaged by this. Usually this will be some version of enjoyment/delight, or annoyance/anger. Both work just fine for the moment. You're getting a rise out of her.

If she agrees to the sex, she agrees, just close the deal and do exactly what you got her to agree to. Don't skimp on what sweetened the deal. If she says *"no"* a second time, sweeten the deal again.

"I'm willing to do some hair pulling and French kissing as well. Plus all the oral, kissing up your body, slow fucking and spanking like we agreed before." And again – you absolutely have to stay playful and

fun in tone when you do this. You have to make it clear that you're enjoying playing the role of salesman here. Also do not offer anything additional that isn't sexual. Don't offer to do household chores, work overtime, drop off the kids to school etc, that will kill it instantly. *You are not offering anything for sex; you're offering sex, more sex and even more sex.* The implication you are creating is that she is fact wants to be laid, but is holding out for more pleasure.

If she still is saying *"No,"* but is in any way showing you a positive response – smiling, hair flipping, laughing, giggling, touching you, giving you lots of eye contact, touching herself across any part of her body – that means she is enjoying the interaction and wants you to continue and overwhelm her sales resistance. Just keep the routine up and play the game with her.

If she is not showing positive interest by this point, just bail out of the routine, and cheerfully, and yes I said cheerfully, wish her a good night, and do the go to sleep thing. You aren't trying to make her hate you. Importantly be as unaffected by the *"No"* as possible. No drama. It's okay to try and overcome a *"No"* with play, but she should be allowed to decline sex without you being negative or turning into a stalker.

So anyway... overcome the sales resistance...

"So what part of the big package I've offered is the problem? I see I've suggested slow sensual sex, would you like something a little rougher?"
"What can I do to get you into a fabulous orgasm tonight?"
"Would you like to test-drive an orgasm?"
"When I spank you, would you rather be kneeling, or across my lap?"
*"I don't usually do this, but *name* I like you... I can do handcuffs, but you have to promise not to tell anyone. It's kind of against the rules."*

Just keep laying it on until she folds. Talk talk talk, play play play. Don't forget to touch her and hold/kiss her if you can as well during this routine. *You're playing with her,* smile at her with your naughty boy smile. Once she folds, you've got her.

If she's still verbally holding out after all that and she's still giving you a positive body language response, you can make one final "desperate offer". And again, I cannot emphasize enough that you have to keep this as light and fun as possible. You pull exactly seventeen cents from your pocket, gaze at the money in your hand with fake sadness for a second, then hold it out to her to take and say...

"Can I just put the tip of my dick in?"

If you do it right she should erupt with laughter, but agree. Importantly, seventeen cents is in no way enough to "buy sex" so it's not really an insult (whereas fifty bucks might very well be an insult – be advised) and that once the tip of your dick is inside her, you both know that the rest of your cock is going to follow and you are in fact a 100% full-of-shit-liar just trying to get into her pants. But she might really like that once in a while.

If you go to the "tip of my dick" gambit, do mess about with just the tip in for a bit, then just groan and fill her up. That will make her feel desired by you, which is a turn on. Also she will always call you on it after you go balls deep. *"I thought you said you were only going to put the tip in."* Correct response...

"I lied."

Chapter 21
Words of Seduction

Saying I Love You

At some point in a LTR and definitely in a marriage you are going to have to say the "L word" and make some sort of declaration of love. You really should be saying this frequently anyway, especially if she clearly responds to it.

However, the first time you say *"I love you"* it can accelerate things or turn her off. Plus every relationship can do with an *"I love you"* that leaves her reeling and giddy once in a while to shake things up a little.

The key is to establish that you are saying something from an emotional state, rather than a rational one. If you're communicating from a rational/logical state, you're actually unwittingly communicating that you don't in fact love her, but that it's just a good idea to love her. If she's a math professor, a CPA, a lawyer or otherwise inflicted with a male typed brain it's ok to give her an Excel spreadsheet of why you love her, but not otherwise. Women want to feel that you feel in love with them emotionally.

So here we go...

Step 1 – Call her over to you and say, *"We need to talk a moment."* It's an Alpha move and it helps with everything that follows.

Step 2 – Run off a short list of some of her very best and most lovable qualities and say that you could say you love her because of these things, but these are in fact just a list of her good qualities.

"I've been trying to decide why I love you. (pause!) I could tell you I love you because you're smart. I could tell you that I love you because you're so caring and kind. I could tell you I love you because you're such a genuine person and so grounded. But these are all simply a list of your good qualities and not why I love you."

See how that compliments logically, but you disarm it emotionally?

Step 3 – Go for complete emotion with an irrational statement.

"The fact is, I don't know why I love you. I just do."

There's no possible way she can deflect that statement's emotional impact. It's not trying to be a logical argument for love, so all she can do is either accept that it is the truth or deny it. Very little middle ground.

Step 4 – Make it seem even more real and solid. Tell her when you realized that you loved her. You can blow up a quite trivial incident into a maelstrom of flooded emotions here. (Hopefully it's true and you're not just a lying sack of shit.)

"What I can do though, is tell you when I realized that I loved you. We were riding the big rollercoaster at Knoebel's together and about halfway around the track I realize I'm not even paying attention to the fact I'm on a rollercoaster. I'm just watching you and your hair flying in the wind. And you looked over at me and smiled and that was it. I just knew."

At this point she should be glassy-eyed and all melting inside. Now is a good time to hear she loves you and go for a long slow kiss close.

Of course this is all very vulnerable and Beta to gush all this emotion and wear your heart on your sleeve, so you can always bring everything back down to reality. With a very naughty boy smile and a twinkle in your eye you can redo the entire routine, but in instead of "why I love you", do it as "why I want to have sex with you"...

"I also need to tell you why I want to have sex with you."

"I could tell you about your fantastic boobs, the boom in your booty, your slutty lower back tattoo. The fact is, these are just a list of your sexy qualities. I don't know why I want to have sex with you, I just do."

"What I can tell you though, is the moment I realized I wanted to have sex with you. You were at the bar and you deep throated a beer bottle and I just knew I wanted to have sex with you."

This should get you a lot of laughter and it's a subtle tease in that you've obviously been gaming her with the *"I love you."* version if both that and the sex version have basically the same script format.

Then gently pull her to you and say that you love her. 100% earnestly with no games, just all heart. Then spank her ass a little as you break the kiss and separate.

*** Disclaimer: Jennifer does not have a slutty back tattoo. She cannot deep throat a beer bottle. ***

Speak Her Love Language

Time to play a little game with the wife...

You each get two pieces of paper and a pen. At the top of one piece of paper write, *"if I was really crazy in love with you, I would..."* On the top of the other write, *"if you were really crazy in love with me, I'd like you to..."*

Then go ahead and fill out at least ten things on each paper without peeking at what the other is writing. You can take ten minutes, or an hour, or a day or however long you want to.

Then you compare each other's lists. Comparing your *"if I was in love with you I would..."* list against her *"if you were in love with me I'd like you to..."* list and vice versa.

The lists would be interesting in and of themselves, but you're also looking for the sweet spot where the same thing turns up on both lists. Meaning if your *"If I was crazy in love with you"* list had buying flowers for her and her *"If he was crazy in love with me, I'd like him to"* list had he would buy flowers for me, well you giving her flowers is a sweet spot.

Obviously you do those sweet spot items. That's a no brainer because when you do things that express feelings, it tends to intensify those feelings. Giving flowers not only expresses love, but it strengthens the feelings of love in the giver.

But don't neglect to do some of the other items as well. If you like giving flowers, but she is somewhat unexcited about getting them, you should still give them once in a while. Just expressing romantic love will reinforce your feelings for her. It may seem to be a little fake for her to happily accept flowers and make a little fuss about them, but she should do so knowing that you're expressing yourself to her and your feelings are intensifying towards her.

Likewise if giving flowers is a total zero for you, but she loves them, you should give them to her once in a while. Receiving them reinforces her feelings for you. And yes it is a little fake of you to give them, but it's also saying that in effect you know what she likes and care enough to woo her.

With enough repetition of in-love behavior, it's very possible to rekindle lost feelings of love together. Yes, it does take some effort and seems a little fake at first, but it's really no different than those first few weeks of heading back to the gym to try and get back into shape. Feels weird, sometimes it hurts a little, but you just have to plow it though and the positive feelings will return.

It works because you are both sending and receiving messages of love in the way you are expecting to give and receive them. Sometimes the love has been there the whole time, but it's just like you've been speaking in different languages and not hearing each other.

And of course everything above about buying flowers applies exactly the same for blowjobs. Just sayin' ladies, just sayin'.

Expose Weakness with Valentine's Day Game

If you're in a very bad place with your relationship – maybe the divorce word has been said, or she's talking about walking out, you have to say something to her and at least buy some time.

Say to her. *"Listen, sometimes I feel like I'm a stupid man."* Generally this establishes common ground as something you both can agree on and build on. It's okay to pause for a second and just hold her attention there too. You should have her full attention before plowing ahead with the rest of the routine.

"And while I love you with all my heart," good place for a pause here as well. Let her feel those words. Straight shoot them.

"I don't really have a clue what to do to you, or for you, or with you, to make you feel loved by me, the way I do love you." Say that "the way I do love you" bit with feeling. Pretend you're in a movie and this is the turning point of the on screen romance.

"I'm embarrassed to ask, but I am asking for your help, so please help me know how to make you feel loved, the way I do love you." This just rocks because you're revealing vulnerability to her (and her only) and this automatically will generate a desire in her to open herself to you.

"So let's pretend today is Valentine's Day. And if today is Valentine's Day, what is just one thing I could do, that would make you feel like you had a good Valentine's Day? And make you feel loved, like I do love you."

Then whatever she says, you go do it. Then you ask her to do marriage counseling with you. Marriage counseling is probably not going to work; you're just using it to buy time to run The MAP more. Try not to book the first appointment too soon.

Every Day is Valentine's Day

You can run the Valentine's Day game as often as you like. The general rule though is that it is "just one thing" you're doing and not a permanent slave collar. If she gets greedy, just deflect demands for more than one thing. Say *"sorry honey I forgot the first thing when you told me the second thing, what was the one thing you wanted me to do today?"* If you do this frequently, you will probably find that the first week or so will be item requests, flowers, card, chocolates etc, and over time as her romance need is met, she'll just turn horny on you and you can just coast along on Ten Second Kisses. Oh well, *just cope.*

When She Asks "Do These Pants Make My Ass Look Fat?"

There comes a time in every man's life, when the woman he is involved with asks the dreaded question.

"Do these pants make my ass look fat?" (DTPMMALF)

Guys tend to be simple creatures with basic needs. Feed us, let us have a place to sleep and some form of entertainment and we usually run at 95% of maximum happiness. Most guys will automatically attempt to answer any question with a one word answer. Unfortunately the only words that spring to mind are either *"Yes"* or *"No."*

Answering *"Yes"* is of course a terrible choice. If you can't figure out why it's a terrible choice then you're on your own, you're probably not salvageable as a male. (Also, those kids calling you Dad probably aren't yours either – just a heads up)

Answering *"No"* is not the relationship suicide that answering *"Yes"* is, but if you watch her face carefully you will not see any enjoyment in hearing a *"No"* answer. *"No"* is not the right answer; somehow you have failed.

Occasionally someone will attempt to answer DTPMMALF by not answering *"Yes"* or *"No"* and advancing a cautious *"Maybe"* as an answer. The Maybe Gambit does work as an answer, but – and this is important – it works only if you are her girlfriend or a gay friend.

You answering *"Maybe"* just makes you seem completely developmentally delayed. You are expected to have strong, well formed opinions on the state of her body. Have you been paying attention to her at all?

The other attempted answer is the It's All In Your Head Defense where you explain that she is somehow mentally unstable for asking the question. This is the best of the answers so far, but is an insult at heart and drives the two of you a little further apart. So no.

The Actual Question Being Asked

Having covered what *not to* answer DTPMMALF with, it's time to find out what to answer DTPMMALF with. Let's break down DTPMMALF into something simple enough for the average guy to understand. When she says,

"Do these pants make my ass look fat?"

You should hear,

"Xx xxxxx xxxxx xxxx xx ass xxxx xxx?"

Removing the verbal clutter, it is summarized as... *"ass?"*

The correct response to that question is your first and natural response, *"Yes of course I'd like some ass."* Remember how the *"No"* answer didn't please her? See how you screwed that up now?

So how do you answer DTPMMALF – and get laid.

Give her your best I'm-a-sly-dog-naughty-boy smile. Hold the smile and make eye contact for at least three to five seconds until she stops whatever she is doing and pays complete attention to you. Then say...

"I don't know. I would have to see your ass without the pants."

Then just wait expectantly, continuing to hold eye contact.

Now What Happens?!?!

One of two things will happen. Either she takes the pants off or she doesn't. If she takes them off... then close the deal. If she doesn't take them off she should have at least smiled letting you know you answered the question correctly. That means good things will happen to you from her in the near future. Don't be a twit and blow it.

Warning about Answering DTPMMALF Correctly.

Women only ask this question when they are in the fertile part of their monthly cycle.

Talk Dirty To Her

Most women enjoy dirty talk in bed. Often this is limited to the bedroom and not an all area pass. I.e. calling her a *"hot little slut"* as you are all hot, sweaty and flinging the covers off the top of you and onto the floor is sexy goodness. Calling her a *"hot little slut"* in the checkout line at the supermarket is another thing entirely. The proper etiquette when standing in a checkout line is to not *say* that sort of thing at all, but to text it.

Some women like being called certain dirty words and not others. (Jennifer for example, likes being called a slut, but reacts quite poorly to being called a whore.) All this is just her inner kink at work and you probably have no hope of changing which word turns your wife on and which words turn her off. There's no real benefit to psychoanalyzing why a certain word turns her on, you just have to keep trying them out until you strike gold. Once you find them though, don't pound the value out of the word by saying it over and over. Use it one to three times a day tops.

If you struggle to come up with dirty things to say, just talk about what is happening. Short positive statements like *"yeah suck me like that"* work well. Tell her to do something, if only a position change, like *"on your back now."* Remember not to say "please" when you do this, just give the order and give her a little push in the direction you want her to go.

Announce your impending orgasm... *"Almost there baby, stay right there."*

Sometimes you don't even need to say anything... just breathe a little harder near her ear so she can hear it. She's going to react as much to you being turned on by her and just saying things to her as by anything in particular you say.

Surprise and Delight Her

Sometimes all you have to do to impress a woman is to do one little thing that surprises and delights her. Ideally that thing you do involves a skill rather than simply giving her something. You writing a song for her, or a poem, or cooking a perfect dinner out of the blue is a greater thrill for her than a straight up gift. Chocolates for example please her for about a tenth of a second, while a memorable moment can imprint deep into her brain and last forever.

Back in the early days of toddlers and chaos I sprung a surprise Christmas present on Jennifer. Jennifer had taken the girls to Grandma's and all three slept there overnight on Christmas Eve so I could sleep in after work into Christmas morning and then meet them all at Grandma's later. I was working the evening shift and came home at about 11:30pm, but instead of falling asleep I went crazy cleaning the house. And not just a little crazy, I rearranged the living room furniture into a new setup that worked better, moved the computers from the spare room into the living room and shuffled the bookcases around and so on. Then I collapsed for a bit and joined them at Grandma's. The first Jennifer knew of my busy night was walking into the house to find my home makeover attempt. She squealed in delight.

The words *"I love you"* are always good, but actions of love can carry serious weight.

Toast Her Marshmallows

At some point you're going to end up by a fire and everyone is going to be toasting marshmallows. Here's how you blow her mind with the humble marshmallow.

Idiots and preteen boys usually just shove a marshmallow on a stick and then hold it way too close to the fire and brown the outside of the marshmallow before eating it. Or worse they will simply set the damn thing on fire and blow it out and consider that a job well done. No son, that's a burnt piece of crap, your woman will not be pleased.

The trick is simple. You stay away from the leaping flames and find a good spot of glowing embers giving off a decent heat. Then while you hold the marshmallow over the embers you slowly keep it turning on the stick. Think rotisserie marshmallow. Just turn, turn, turn, turn. If you do it just right you can cook the marshmallow so that while the outside doesn't burn, the inside of the marshmallow heats up enough to turn into a gooey liquid.

You know that the inside of the marshmallow has turned into a gooey liquid when the marshmallow stops turning on the stick. You can turn the stick and it just kind of stays in place. If you continue on cooking the marshmallow much beyond this point it just falls off the stick into the fire. (Oh and it's not terribly hot either as marshmallows liquefy at a moderate temperature. Try one yourself first and see.)

Now confidently stride up to your wife and present your marshmallow. Importantly she needs to take the whole thing into her mouth. The marshmallow will have a little mini explosion when she pushes it against the roof of her mouth with her tongue. The technical term for this is "Splucking". Toasted marshmallows should spluck. Anyway if she bites into half of it, half of the gooey white stuff will end up dripping off her lips and chin. Which is a good look, but you really want to train her to swallow the whole thing.

You should get a look of genuine surprise and delight from anyone that hasn't been previously splucked. Just maintain eye contact and smile a crooked naughty grin...

... *"Now imagine what I could do to you."*

Post-It Notes

You can always leave her a Post-It note saying you love her and leave it where she will find it. Recently at work when I went down to say hi to Jennifer she wasn't at her desk, so I scribbled *"I love you – no reason."* on a Post-It and put it on her computer. As I was stealing some of her pens, I realized that pinned to her cubicle wall were another two nearly identical notes that I must have written years earlier. So they were stupid little Post-It notes that took five seconds to write, but if she keeps them it means they have meaning to her.

I think Post-It notes work because they have a perfectly incidental quality that means you really were just thinking of her impulsively, but you're unaffected by her enough that you aren't weak to her. It's a nice Alpha and Beta mix.

Love Letters

Once in a while an old fashioned love letter can strike a chord where mere talk or cards cannot. For the most part everything that we get in the mail is boring, a bill, or just plain nasty. Written documentation is usually serious in nature, so getting a love letter carries a little additional weight.

One thing that a loyal spouse does in combating the affair of the disloyal spouse is write them a letter essentially telling them to cease and desist the affair or suffer the consequences. A letter is used because it is a clear and direct form of communication with little wiggle room for misunderstanding.

So why wait for an affair to write her a letter like a written warning? Tell her what she's doing right and give her a written *warming*. These are the sort of things that she might just hold onto forever.

Chapter 22
Sext Messages

I Wanna Sext You Up

Cheated-on husbands *always* discover their wife engaged in lurid sexting, email or Facebook messaging with the other man. Really – this is not something that *sometimes* happens in affairs, it *always* happens. There can be *thousands* of messages between affair partners in just a single month. The husband is usually appalled because *"she isn't like that"*... but apparently she is. Women love sex just as much as men do and they clearly do enjoy sexual flirting and playing. Also to be completely blunt, *some* women are attention-whores and if you don't give them regular attention they will take steps to go find it. If another man supplies her with sexy attention, he's on the fast track to a final seduction with her.

The obvious solution is for you to step in and "act like her lover" would. Just start supplying some daily interaction via text, email or Facebook and engage her attention and sense of sex and fun. This all returns to the basics of *"Instigation, Isolation and Escalation"*. When you message her playfully, you are instigating. Because she is getting a personal message that only she can see and respond to, she is already effectively isolated with you, even if she is in a crowded room or having dinner at her mother's. That means there's plenty of ability to kick things up a notch and turn the conversation sexual or get her to do things for you sexually... like snap a shot of her boobs and send them to you. Bam! You're escalating her.

Play with her and have fun! *You* be her lover.

Text Her Incidental Things

You can update each other during the day of whatever is going on that's nice. I often text Jennifer a *"How is it going?"* during my lunch break. If I see something funny happen I'll text her that too. The whole purpose is simply to keep up a relationship by regular contact.

My work schedule is very flexible, but also demanding in that if something comes up last minute I really can't walk out the door. I also tend to be somewhat distractible. So when I'm doing kid pickup or coming home, I text Jennifer. She's not keeping tabs on me, she just worries that I'm stuck somewhere and a two-second *"On my way"* relaxes her.

Change Your Name on Her Phone

Upon occasion I have snuck access to Jennifer's phone and reprogrammed my name in her contact list to; *"Big Daddy," "Cockzilla," "Sex Toy"* or *"Lord and Master."* It shows the caller's name on the outside of her phone, so I try to avoid this for important business meetings, but it always gets a reaction. If she reads this book... *"Captain"* works as well!

Ask What Color Her Panties Are

Women love to be treated like sex objects if they are interested in the man, so treat her like one. At random I'll just ask Jennifer what color panties she is wearing. It's fun, it's flirty and fairly quick. Also, picking days when she has a little more privacy and opportunity, it's possible to wrangle a few photos out of her as well. (Especially if you timed that with her ovulation.)

The trick with asking for panty color or photos is to ask for them, then just wait. Don't fold and apologize for asking, just ask and wait. Very frequently they will come. If she doesn't give you what you want, just don't reply to her next text. If she tells you off for asking, just laugh it off and text back *"I'd apologize but I'm obnoxious."*

She Speaks Another Language Text

Jennifer speaks reasonably good French while I only know how to say *"dog"* and *"cat."* But despite Jennifer having me beat on this one, I still send her texts in French once in a while. I just use an online translator to assist me. Jennifer tells me that the www.Babelfish.com

site is the best one... I have no clue of course as everything translates *"dog"* and *"cat"* correctly.

Some examples;

"Je tiens a la livre a votre chat ce soir"
(I want to read a sturdy book to your cat tonight)

Ok that just blew. I was trying to make a joke about pounding her "pussy" tonight, but I have no clue what happened there. Try again...

"Vous êtes trés belle dans la cuisine quand nu"
(You are very beautiful in the kitchen when you are naked)

Better.

So go hunt up a few good phrases and save them to templates or outgoing messages, then you have them on a whim during the day. Just launch a couple at her during the day. If she doesn't speak French then you can still do it, just make sure she knows about Babelfish.com. Little compliments and/or sexual requests. She'll eat it up.

One more...

"Je veux avoir le sexe chaud de singe avec vous ce soir"
(I want to have hot monkey sex with you tonight)

...and it retranslated *"Je veux avoir le sexe chaud de singe avec vous ce soir"* back into English as "*I want to have the hot sex of monkey with you this evening.*" This wasn't exactly what I ordered, but I did enjoy it anyway but the pet monkey we bought refuses to come out of its cage now.

Simon Says

After a text or two generally opening the conversation, and making sure she has some privacy and ability to respond, you start the game with texting...

"Simon Says..."

This clues her into that you are playing a game with her and unless she had some sort of bizarre childhood, she will know the game and be almost automatically driven to comply with demands from "Simon."

"Simon Says, text that you are IN to playing Simon Says."

If you get an "IN" reply, you're in, and can just start issuing commands as you think she would comply and enjoy. Suggestions:

Simon says find a private area of the house
Simon says remove an article of clothing
Simon says take a photo of your boobs
Simon says take a photo of your panties
Simon says rub your nipples
Simon says take your panties off
Simon says turn the lights down low
Simon says finger yourself
Simon says have an orgasm
Simon says come open the front door and let me in

Generally just start from simpler less daring requests and work up to more daring ones. Of course if you're a single Bad Boy you can text Simon Says requests to multiple women at once as long as you can keep up with the texting speed.

The Star Trek Game

I'm a big believer in play. Playing with your wife, and playing with your kids. Life is getting so serious these days. Play is the antidote to serious. You don't have to turn into a big immature kid to play, just add a helping of goofball and lose a little of the frown.

Both my wife and I work full time jobs, plus we have busy and social kids. We have to schedule pickups and drop offs with school, and it's getting to be a lucky dip how many kids you come home with when you go to pick them up. You get two kids some days, sometimes four kids, others none. This is by no means a complaint, these are a great group of kids in our neighborhood and we love all of them. They just move as a pack from house to house it seems.

We have two daughters and all four of us have a shared cell phone plan, with unlimited text messaging between us. And as all good geeks should know... a cell phone is really a Star Trek Communicator. So obviously there needs to be a geeky Star Trek Text Game.

The first step is to define a few terms. Take your street name, add *"The"* or *"USS"* to the front of it, and then drop the street/road from it. So *"Redstone Hill Street"* becomes *"The Redstone"* or *"USS Redstone Hill"*. And bingo you have the starship name of your house.

The cars are more easily named affectionately. These are shuttlecraft and the owner/primary driver's middle name is the name of the shuttle. That or simply refer to them as shuttles or runabouts.

Naturally I am the Captain with the rank of Captain. If you're properly geekish and want me to pick an actual character, I'm Spock. Most particularly the middle aged Spock who is no longer purely logical, but more in touch with his emotions and even goes so far as to talk of faith. He is quite illogically loyal and concerned for his friends.

Jennifer is the First Officer and rank of Commander. Geeks might enjoy thinking of her as Deanna Troi, but not so much the bimbo-early-seasons-Troi stating the obvious *("You feel profoundly sad")*, more the final season or two where she is a full bridge officer and uniformed and packing a phaser for away missions. She has a social fluidity, emotional balance and genuine charm that still astound me to this day. Plus she has the bedroom thing down.

Daughter #1 is an Ensign. She is more fully my daughter than her mother's, but she interfaces with technology superbly, is always connected to something...computer, iPod, phone or all three together. There's a struggle for individuality from the collective. So she is clearly 7 of 9, our resident Borg. As Ensign she is capable of performing away missions without direct supervision. (Though shuttlecraft training is a few years off.)

Daughter #2 is a newly promoted Ensign. Like her mom she is socially adept, sensitive and hard working in the extreme. But she has a wide variety of skills and interests too. She'll play fight like a Klingon one minute, love money like a Ferengi, then want to read for hours like a Vulcan. There's a multitude of talents and skills in there.

And in time she could possibly be the wisest of us all. So she's a Trill. But young, button cute and a little shy...so Ezri Dax.

So that's the Ship and the Crew...

Neighboring kids' houses are referred to by street name, but changing the word denoting street to that of "*system.*"So someone living on "*Duke Street*" becomes "*The Duke System.*"

Another option if the street name is horrible for usage, "*22 Peach Road*" for example is awful, then just ignore the street name, and use the house number and switch it up to "*Starbase 22.*"

So we text each other a lot; kid pick up and drop offs, where are you going? When are you back? I'm on my way and so on. Here's a list of playful terms and verbiage to kick start things.

Fleet operations complete: All kids are dropped off and we are home now.
Understood: Ok
Ensign away mission to Pine System: Daughter is going to her friend's house on Pine St.
Creating resupply manifest: I'm going to the store, you need anything?
10 Forward?: I really need a drink tonight, want to hook up?
ETA The Redstone 10 minutes: I'll be home in ten minutes
Call for extraction by 2100: I'll come pick you up from your friend's house when you text, but I'll just show up at 9pm if you don't call earlier than that.
Educational delegation on board: I am up to my ass in freaking kids.
Report: Where are you? How is it going?
How was the diplomatic conference?: How did the meeting go?
Keep a channel open: Stay in touch.
Report Overdue [Rank]: If you shut your phone off or refuse to answer my texts I will ground you young lady. Don't think I won't do that just because I'm capable of being playful at times.
Life support critical: We are very, very hungry, please bring home something to eat.
Yellow alert: I'm not feeling comfortable here. Please come get me right now.
Red alert: HELP NOW.

So that's the basics, just play and have some fun with it. The kids love it and I'm the cool fun dad. But also one that's in communication and paying attention. I've totally been training the kids that they can dial mom and dad and be automatically dragged out of any situation by their parents. Don't forget that this entire thing of playful attention to wife and family works for my wife and builds her interest in me. Maybe Star Trek doesn't work for you, it does for us. But then we're a little geeky at times.

How Not to Ask Your Boss What Color Her Panties are by Accidental Text

My female boss has a first name that starts with a "K". In my address book my contact list went "Jennifer" and then immediately "K". I'm a little fast and careless with my texting occasionally and I'd prefer not to accidently ask the Director of Nurses what color her panties are.

For myself, I use a number system and rank my most valued female contacts. "1 Jennifer" sits at the top of the list. It's actually cool because about 40% of my outgoing calls and 75%+ of my texts are to Jennifer, so I get a lot of ease in quick keying replies etc.

"2 xxxxxxx" is my primary coworker and we do have a lot of contact with each other. Our work group is geographically spread out, but we're a small team, so we do a fair bit of calling and texting each other.

"3 xxxxxx" is my female boss who I both love dearly and have a lot of respect for.

"4 xxxxxx" is daughter #1

"5 xxxxxx" is daughter #2

Basically this group gets 90% of my outgoing calls, and 98% of my texts and they just all sit at the top of my address list. See how that's all easy phone management?

On discovery of this ranking... #2 was quite flattered that she out ranked #3 in my phone, though I pointed out immediately that I do occasionally text a little too quickly and she was the only one in the top five that I could accidently send a filthy text intended for 1 Jennifer to and not get in serious trouble with. So she's technically the buffer to the people that really matter.

I do find it very helpful to have my #1 ranked female flashed in front of my eyes as such at least four or five times a day. More important than the kids. More important than the boss. More important than female coworkers.

See I told you she was my *"Number One!"*

That's What She Said

This one is simple but effective. Whenever your wife says anything that could be misunderstood as sexual, you just draw attention to it with the line *"that's what she said."*

As an example; I'm driving my wife's car and there is no windshield washer fluid left, plus the driver's side wiper looks half broken and finishes all wonky right across my field of vision. So by text...

Me: *"No washer fluid and the wiper looks broken."*

Jennifer: *"Yeah it gets stuck halfway when it isn't wet."*

Me: *"That's what she said."*

Jennifer: *"LOL."*

So yeah... it's juvenile and needlessly sexual, but that's why it works so well. It's funny, it shows a one track mind and it's hard to find a more reliable joke.

Same Room Texting

If you're in the same room, you can still text each other. Especially if you have some private joke you want to share. Or maybe the kids are in the room and you're putting in your orders for bedtime...

It Can Be Short

Jennifer: *I'm on my way home we need anything?*

Me: *Raw dog sex*

Jennifer: *LOL oh really.*

Me: *Woof.*

Chapter 23
Date Night

It's a Date and it's at Night

Now we're into the fun stuff, some practical things that you can do to boost your wife's interest in you. These aren't just ideas like "light candles in the bedroom", but are specifically designed to play off either or both Alpha and Beta traits.

The much praised weekly "Date Night" is supposedly the touchstone of marital bliss, but many couples find it lackluster and less fun than it should be. Personally, I think it's hard to come up with clever and novel dates on a weekly basis and for many couples the expense of eating out cuts into the budget. Jennifer and I do a proper Date Night about once every three months, but we execute them well together.

The most important thing for a Date Night is that you have some sort of plan for the evening and don't just flounder around without a clue what to do next. Women generally like their men to lead them, so you asking *"Umm, what do you want to do?"* for the special night out just turns them off. It's ideal if you can time Date Night to sync up with her ovulation.

The idea is to put into practice the core of pickup by touching on the basics covered in the chapter *"Instigate, Isolate and Escalate."* What follows below comes in two parts for an actual Date Night Jennifer and I had together. The first part is my plan and the second part is how it actually played out. Jennifer naturally got to read the first part on my blog before the actual Date Night, so things had a slight variation along the way...

The Plan for Date Night

The plan is to drop the girls off at Grandma's house for an overnight and then have a proper Date Night. The entire point of getting rid of the kids is to create an isolation play so that we're alone together properly. It's one thing to have sex in bed after the kids are asleep, but you can't exactly rampage naked through the house squealing and rutting without waking up the little dears. As we drive to Grandma's, I will most likely reach over and touch Jennifer on the thigh about three times and give it a gentle squeeze. She'll put her hand on top of mine, letting me know she likes it.

We'll head to the mall and watch the movie "Date Night" together. It's a 6:55pm show time, so we'll probably have a snack and drink before the movie at one of the places inside the mall. Hopefully the movie will be good, a little sexy and funny—a grown-up movie we can't see with the kids around. There will probably some hand holding as we're walking through the mall. At some random point I will likely physically pull her into a store to look at something - I mean simply say *"Oh look at that!"* and walk into the store still holding hands making her follow. The other subtle move is the lower back push to go into a store. The tactic depends on whether you are closer to the entry of the store or she is. It should be as natural as possible - it's just something that's happening.

After that will be a location bounce to get sushi (her favorite) and possibly another drink. Sushi always makes her happy; the exotic and the erotic are kissing cousins for most women. (As an aside, sushi girls rock... I mean, if she'll put raw fish in her mouth....) The location bounce is usually to further isolate her, and a small sushi restaurant is more intimate than a shopping mall. There will be lots of opportunity to touch on the way in and out of the restaurant. While sitting across the table from each other, I'll compliance test her by reaching across the table with my palm upwards, seeking her compliance to put her hand in mine. It's leading her into a subtle physical escalation.

The next move will be another location bounce in the direction of home. Obviously the point of Date Night is a long session of sex, but I've been instigating this further by picking out a "couples oriented" DVD for the evening. Jennifer already knows about this, she agreed with the choice when I ordered it on Sunday. When it arrived on Tuesday I saw the mailman come and I purposely left it in the mailbox so *she* had to handle it and take in the house. It pretty much forced her to walk up to me and say *"Does this box contain the pussy plutonium we need for the bomb we're making on Friday?"* *"Yes dear, it does."* Okay so she phrased the question differently, but that's what she meant.

After that, the plan is that the night turns into a long slow session of making out in the living room, fondling and squeezing as many orgasms out of Jennifer as she can manage without damaging her basic life support functions. She watches adult movies pretty much only on Date Night so they really get to her. Also the movie is apparently all my idea, so it bypasses any remaining anti-slut defense and allows her to enjoy it more. She's just tolerating me being a bad man or something. When she can't handle anymore orgasms, it's my turn. My turn being me on top and riding her to a firm finish with just a touch of the spurs at the end; I am, of course, very overconfident with Jennifer.

For this Date Night, Jennifer also went out and hunted down something *less comfortable* to wear. I had no clue what it was going to be exactly, but I did praise and positively acknowledge what she was doing. Whatever it is will be fine. The point is she's trying to please me, so I'm telling her I'm pleased. When a woman who enjoys being at all submissive to you does something nice for you and you say thank you... her vagina tingles a little.

How It Really Played Out

Because she reads my blog, Jennifer knew all my plans, so I was naturally assuming that things would not go exactly to plan.

So I had said...

"...as we drive [the girls] to Grandma's, I will most likely touch her on the thigh about three times. She'll put her hand on top of mine, letting me know she likes it."

After about a minute driving, I very obviously reach out and pat her thigh and gently squeeze it. She looks down, looks at me, bursts into hysterical laughter and then puts her hand on top of mine. It's supposed to be a comfort building move that just subtly works its magic, but obviously I've tipped my hand here. Now my move is purposely goofy; *"Hey baby I'm gaming you, I'm a pickup artist!"* It only works if she wants to be gamed... and she does, so it works. She's laughing, my hand is on her thigh, and her hand is on top of my hand. Don't forget that after a certain threshold women actively enjoy being seduced and can be in on the game. They aren't stupid.

Later on in the thirty minute drive I repeat the move, but in the standard variant. It's just a touch and a squeeze and she pats her hand on mine. It's just something we do together. *Hi there, I like you, I'm happy to be driving somewhere with you.* She's right there and I like her, so I touch her.

With the kids dropped off at Grandma's, we are off to the mall. We get the movie tickets then eat at the Olive Garden (She had coupons to use, which makes her very wet, so I roll with it). I tend not to be an adventurous eater, I could probably just order cheeseburgers everywhere and be perfectly happy, but Jennifer likes food variety and new places. Neither one of us had been to the Olive Garden, so I gain valuable points for taking her there. We share an appetizer and then swap some food off each other's plates and generally yap about work, the blog, life in general. It was a fun conversation.

After dinner we have an hour and a bit to walk the mall before the movie. As we go up or down the escalators we always kiss and cuddle a little. I'm six feet tall and Jennifer is five feet tall, so escalators are always exciting to us because we get a fifteen second make out moment with our height differential adjusted. Again it's just something we do together. Yep... escalators are sexy time in our marriage.

So we walk the mall together, remembering that I've said...

"There will probably some hand holding walking through the mall. At some random point I will likely physically pull her into a store to look at something - I mean simply say "Oh look at that!" and walk into the store still holding hands making her follow. The other subtle move is the lower back guide along push to go into a store. The tactic depends on whether or not you are closer to the entry of the store or she is. It should be as natural as possible - it's just something that's happening."

We're walking and looking in stores and holding hands at times and generally just popping in and out of stores and window shopping. I've still not really done "the big move" as we come up to Victoria's Secret.

Obviously, I am going to turn my head and look into the store... I'm caught looking and she doesn't get the hand yank move. Next thing I know Jennifer puts her hand in the small of my back and *shoves* me into Victoria's Secret!

So we snoop and look. Jennifer is a picky shopper so she's trolling for sales. At the underwear area one of the five "ass mannequins" in the center of a display catches my eye. *"I wanna see you wearing this one"* I say pointing to the ass mannequin with no panties on. I get a mock groaning *"Dude"* plus a fake eye roll of disgust coupled with a smile. *"It's a good look for you though..."*

So we walk a little more and then head up to the movie. We're in a little early and have the movie theatre to ourselves. I'm tempted to make a very naughty suggestion or make inappropriate attempts to get my hands inside her shirt, but this would probably backfire, so I behave. Within about one minute a few more people wander in, so this was a good decision. The movie *"Date Night"* was a little silly in places, but generally good. Jennifer liked it too, so it's all good. After that we leave and start heading in the general direction of home.

The original plan was a location bounce to get sushi because she likes it but we're actually both still a little full from the Olive Garden. We decide on coffee and dessert at the Ninety-Nine (bar and grill chain) but make a last minute detour to Wrapsody which is a little more grown up. Jennifer has never been there (I've been once for a work thing) so again this gets me points for "variety and interesting". Jen gets spiked coffee, I have regular coffee and Tawny Port and we share cheesecake. Her coffee is a Raspberry White Chocolate thing and is amazing.

So after that we head home and start a long, slow session on the couch together watching *"Bodies in Unison"* from the Playgirl DVD line. It's basically vanilla porn, boy-girl, oral/vaginal, no crazy ass to mouth scenes, no stupid cock gagging blowjobs. The guys and girls looked pretty good and it's standard porn with terrible dialogue/acting, with the music mixed a little loud. I can go a little harder core and like it, but not much further than that. Maybe I'm odd, but I still like vaginal sex and women. I've got my silk boxers on, Jennifer in a silk top and filmy thin panties and we cuddle and fondle under the blanket. Then we do it like they do on the Discovery Channel.

Make Sure Date Night Is Special

As final thought, we all have a variety and interest gene that needs satisfaction. It's the dopamine based thing again. If you were single and dating, you can go to the same place and do the same thing every time, but with a different woman and still get your variety needs met. When you are married though, you can't get your variety need met from the same woman, unless you frequently do something different with her. It's very important to inject variety and newness into a Date Night, or maybe it's better to not go at all. Don't make a special night a boring night for her. Variety is the spice of wife.

Chapter 24
Rough Stuff

This Chapter is Different

This chapter is a little different from the rest of the book, because everything I've covered before now, you can just go ahead and do without asking her about it first. She isn't going to have a problem with you kissing her, or asking her out on a Date Night, or even having a strong pounding in the missionary position. She isn't going to react badly when you start doing your laundry, fixing up the house or losing twenty pounds either.

But when you start moving into the realm of trying to tap into the raw erotic potential of being *physically* dominant with her, you need her active consent and cooperation to do this safely together. Neither one of you should be getting hurt from exploring this, nor should you create a situation where someone could be arrested because you failed to communicate and agree beforehand.

You can't *make* her physically submit to you without it becoming a violent assault. But she can *choose* to physically submit to you willingly, to experience the sensations that doing so brings. When you explore this together, you should see it as playing a game together; it should be as different as a *fight* and a *play-fight* are in both of your minds.

When a father play-fights with his young children, he is clearly bigger, stronger, more powerful and in control. He is clearly dominant over the children and can tickle them, pin them, hold them upside down and playfully rough them up; but he doesn't seek to hurt them. The kids on the other hand get huge enjoyment from being dominated and toyed with like that. It's exciting but safe. A father that just beats his children though is a monster.

Because of all the programming built into us from The Time Before Writing, most women respond to a physically dominant male with unconscious sexual attraction. It's just her Body Agenda at work seeking good genes for a possible pregnancy and making her responsive to him. So while very clearly no woman wants to be sexually assaulted by a man she does not want, there is an erotic thrill to be had from submitting to the physical dominance of a man she does want. It can be exciting and safe. A husband that just beats his wife though is a monster.

And like everything else you try in the bedroom, only 30% of it will work for any particular couple. So talk about it, try it and see how it goes.

Hair Pulling

Hair pulling is a physically dominant move in that once you have a good grip on her hair, you have control over her head. Once you have control over her head, you have essentially gained control over her entire body and can lead her anywhere. If you remember anything from playground fights when you were little, if someone had your hair good, you were pretty much on the losing end of the fight.

So when you get a good hold on her hair, her body experiences a sensation to either fight you off, or submit to you physically. Seeing as you already have a fist full of her hair, you've already established that you would win a fight with her, so her body opts for submission and greater sexual response to you.

In general the more hair you get hold of, the better enjoyed it is by her. If you just get a hold of some of her hair, you risk pulling it out, plus it will hurt if you have only some of her hair. If you can get almost all her hair in your hand, it spreads the pull over more of her head so it's a greater sensual experience, and the pulling is spread more evenly so it doesn't hurt either.

Hair pulling is something that you can just add in to most sexual positions. Maybe not for the whole time of intercourse – it can start to get painful after a while – but adding it into the final run up to your orgasm can be amazing. The physical message being, *"I am about to cum inside you. I'm going to hold you so you can't possibly escape it."*

Bondage

Some women enjoy being tied up during sex. It's really a continuation of positioning in that she is placing herself at a combat disadvantage, so she triggers greater sexual response in herself. Bondage can be a little frightening to some people, so this can be eased into slowly. One starting point is to simply have her lie on her back and be ordered not to let go of the headboard, or to loop one of your business ties around her wrists and order her to not let it go. Obviously she could let go at any time, but she probably won't. It's all just a mental game in that she can just as easily consent to handcuffs as she can consent to not letting go of the tie. You're not actually forcing her do anything even if she is tied up.

Once she's enjoyed the baby steps, there are hundreds and hundreds of bondage sex toys available in stores. Pick some out and play with them. Extended foreplay can be erotic play-torture on someone who is tied up. When you allow their orgasm finally, it can be exceptionally intense.

Body Positioning

There are a number of body positions that a woman can be placed in that evoke submissive feelings and attraction to a dominant partner. The most common position is the "boring old missionary position," where she lies on her back with her legs open, while you are on top of her. But once in this position, she really has no physical ability to push you off the top of her. She's pinned under you for as long as you want to be there, which is why most women love the missionary position so much.

Being in a kneeling position is purposely putting yourself at a combat disadvantage, so generally anyone that is kneeling is displaying submission to whoever they are kneeling to. So when she kneels for you, simply having her take up that body position evokes a submissive feeling in her.

If she's kneeling in front of you, it's a short step to having her suck your cock. If she's on hands and knees, she lets you have full access to whatever part of her body you want to touch, for as long as you keep her there. Knees do start to get sore after a while, so she can probably kneel much longer on a bed than on a hardwood floor.

Neck Holding

Covered a little bit earlier in the Kissing chapter, holding the back of her neck is an easy dominant move that most women would have no problem with. It works on the same principle of being able to control her head as the hair pulling does.

Hold the back of her neck as opposed to the front of her neck. It doesn't take too much to make a front neck hold feel very uncomfortable for her and want to stop the sex completely and afterwards feel very creeped-out about what a future with you would have in store for her.

Spanking 101

Spanking can be very powerful in playing with dominance and submission. The woman is usually in a submissive body position, like bending over something, on all fours, or across the lap of her husband, so that triggers a submissive reaction by itself. But what really creates the emotional intensity of spanking is that it removes the *implied* ability of the male to dominate the female on a purely physical level, and he proves he can physically dominate her in *reality.* There is little question about who is being dominant and who is submissive when a husband spanks a wife.

However, this comes right back to the huge difference between an actual fight and a play-fight. Spanking is meant to be an exciting but safe demonstration of his potential physical power, and not his full power. The intensity of being spanked is an extremely stimulating experience and will usually result in a dopamine response in the woman. She may not enjoy the actual experience itself as much as she enjoys the after effects on her mood and intensity of feelings for her husband. Spanking is the most primal Alpha move there is, but it can't be used until she consents to it.

Safely Spanking

There are thousands of spanking porn movies to watch out there and I find them showing things well beyond anything I would ever do. Spanking porn keeps trying to top itself and has escalated into bigger and bigger bats to spank with and bloody, raw, wounded bottoms. Spanking porn is to safely spanking as waterboarding is to taking a bath.

To start with, limit any spanking to just the use of your hand. No belts, whips, floggers, straps, canes, crops, paddles or slippers. You can't feel the depth of sensation you are giving without having your own hand involved. You can progress to some of this stuff if you want, but as a starting point, *just your hand.*

Before you ever spank her... spank you. You should practice on yourself before you ever spank her. Get used to the sensations and sounds you can make. If you can't reach your own ass, do your legs. Learn the difference between the tingle of pain that's kind of like eating hot-sauce and just plain old *"That hurts!"*

Agree on a safe-word that instantly brings the session to an end. "Stop" is usually a good choice. If she forgets her safe-word, yelling out the name of a local law firm is remarkably effective as well.

Be relaxed about it. If you are tensed up, you will also tense up your hand, changing it into something harder and less forgiving. You'll end up "thumping" her with your hand, rather than "smacking" her. That means more of a bruising impact, rather than that hot-sauce-like tingle sensation.

Rather than hold your hand flat, cup your hand so that it meets the curve of her ass better. This is to spread the contact out across a greater surface area, so it will hurt less, but also so that it creates a much louder *sound* when you spank her. If you can make it *sound* like she is getting a big spanking, she can often be turned on by just that alone, while you keep the pain to a minimum. Think of it as "one hand clapping" on her ass.

Only spank on her butt. It's big and padded compared to any other area of the body. Use up the whole surface area, don't just spank in the exact same spot over and over. Spank both sides, upper and lower, in an even spread.

Rather than taking a "six of the best" approach where you just wallop her with a small number of big whacks that could injure her, go for dozens of *little* spanks in a session. Take your time, there's no hurry.

A bare bottom spanking is safer than a clothed spanking. You have to spank harder through clothes to get the same sound and sensation as a bare bottom spanking. That extra force turns into more of a bruising spanking. Also you can see her skin color if she has a bare bottom.

As you spank her bare bottom, pay close attention to her skin color. There is a pinkish flush that can come from increased blood circulation to her bottom, but once her skin starts changing color to pink, it's time to slow right down or stop. If you're seeing reds or purples, you are well beyond the limits and she is becoming *injured.*

Erotic Spanking

With an erotic spanking, you are generally mixing up both spanking and sexual play at the same time. If she is on her hands and knees for example, most of your attention is going to be on playing with her clitoris or vagina, while you occasionally give her a few safe spanks.

You can also be on your back with her on top of you in a cowgirl position and spank her occasionally as you are having sex. This is usually the easiest spanking position to first experiment with as the spanking action can be very infrequent as there is already a lot happening sexually. Generally if you give her an occasional light spank while she is on top, you get a pretty good idea of whether or not she is sexually turned on by it. Some common giveaways being her sighing in pleasure, moaning, becoming more turned on, shutting her eyes, saying "Yes" and it can even be felt in a tightening of her vagina around your penis.

Another good position is you sitting on the sofa, with her lying across your lap. That way you can both finger her clitoris and vagina, plus also occasionally spank her ass. It's a slow relaxed position and also good for first attempts.

It's Not For Everyone

As I've said before, only about 30% of what you try in the bedroom will ever work for you as a couple. For many couples, nothing in this chapter will work, for some couples, a lot of it will work. It's worth a try to see if it works for you, but as I made plain at the start of this chapter, these can be quite potent, so you should discuss and agree with each other before trying them.

Part Four

When Push Comes
To Shove

Chapter 25
<u>Oneitis</u>

But She's the Only Girl for Me!

Oneitis is the state of being emotionally hooked into one woman as your entire romantic and sexual life. This sounds an awful lot like what marriage is supposed to be like, but if you're feeling emotionally and sexually attached to her, and she isn't to you, then you're going to be completely owned by this woman. Oneitis can take all your very positive and good emotions for her and use them against you to lock you into the relationship.

Just as I've told you about the Alpha and Beta Male Traits triggering dopamine and oxytocin reactions in women, they do the same to us as well. What is Alpha for a woman are her physical body, appearance and obvious sexual interest all of which can trigger the dopamine reaction in us. Most times a guy with Oneitis has it about a very beautiful woman and not a plain looking one. The female Beta Traits cause a vasopressin response in a man and those are the ones that create the pair bond in him to her. Witnessing the birth of children and orgasm are the best creators of vasopressin in men.

As a woman can go crazy over a guy, so can a guy get emotionally and sexually fixated on a single woman. The trouble being that because his love interest is so important to him, he tends to not want to risk the relationship by upsetting or troubling her in any way. Plus he likes to gift her things as expressions of his love for her and deferring to her. All of this is a very low Alpha approach to her, so usually he stops triggering her attraction to him by being Betaized.

Many low sex marriages have a husband that is cupid stupid over the wife, while she can barely tolerate his existence in a romantic sense. She's usually perfectly happy to have him wait on her and bring home a paycheck though. She just doesn't want to have sex with him, save an occasional drip feed of sex to keep him on the hook and make him still bring her stuff. *It's a tragic twist when your love for her, kills her love for you.*

Oneitis is an Addiction

If a basically healthy wife can't hold a job, keep a house or have sex with you with any degree of functionality, she's just dead weight. From a purely rational point of view, you may as well just cut her loose and go on with your life. But the husband with Oneitis for his wife can rationally know that she is a giant millstone around his neck, *but he can't leave her anyway.*

He really is addicted to her. The dopamine and the vasopressin literality tether him to her. The traditionally suggested Pickup Artist method of dealing with this addiction is to sleep with ten other women... and then see how you feel about your crush. That's a little bit beyond my advice as obviously I'm trying to save marriages by jumpstarting sex lives. If you're married, having sex with ten other women isn't even remotely an option you can use. Plus I wonder how you can feel about *anyone,* after ruthlessly sleeping with ten women just to forget the first one.

What I would suggest though, is that you purposely stop all the extra lovey-dovey catering to her. This is to undercut her reward of having you do stuff for her, and it stops you looking so weak to her and starts to unplug you from endlessly pouring dopamine and vasopressin related to her into your system. You're actually starting to give yourself some space from her. You may even wish to decline sex from her if she offers.

If You Have Oneitis The MAP Will Fail

This is the really critical point of this chapter. You can up your Sex Rank and get all the way up The Timeline into phase three and four and do really well with it. But once you get into phase five, you can't actually follow through with looking like you might really leave her if pushed hard enough. You're still tethered to her; so you fold.

As soon as you fold and stop acting like you really might leave her and go running back, she will perceive your Sex Rank to be lower than her Sex Rank. It won't matter that to an impartial observer you might be an 8 and her a 6. If you go running back, *she will perceive that you failed your own ultimatum because you are a male 5-* which is to say that you would have run all the way back to phase one. If The MAP is a game of chutes and ladders, you just rode a chute all the way back to the start.

Note that she will be pleased that you have returned to her, because she has her servant back. She will probably have sex with you once. *Just once.* Then you're back to the endless waiting for another special moment and her whim. If you can't ever get it into your head that you really can find another woman to replace her, you're going to be trapped with the one you have.

Women Are Replaceable

It's a fairly cynical point of view, but any one woman can be replaced with another woman. All a woman needs to do to make you happy is do some mix of working a job and keeping house, be reasonably enjoyable company and have a functional vagina that she happily lets you use. The job description really isn't all that hard to do, or all that confusing. Most women would make a reasonably good wife for you if given the opportunity.

I don't mean to make women sound like chattel here. Men are no less replaceable than women are. Men sell "husband" and women sell "wife" when it boils down to it. This book is aimed for men who live with women that want to get paid for selling "wife" but don't want to part company with the goods. The solution for this is that you start shopping around and stop buying "wife" from her and buy "wife" from someone else; the essential threat of running The MAP.

Objectively, there is nothing special about your current wife. The only thing that makes her seem special to you is a bunch of hormonal markers cycling around your body telling you to think she is wonderful beyond all reason. She's not all that wonderful. If you met her today for the first time and she told you she wanted to marry you but only have sex five times a year, you'd just laugh and walk away. No one would agree to that. You just can't see that because you're so drugged on dopamine and vasopressin. It's like your body is jacking you up on a bad cocktail of emotional cocaine and valium.

Even sex with a new woman isn't going to be all that different. It's not like you get to have sex with a new woman, or even ten new women, with a new penis. Your sensations and orgasm are going to be much the same no matter who you are with in bed. If you're a 7 and leave your 7 wife and remarry another 7, the sex is going to be about the same. But you might have ten times as much sex with a new wife.

Get a Massage

Oh relax. I didn't say go have hookers stroke your back for ten minutes and then blow you. I said get a massage. Go get a real proper therapeutic massage – from a female masseuse of course.

Just enjoy it.

Just soak in the sensation of another woman physically touching you all over for an hour. If you're at all undersexed or under-touched, you'll probably get hard as a rock at some point in the session. Just don't worry about it, that's all perfectly normal and nothing will happen to you. Massage therapists do not suddenly decide to give up their licenses and start jerking on your dick.

But think about this. How many weeks go by before you get as much physical touch from your wife as you got in this single massage session? Massages cost fifty to one-hundred dollars, depending on where you live. How much comes out of your pocket for your wife over those weeks? Does it seem to be a fair comparison?

I'm not even talking about *sex* here, I'm just talking about *touch*.

Hooker Math

Okay, let's do the hooker math now. Figure out how much money you spent on your wife in the last year and divide that by the number of times you've had sex in the same time period. That's your cost per lay. Is that more or less than the price of a nice hooker?

Now this is a pretty loose and highly offensive way of assessing your wife and I don't advise making too much of it. But if that number is much larger than you feel comfortable admitting to, maybe you need to really consider what you are getting from the relationship. If everything flows from you to her and nothing much flows from her to you, why bother?

Now I know that you're not going to bail on your wife and plan to eat Ramen noodles to maximize your hooker money. That seems like it might be fun for a week, but after that it's all a bit impersonal. I'm just trying to get you thinking clearer and trying to get some perspective on your situation. Like I said before, you're really probably looking at the possibility of leaving your wife to remarry someone that's actually interested in you. If you have Oneitis, you're like a drug addict for her; I'm trying to stage a mini-intervention here.

And let's be serious, if the Hooker Math for sex with your wife comes to over a thousand dollars a lay, it sounds like you're partying with Charlie Sheen a bit much.

Take a Vacation Alone

One way to try and clear things in your head is to go on a vacation without her. Just go do it for you. It has to be for at least a week. Go have fun. How do you really feel without her around you? If everything flows from you to her, a real vacation for you is actually *being away from her*. So think about that for a bit.

Are You Captain-Save-a-Ho?

The purpose of marriage is not to save a woman. The purpose of marriage is to have a productive, functional and happy life together. It's not your job to act like her paid 24/7 support staff and bail her out of every mess she gets herself into, or endlessly cater to her every whim without hope of you ever getting you needs met.

Balanced Relationships

Don't get me wrong on this chapter. I have a good case of Oneitis for Jennifer, but she also has Oneitis for me, so it's a balanced relationship. When both sides of the marriage are really into each other, it's how it's meant to be. But when only your side of the marriage is into her, all those wonderful feelings of love and intense attachment become a *liability* to you and trap you into the relationship.

Jennifer and I don't blindly believe we're soulmates. I sell her "a pretty good husband" and Jennifer sells me "a pretty good wife". It's a balanced, fair exchange and we're great together, but we both know that if we didn't have each other, *someone else would probably do.* If we hadn't met each other, we would have gone on to marry other people and very likely had happy lives.

We're also both loaded up on hormones for each other too... so there's *real love* between us. That may be distressing to think of, but hormones really do act as real world physical counterparts to actual feelings. Your brain is a meat computer and the hormones act like software. Emotions are, on one level, actual physical *things.*

This is all rather clinical and unromantic, but once you get used to thinking these thoughts, you realize that your romantic feelings and love for your wife aren't actually affected by knowing that you have a bunch of hormones inside you making you feel as you do. Dr. Helen Fisher has a wonderful story she tells to explain this. She says that you could know everything there is to know about chocolate cake – how to make it, what all the ingredients are, all the chemistry that happens when the cake is baked and so on. But that knowledge doesn't affect the sensation of enjoying eating chocolate cake. Once the cake is in your mouth... you just *experience* the chocolate cake.

For Jennifer and myself, we've actually felt deeper feelings for each other since taking this journey into knowing the contents of this book. It explains why our constant sex with each other bonds us so well to one another and we consciously do fun things together and feel more in love because of it. *Plus if women are essentially replaceable and all much the same... that's why the grass is always greener on the other side.* So I may as well keep nailing Jennifer then.

Chapter 26
Common Mistakes

Cheating on Your Wife

Imagine you're a humble male 6 married to a female 7 and the sex life is mediocre at best. Then you buy this book and discover the basic principles I cover and start putting them into action.

You work out, are nicer at home, earn a little more money, dress better, play with the kids and so on. When you go from a 6 to a 7 life is great and your sex life gets better. So you keep plowing ahead and continue to develop yourself further. When you hit Sex Rank 8, the sex at home starts getting really good. Your wife loves the new you and can't help but respond to you.

Then comes the test. Failing this test will probably undo, in one easy move, everything you've done to improve things with your wife.

Here's how the test occurs. Say you know another female 6 or 7; your sister-in-law, your wife's best friend, your female work friend, the chick behind the counter at Starbucks, one of the moms at your kid's school, or any woman in your sphere of influence. When you were a 6, you were off the market and she wasn't interested in you. Pulling you off your wife would have taken a lot of effort, and let's face it, you were just a 6, so why should she bother?

But now... now you're an 8 and that's a whole different deal because she's a 6 or 7 and you're a sexier than her – a quite different experience for her to think about. She can't help feeling attracted to you because attraction isn't a choice. She may not even be consciously aware of it, but you are far more sexually interesting to her now. Then you'll start noticing some of the dozens of "Indications of Interest" she's throwing out at you:

Dressing better when she expects to see you.
Hair flipping and stroking.
Reapplying lipstick. Licking lips.

Smiling.

Eye contact.

Touching her body, especially her neck area.

Sitting with her body oriented towards yours.

Sitting with her legs open towards you.

Laughing easily at your jokes – even if they are not particularly good.

Taking an article of clothing off in front of you.

Small acts of service that aren't required.

Seeking to stand or sit near you.

Increased breathing rate.

Being eager to see you.

Unnecessary phone calls, emails, text messages just to create contact with you.

Touching you in any way.

One day you're going to be having a great conversation with this woman, not even trying to consciously to seduce her… and you'll suddenly realize that she's doing half the things on the list above. Then you realize all you need to do is *"Instigate, Isolate and Escalate"* a little and she would very likely have sex with you if you can be discreet.

As an aside - being discreet is the key to seduction. I once answered a phone call as a female friend was laughing at one of my jokes. The caller asked me, *"Who are you with?"* and I replied *"Oh I don't kiss and tell."* Just that phrase alone turned my friend positively crimson and then she completely took down her hair, shook it out and tied it back up again, then removed her scarf and just hung out with me longer than she needed to. If I had made a move in that moment, she would have very likely responded to me.

So it's not going to be some super hot 10 wanting to get back at her boyfriend who will be your test. Megan Fox won't be your test. It's going to be someone close to you, someone you probably have known for a while, even feel friendly and emotionally connected to, that is going to be your test. You may not see it coming until it's close to the point of no return.

You will absolutely love every second of her company as well – you're biologically programmed to like it. The great difficulty of temptation is that it's… tempting. No matter how wonderful sex at home is, new pussy is incredibly tasty. Once you can read a woman's indicators of interest, and you know the basics of seduction, having a little piece of something on the side becomes not just a fantasy, but real possibility. Emotions can run high. You may be more hooked on the other woman than you know...at least while you're standing next to her anyway.

And all this will be happening just as everything you've worked for with your wife responding to you is coming together. If your wife is even halfway paying attention to you, she'll know something is up.

So while I'm not telling you what is right and what is wrong, be aware of what you truly risk for a little extra fun on the side. If your Sex Rank is higher than your wife, you have her full attention on you, so getting away with things is probably harder than it seems on the surface. Wives hate being cheated on and the damage you do to your relationship may be permanent. What may seem a little harmless fun to you, will be seen as an affair by your wife and provoke the most serious of marital crises. Any illusions you have of an easy resolution to a discovered affair are laughable.

Also you're assuming that the other woman isn't going to turn nutty on you and call your wife up. In fact if the other woman thinks she has a chance at being the new Mrs. You, she might actively seek to end your marriage by revealing the affair to you wife. I mean if she's a 6, and you're an 8... wouldn't wrecking your marriage for a shot at having you permanently be... *smart?*

Facilitating Her Affair

One thing that constantly surprises me is how frequently a husband plays an active role in creating an environment where his wife is tempted to cheat on him. If you constantly leave your wife alone with a man she finds attractive, there are fairly logical consequences that could kick in. Some examples I've come across:

One - The wife strikes up a friendship with the builder working on the neighbor's house and this goes on for several weeks. They both have a mutual and clear attraction for each other and the husband becomes aware of it and is uncomfortable with it. His solution... "Not to show fear" and he asks the builder to remodel the kitchen in his house. Now the stay-at-home wife and the builder are alone in the same house for a couple of weeks. So in this case the husband actually *paid* a guy to be around for a potential affair.

Two - The husband has a younger body builder friend who is a known player. Yet he continues to see this friend frequently - with his wife in tow - *and* often has him over to the house. When his wife starts to lose a ton of weight and dress sexier, the husband just thinks it's great and loves it, but too late he discovers that the weight loss was not for his benefit... but his friend's. The communication between wife and friend all happened behind the scenes via Facebook.

Three - The husband opens his home for three months to a young specialist sports coach from another state. The husband is at work all day and the coach works at night running sports practices. But all day the coach and the wife are home together. The husband finds out about the affair when the coach, the wife and all four of his children are at a water park together. He was the last to know.

Four - This one is so common it's insane – the husband takes in his "best friend" for a couple of months to help his friend out. Fast forward a few months and the best friend takes the wife, the kids and the house... which was his plan from the beginning. Absolutely do not trust another man not to make a move on your wife, no matter what he says about loyalty, honor or the right thing to do. Men will say nearly anything to get access to the good pussy.

In short, when you frequently leave your wife alone with an attractive man, *you're running an isolation play for his benefit.* If he has any sense of confidence he'll start making moves on her, and sometimes a wife will rationalize that you have essentially given permission by setting the situation up like this. Be warned.

Doing Nothing About Her Interest in Another Man

Don't make the mistake of viewing your wife becoming seriously interested in another man as a Fitness Test. By playing it cool and unaffected you can effectively defuse a real Fitness Test, but the same approach with a serious potential competitor is the complete *opposite* of what you need to do.

Recapping some of the Body Agenda chapter quickly... many women are attracted to dominant men and enjoy feeling excited when they are reacting to such a man. Women who lack stimulation feel bored and can create a Fitness Test for their man to pass. Once he passes the test, she enjoys her own body producing the dopamine hormone and feels attracted and stimulated again.

Men pass Fitness Tests best by not over-reacting to them. The tactics of reframing the test so that it seems silly, responding with humor, responding with boyish sexual interest or just saying "No" work very well. (Remembering that simply her asking you to do something isn't always a test. It's a test when she is asking you to allow her to treat you badly, or have her gain something at your expense.)

By not feeding into the test and over-reacting to her, you retain the locus of control in the relationship and she, despite the initial upset at being denied her request, ultimately responds with attraction to your display of dominance.

However, when another guy is starting to make traction on her, she's starting to get a dopamine reaction to *him*. So she's not actually bored anymore, so she's not trying to get you to do anything for her. What she actually wants you to do is get out of the way and leave her alone with him.

So if your approach is to generally show that you are unaffected by her and take a view that you'll just display higher value instead of taking direct action, that just gives her more room to interact with the other guy. *The classic line given by cheating partners early on is a request for "space."* So if she asks for space and you give it to her, what you think is her "alone time" is in fact a beeline to the other man. Any time you hear a request for "space" you need to immediately figure out if you're being clingy, or if she is up to something; either way, it's bad.

She may or may not be having sex with the new guy. She might just be hanging out...many intense relationships outside of marriage can go months or even years before turning sexual. Some never turn sexual but can do damage just the same. The energy that could have gone into making your marriage more enjoyable gets diverted and lost into another one. An emotional affair can end a marriage just as a physical affair can. Once she starts getting her addictive dopamine fix from him, a few harmless little meetings can snowball into a full-fledged crush and obsessive thinking over him, despite being married to you.

Back in the Time Before Writing, the textbook method of dealing with a man interested in your woman would have been a spear tip shoved repeatedly into his chest. Or maybe using an early Ninjitsu technique and smashing his head in with a rock while he slept. This still retains some appeal today, but it generally results in extended jail terms, and while you're inside your wife will probably divorce you and hook up with someone else anyway. So the idea of putting Mr. Loverboy in a burlap sack and playing Home Run Derby is tempting, but not really a good one.

Likewise, if you use violence on her, which could be regarded as something as simple as pushing her off the top of him, you may find yourself punted into the court system. So violence, despite its natural appeal, is a poor solution for the modern man.

The solution is that the relationship with the other man needs to be interrupted as best you can. Plain English – you have to cockblock him. The longer you let it go on, the worse things get. You need to very firmly and clearly intervene and make it clear that she is risking the marriage. She either has to break it off, or get out. (If she's actually cheating, I cover your response in the next chapter.)

Blindly Believing She Would Never Cheat

A few too many men put their wives up on a pedestal so high that they lose sight of the fact that she is flesh and blood rather than a divine creature. You really have to break your mind of the illusion that when she's done taking a bath, the church comes over and takes it away as holy water. She's a normal human being and we all have our price point where we become capable of almost anything.

Trust her enough that you don't climb up her ass trying to find out where she is every minute of the day. Just don't be blind about her being a normal woman with sexual desires. If you get that sick feeling in the pit of your stomach that something isn't right, don't just rationalize it away. Trust, but verify.

Believing that You Are Soulmates

While Jennifer and I have a wonderful relationship, I don't see her as my soulmate. She's my *wife*, which is a far more powerful and meaningful thing.

With a soulmate there is a sense of powerlessness that goes along with it. We *just are* soulmates, it *just is* magical, it's so *effortless together*, we *just know* what the other is thinking, and we were *just drawn* to each other. It's as if the relationship has a power all of its own and the couple involved are passengers in that relationship. It's a wonderful experience, but it relies on the strength of the hormonal attraction to sustain the relationship.

With a husband and wife though, there's an active sense of empowerment that goes along with it. If there is magic, *we made that together*, if we know what the other is thinking, it is *because we have* listened to each other, if we have a special bond together, it is because *we have* gone to each other and joined. We drive the relationship and direct it. It's a little more rational in approach.

Being in a soulmate experience is more typical at the start of a relationship and is a heady experience. Let's just call it what it is – it's two people crushing on each other. It's all hormones and biology. The experience is amazing and some people crave that like a drug... which... is probably because *it is a drug,* and the drug is called dopamine. Being a husband or a wife, though, is about creating a long term, meaningful, deep, emotional pair bond. It's less dramatic, less in your face, but it's vitally important and smooth and deep in flavor.

Accept that crushes for each other, or even other people, are temporary and erratic. They can spring up from nothing, burst over you for a moment and then be gone. They can simmer quietly in the background for years, or suddenly fizzle out. They can ebb and flow as mine does with Jennifer. Up and down and around and around. I still crush on her after all this time and then I don't. And then I do. (Jennifer is the stable one in our relationship; I'm the more random one.)

However, as long as you are being actively good to each other, the pair bond will strengthen over time. I can hardly remember life before Jennifer. It's like she was always a part of me. I halfway expect to go back to the photos of me before we met and still see her with me somehow.

One of the reasons I am so serious about couples having regular sex – even below average sex, is that sex is one of the most potent ways to strengthen and maintain the pair bond you have together. Half the reason long distance relationships fail is that you can't have sex with each other and maintain the chemistry exchange program together.

If you keep the sexual frequency high and keep being good to each other, you will likely experience crushes on one another more often. Crushes are a neurochemical reaction in your brain most likely designed as a Mate Replacement Program hold-over from The Time Before Writing. If you are in constant intimate contact with your wife, when the Mate Replacement Program gets run, she can be the best option available to you and so you experience a crush on her again.

If you aren't in such frequent intimate contact with your wife, maybe your Body Agenda decides someone else might make a better prospect for a sexual relationship. Which explains why "fairly happily married you", suddenly has this epic crush on the hot young girl with the perfect breasts that serves you coffee at Dunkin Donuts.

If you rely on the feeling of being soulmates and need that emotional "in love" high all the time, eventually it's going to cut out on you and not be there. You may have a perfectly functional relationship end, simply because one of you doesn't feel in love anymore. In love feelings can be very temporary and erratic, so a relationship based on them alone can burn brightly for a time, but then blink out of existence. This stuff happens and it's a completely normal biological event.

Quite often, the entire concept of a soulmate is just the Rationalization Hamster justifying taking action that someone's Body

Agenda suggested. If your wife ever says that she feels another man is her soulmate, take that extremely seriously.

Playing with Non-Monogamy

I'm going to lump in cuckolding, swinging and polyamory as essentially all the same thing. I'm sure devotees of all three varieties of non-monogamy would feel uncomfortable with that, but all three boil down to legitimizing women having sex with multiple men with their primary partner's consent. In none of the three groups is there any sense that a woman could be forced into a sex act that she didn't want and the men in those groups only get to have sex by the choice of the women.

So while I don't have a particular *moral* concern about people engaging in consensual sex, there are obvious *practical* dangers to your marriage when a man more attractive than you has sex with your wife. If you're a 7 and you go to a swing party and your wife has sex with a 9, there's a good chance that she'll get a huge rush and start to develop an attachment to the other man. After all, this is exactly what her Body Agenda would want to happen.

Books and websites on swinging and polyamory discuss managing jealousy in huge depth. Jealousy is a powerful emotion, and it takes a fair degree of social reprogramming to have a jealous lover not act on that emotion. The person most likely to experience feeling threatened and therefore jealous, is the lower Sex Rank half of the couple. The practical purpose of this social reprogramming is to make the lower Sex Rank half of a couple become passive in the face of risk to the relationship. So if the male 7 watching his wife have sex with a male 9 gets jealous and upset, *he's framed as the one with the problem*. He has to struggle to behave himself and she gets pumped by a 9, so she's is a clear winner. In cuckolding there are no illusions about this, as the erotic humiliation of watching a higher Sex Rank man take his wife is channeled as the turn-on for the husband.

Husbands do tend to float the idea of non-monogamy first in a marriage and it may take quite some time to convince the wife to try it. But if the interest and activity persists, eventually the driving force becomes the wife's. If a wife is married to a 6 or a 7 and she's allowed to have sex with an 8, 9 or 10 in sanctioned hook-ups, she will almost never stop that contact. This is exactly what her Body Agenda drives her to do. Then if you're the 6 or 7 husband, should one of those 8, 9 or 10s take a bit more of a shine to your wife... she'll very likely leave you for him. Well... it would be *rational* for her to do that wouldn't it?

It is a weakness display of the highest order to allow another man to have sex with your wife, and a turn off for almost all women. In fact most wives don't agree to start these activities until their husband's begging for them reduces her attraction to him. Don't confuse the wife's sexual excitement for her husband after having sex with another man as an increased attraction to her husband; it's simply carrying over from the rush she felt with the other man and her desire to have sperm competing inside her.

Likewise, when you allow another man to have sex with your wife, you're making a weakness display to the other man as well. He will gain enormous confidence in his ability to best you and you are actively encouraging him to move against your interest in your wife. Your best friend may have desired your wife for many years, but never thought he could steal her from you. Once you allow him to sleep with her, he knows he could probably take her from you.

In the end, the purpose of non-monogamy groups is to try and create a small sub-group where the women have sexual access to the best men and are sexually unbothered by the rest of them. Of course, if you're a super hot guy, then there is no problem with chumps handing over their wives to you is there?

Trying to Stay Married to Someone who is Batshit Crazy

When you run The MAP on a normal woman, she generally responds positively to your efforts. If you're being Alpha she normally feels more attraction to you, if you do something Beta she normally feels more comfortable with you. You just ping pong her with Alpha and Beta and pretty soon she's in love and loving you. She doesn't mind lying down with her legs apart while gazing at you with bedroom eyes because this is normal behavior for a woman that is highly receptive to a particular man.

Unfortunately some women are batshit crazy, as in really diagnosable as mentally ill with a personality disorder. Which leads to the question, *"What happens when you run The MAP on a woman who is batshit crazy?"*

Well if you are doing something Alpha, this threatens them, so it triggers an acute episode of being batshit crazy. This will look like a Fitness Test, but it's not a Fitness Test, *it's just them being batshit crazy.* In a Fitness Test there is some sort of subconscious plan being run by her Body Agenda, to test to see if you can respond to her with appropriate dominance. When someone is formally diagnosed as being batshit crazy and is having an acute episode of behavior, they aren't caring whether or not you pass their test; *they are just being batshit crazy.*

When you do something Beta for them, they quite enjoy it and lap it up because being batshit crazy actually takes up a great deal of effort. However you get no points for doing anything Beta as their relationship comfort with you can't ever improve properly. Batshit crazy sufferers are always deeply disturbed and can't be pleased or comforted, so you typically waste your efforts in doing Beta things for them.

Generally with someone that is batshit crazy, you don't even really have a chance to really do The MAP, as you're too busy coping with them being in one of the five stages of being batshit crazy:

Phase 1 - Threatening to be batshit crazy.
Phase 2 - Acute Crisis: Actually doing something batshit crazy.
Phase 3 - Recovering from the effects of being batshit crazy.
Phase 4 - Being really nice to you.
Phase 5 - Suddenly realizing that you are an asshole for not meeting their demands in Phase 1

This cycle repeats endlessly and Ten Second Kisses, sexy text messages, flirting, cooking dinner and playfully fondling her in the shower will not work on someone that is like this. You can try and be the Captain all you like, but if the First Officer tries to smack you with a hammer, it's time to stop the madness.

The only really effective way of dealing with someone that is batshit crazy is some combination of, leaving the relationship, finding an effective medication regime, therapeutic support and using emergency services as is appropriate. Should they become violent or engage in property destruction, call 911 for your safety and that of the children. Even batshit crazy people understand tazers.

Chapter 27
Dealing With Her If She Cheats

Signs of Cheating

There are four general signs of cheating.

A change in behavior – There are hundreds of things that books and magazines say cheaters do as tipping off behavior. However a far simpler way of noticing a cheater is to pick up on their *changes* in behavior. If they had been reliably doing A, B and C, but suddenly they start doing X, Y and Z, it doesn't matter what A, B, C or X, Y, Z actually are, you're just looking for the change in behavior. Once you see that, then you should dig deeper and find out what is going on.

Cheaters lie – Cheaters lie endlessly and their lies are like rats; for every lie you catch, there are usually a hundred you didn't. You may catch them in a fairly minor lie that may not seem to directly relate to cheating, but you never know. The lies can start small, like simple omissions of information – like *"I had lunch with a guy I'm very attracted to that I work with."* Then slowly ramp up to bigger things like secret bank accounts, *"I can't leave work the boss is making me stay,"* *"It's your baby,"* and so on. If you catch your wife in a lie of any sort, you need to see that as a big red flag.

Cheaters live in a fantasy world – Cheaters base their entire decision making framework on the belief that they are able to get away with it and not experience a negative outcome. As an example, I can very much enjoy a fantasy experience of dreaming about robbing a bank and loving all the money – but I don't rob banks because I believe I'll get caught. Actual bank robbers believe they can get away with it and getting caught is a horrible shock to them. For the most part robbing a bank these days requires someone completely delusional considering all the cameras and security. Likewise, people who cheat assume they can get away with it. They can't perceive that there are consequences for their actions like divorce, not seeing their children and the emotional devastation of their spouse. The delusion also extends to thoughts like *"I love them both, just differently,"* *"I can't help myself"*, *"The children will be fine,"* and so on.

Cheating is addictive - The whole thing of *"It just happened"* really does happen, but usually it gets spread over many small occasions rather than one bizarre event. Usually the cheater experiences something pleasant with a member of the opposite sex...a flirt, a smile, something nice, a little attention and it's all completely harmless. So they go back for another little nibble on the good feelings. Then they go back for another little nibble. Fast forward a couple of weeks and the dopamine has kicked in and the full OCD-like symptoms of interest in another person have started to take over their thought process. Now they can't live without lunch with the love interest, they have to call them repeatedly and they need their texts every twenty minutes. The more serious it is the more evidence will pile up.

As an aside, should you ever get involved with another woman, these four signs of cheating will also apply to you. If you ever find yourself both lying to your wife and somehow magically thinking that seeing the other woman isn't that bad, you're probably already changing your behavior and starting to tip your wife off that something is up.

Gather Information

The answer to this combination of changed behavior, lying, delusion and addiction is to drag it all out into the ugly light of day. To do that you're going to need information and documentation, so you have to spy on them.

I do have two serious warnings about spying though. The first is that it will drive you paranoid and half crazy just doing it. As you spy even an innocent thing can seem more than it really is to your crazy thinking. The second is that if you get caught spying and your spouse was doing nothing with anyone, you're going to look like a lunatic and that could damage the relationship. So never get caught and never start this without at least some evidence that they are being shady.
As a serious warning, some or all of this may be illegal in your state. I do not advise breaking the law.

Some possible options are:

Keyloggers – by tracking their internet use you can often quickly find sexual emails or online chats. Just print everything off that you find that is evidence of the affair.

Phone records – if you get your phone bill, often there will be evidence of endless calls and texts between the cheater and the lover. Again, all of this is evidence and can be printed off.

Cell phone monitoring – there are some services that enable you to tap cell phones and get text messages. Also some services can GPS track the phone.

GPS tracking – there are GPS trackers that can be attached to cars or put under the seat.

Voice activated recorders – these are also good for use in cars. Very often the cheater will call the lover while in the car.

Video cameras - If you're suspecting the relationship is physical and happening in your own home, you can go for a huge variety of nanny cams that are motion activated. If you're catching her out and about, there are a variety of spy cameras or most good cell phones take decent pictures or even video as well.

Private investigator – Sometimes you just have to go with the pros and get it done that way.

Then you lay low and collect information. Print a hard copy of anything and everything that looks bad. If she's going to some guy's house (GPS tracked her there), snapping shots or video of her going in and out is good too. Absolutely do not tip your hand that you are spying until you have solid evidence against her.

You need to visit a few attorneys' offices and grab a few business cards and whatever divorce handouts they have. Also do the same thing for marriage counselors.

Expose the Affair

Once you have solid proof that something inappropriate is going on, you unload the whole thing on her and drag it all out into the open.

Here's your list of fifty-three phone calls to Mr. X in the last two weeks. Here are all of your texts to him. Here are the photos of your breasts you sent him. When you said you were at the movies with your sister on Friday your cell phone GPS was at his house for two hours. You've been to his house four times in the last two weeks. Here are all the emails where you said he was fantastic in bed. Here's a photo of you both holding hands in public. Whatever it is just lay it on with a shovel.

Then she has a simple choice...

Choice one – She breaks it off with the other man, as in completely off, *No contact whatsoever* beyond a final joint message to him, *"Sorry, my husband caught me, I'm going back to him, this is over, don't contact me."* This all happens in front of you by the way. Any repeated attempts by him to contact her need to be ignored, or if they become threatening in any way, it becomes a police matter via 911 and/or a restraining order. The no contact rule is absolutely vital since she needs to be weaned off the addictive (dopamine!) effects of contact with the other man.

Until she can be tested for sexual diseases, condoms should be used if there is any possibility of it being a physical affair. If there is any possibility of pregnancy I'd advise testing that as well. This is one of those "reorient her to reality" things. It doesn't matter what she says happened because cheaters are liars and lying liars need to pee into a cup. You don't have unprotected sex until the results are in.

Depending on circumstance it may be worth paternity testing any and all children you have with her. If you're catching her *now*, what's to say she wasn't cheating *then*? She also needs to agree to attend marriage counseling together.

Choice two – She needs to pick a divorce attorney from one of the business cards. There's no allowable middle ground; if she can't stop cheating she's made her choice and it's over. She also should be asked to move out if she chooses option two. You shouldn't move out of the home because once you are out, it is very difficult to move back in. If you want to move back in, she simply may not let you, and the courts may view you as having abandoned the family home, and simply award it to your wife in settlement. The party that is in the wrong should be the one to leave.

Then you go no contact on her unless she's willing to do option one, or you have a divorce issue to discuss.

Following Up

Usually all this should stop her in her tracks cold. When you reveal your proof of the affair, you're going to get a huge emotional reaction...crying, screaming, wailing and even puking for a full-on remorse display. This is typically a very genuine reaction and she is not trying to lie. What happens is The Time Before Writing "Oh SHIT!" software routine gets run and she immediately becomes extremely docile and submissive to avoid being killed by a jealously enraged mate. In this moment she will be 100% believably distraught and you will probably feel moved toward forgiving her by this display. Women's tears are proven to give off a chemical that reduces testosterone in men, so her bawling really does make you weak to her.

Of course that's all a setup... what very likely will happen is that she's going to say she's opting for option one, and then because she is still hooked into the other man emotionally she's going to try and wriggle out of it and continue things. She likes her dopamine and the other man is the supplier, so like a crack addict she's going to go crawling back to him.

Also remember that the other man is usually doing the same dopamine roller coaster thing as well and is going to want to try and keep seeing her. Plus your darling wife probably painted you as some sort of monster/asshole/total loser to him, so he's possibly got it in his mind that he needs to rescue your wife from you on some level. It's very important to keep them apart and out of contact.

At this point your surveillance is going to need to intensify in a direct face to face manner while things are being rebuilt. She will have to be completely open about where she is, who she is with, what she is doing and on a case by case basis you may have to alter some of her commitments. If this all happened via a gym membership, then she needs to find a new gym. If it happened via church group, she needs to find a new group. If it happened via online group, then she can't go back. If via her job, well this can be tricky... but if possible a new job or transfer can be very helpful. You're dealing with an addict and she still can't be trusted.

Ideally this sort of additional control is a short-term thing until her feelings subside. This may be a few months and generally I advise additional professional help with this. You will get emotionally involved and it's hard to maintain perspective without help. Also at some point you will need to relax this level of control, because the control itself will become a sticking point and cause problems. Once the in-love feelings subside and the wife sees her prior love interest in the cold hard light of day, she can often experience acute embarrassment and even revulsion for him. (I'm sure you've all experienced something similar for someone you've fallen out of love with at some point in your life).

Expose the Affair Further if Needed

If this isn't working and she continues to have contact with him, you simply step it up to the next level. Everyone with an influence over her should see the proof of the inappropriate behavior, along with your request to ask them to talk sense into her. And by everyone I mean, her parents, her siblings, her friends... basically anyone with influence.

The important thing is that this isn't framed as *"Your daughter is a whore and here's proof of your little whore whoring,"* but as *"I'm willing to go to counseling and work on things, but she has refused to stop seeing him or work on this with me. I don't want to divorce her, but obviously this just can't continue. I want to save our marriage and life together, but she isn't listening to me. Can you please talk to her?"*

Naturally if the other man has a wife or girlfriend, you inform her of everything as well. There's no point letting him sleep easily. Seriously, screw him over as well as you can with the proof. No hitting him though... which is a pity, but there we go.
So anyway, telling everyone brings it all out into the open and into the light. If that doesn't break her cheating then nothing will and I firmly advise you to just get STD tested yourself and divorce her without flinching.

Do be careful about telling your own family about her cheating though. Even after you have moved on and forgiven and healed your marriage, your family will very likely hate her for all eternity and that may cause longer-term problems.

The Other Option

All of this assumes that you even want to save the marriage after discovering what you uncover. These are serious choices; a knee jerk *"Kick the bitch out!"* usually ignores the difficulty of unpacking a long marriage relationship. There are children, money, house and savings to consider. It's not an easy road no matter which you choose. Some marriages can recover from affairs both emotional and physical and end up stronger for it. Others don't. Affairs suck. I can't make the stay or go choice for you, everyone is different.

The Aftermath

In the aftermath of the affair, you do need to look within you to find out what you were doing wrong in the marriage that helped create the environment for the affair. No man is perfect. Maybe there is something there that you can look back on and decide that you need to change.

I'm not saying you caused the affair, she did after all have the ability to choose not to be involved, but if something you did created the environment for the affair to grow, it would be stupid not to fix that.

Trial by Facebook

When your wife learns of this contingency plan for dealing with her if she cheats, it's a huge deterrent, and could be the difference between her being tempted by someone and actually jumping into his bed. It's one thing to sneak around on a chump, but if she thinks her cheating will result in a video of her uploaded to YouTube, posted on Facebook and divorce, that's another. One does not wish to use such nukes of course. But one does wish to have nuclear *capability.*

Chapter 28
How To Choose A Wife

One and Done

Getting married is serious business. Ideally when you get married, it's the one marriage you have your whole life, thus "one and done". That being the case, you're marrying a woman not just for what she is, but also for who she will be, *decades* from now.

I expect most readers are already married, but for the younger men who aren't married yet, I'll cover here some possible ideas for what you should be looking for in a wife. Consider this aimed at a twenty-year-old, if you're middle-aged and remarrying some of it won't apply exactly the same. In short though... don't just vote on her with your penis.

Women That Aren't Wife Material Waste Your Dating Time

A key problem is that most men do not go looking for a wife. They start looking for a date, and then try and turn the date into more dates, then the dates into a girlfriend, then a girlfriend into a serious relationship, and then and only then worry about whether or not to bridge the relationship into marriage. Of course by then you may be realizing you've been backing the wrong horse as what was great for a few dates (that would be tits, ass and easy pussy) isn't always the best woman for a lifetime together.

If you're really looking for a wife, kids, the PTA, ER visits, Thanksgiving Dinners, a joint bank account and someone who will hold your hand until the last minute as they push your bed into surgery, then you need to start with that somewhat in mind. By all means date around, but when you start to see major red flags, just stop dating them and move on. If you're dating within any sort of coherent social group and you are passing on women because you are *"looking for a woman with wife material"* that will likely make all the women in that group sit up and take notice of you.

The truth is that men willing to commit to a woman in this day and age are in short supply, and by being willing to express interest in commitment, your value goes even higher. You might land a highly attractive woman simply because you were willing to commit to marriage, when supposedly better men than you were available to her.

So start with the end in mind rather than blundering into things just because you can get laid.

Height and Weight Proportional

Something to be aware of is her being height and weight proportional. A twenty year old carrying an extra thirty pounds might be bubbly and voluptuous, but it can reveal an inability to exercise self-control. An extra thirty pounds at age twenty can turn into an extra hundred pounds within a year of having the first baby. That's a decidedly different effect on your sexual interest in her.

The old trick is to look at her mother and older sisters if she has them. If there's a family pattern you can pick up on, then that's probably what you should expect to happen with your potential wife as well.

If you are unsure of what to do on this front, simply go for a woman with A, B or C cup breasts. Young women who have D cups before ever getting pregnant tend to start morphing larger and larger, Miss D Cup at twenty-two is Mrs. EE Cup at forty-two and her back always hurts and she's cranky from the pain half the month. Her ass is wide as well. Be advised.

The general expectation you should have is that a woman is going to go up a bra cup size after having her first baby. Also, you should expect that she immediately gains around fifteen pounds after the wedding. She does that because her body is laying in a calorie store to prepare for a possible pregnancy. It's actually an expression of positive sexual interest in you.

Non-Smoker

Smoking is a nasty habit and a serious health risk. The woman that smokes will age much faster and become less sexy quickly. She may be pretty at twenty-five, but by forty the wrinkling is getting pretty bad. Also you risk lower weight babies and birth defects if she can't stop during pregnancy.

Women that smoke smell so powerfully bad, that it overrides even their own sense of smell and much of sexual attraction is smell based. Imagine that your wife can't even smell your pheromones over the smell of her own cigarettes, how is she going to react to you sexually? Badly that's how.

People that smoke just die earlier. If you're signing up for 50+ years together with a non-smoker, it's really like 35+ years with a smoker with the last five to ten years being them dying by degrees in front of you, and then you living alone and sad as your kick off to retirement.

Because smoking is such an obvious health risk, her inability to stop smoking reveals a great deal about her lack of self-control. That's a major red flag right there. I know this seems harsh, but as soon as you see a woman light up a cigarette, just cross her off the list and move on.

Reasonably Beautiful

There's really no good way to spin this, but yes indeed looks very much do matter. You should be trying to find the most physically attractive woman you can marry. Being physically attractive is a great marker for the ability to have healthy babies and seeing you're getting married, you're far better off having healthy children than unhealthy ones. To be sure there is an element of luck with health, but a physically attractive wife is a major influence on birth outcomes.

Good skin tone, long healthy hair, good teeth... these are all absolutely *not superficial* things to be concerned about. We aren't all going to marry supermodels and even the prom queen is out of reach for all but a few. Just look for someone that is as attractive as you can reasonably get and *who cares about her appearance*. It's okay to want her to be attractive as a requirement.

Good General Health

If a young woman is on routine medications for various ailments, you need to ask some serious questions about her health. Find out about her health as a child. Find out about any special complications or difficulties when she was young. None of these are deal breakers of course, we all get sick from time to time, you're more looking for *chronic* medical conditions. You don't care that she had the chicken pox when she was eight, you do care that she had cancer when she was thirteen.

If you find a history of basic illness you can bet that this will be the pattern into the future as well. It's not the job of your marriage to save the world or even any one woman; it's to have a full productive happy life. If you want to save people, be a fireman or an EMT worker or something. So if she's constantly sucking an inhaler when she's twenty-four, you can bet it will be worse at thirty-four and your children will probably be much the same as well.

You really have to ask serious questions about any psychiatric medications she uses. If there's an apparent family history of mental illness, you need to be able to carefully rule out the possibility that your potential wife is going to be affected by mental illness at some point in the future as well.

Simply having a medical issue doesn't need to be a deal breaker, but you should go in with eyes open. Jennifer had braces as a kid. Both of my daughters needed braces too. That's about all I'm saying here.

Positive Family History

Does she have a reasonably intact family home and childhood? If she's from a divorced family then you will have a higher likelihood of divorce in your marriage to her. Again, the purpose of your marriage is not to save a woman, it's to have a happy productive life with someone. Is the rest of her family basically normal and generally free of mental illness, developmental disabilities, crime, cancer and drama?

By all means make allowances for the few black sheep in every family, but a coherently bad pattern is a stumbling block. If meeting her family starts making you feel like you're a social worker, it's possibly best to step back, or bail and start over.

Minimal Prior Baggage

If she has a kid and she never got married to the guy that got her pregnant, or a failed marriage, or anything large and dramatically negative in her life with ongoing consequences, then that's baggage. The more baggage she has, the worse of an option she is to marry.

Sometimes baggage is a major red flag that she's capable of making really bad decisions or incapable of self-control. Sometimes baggage is just the result of shockingly bad luck, but it's still baggage nonetheless.

Having a simple family life of just you and her and having all the children sharing the same parentage in an intact home, makes life vastly easier than the endless juggling of who has custody this week. Where Thanksgiving is going to be is easier too.

Plus her prior kid(s) and whatever kids you have together may not always go smoothly and easily as if they were all your own children. Also there's a "baby's daddy" out there that she still has an eternal connection with. (Middle aged people always have baggage of some sort. No baggage means they never did anything of note their whole life. Just evaluate if it's basically under control or not.)

She Has a Clue

I don't care what it is that she does at college, or even if she doesn't go, but either way she needs some sort of direction and purpose to her life. You want to see that she is able to do something that doesn't really require you to be attached to her, for her to have a life of her own that's functional and productive. You need to see some sort of ability to hold a job and responsibilities together as an adult.

If the whole point of her life is simply to meet a man and be a Stay At Home Mom, that's fine as long as she is displaying a top notch SAHM skill set already. I'm talking baked goods, knitting, cooking, child care, cleaning, decorating and social planning skills. Or put another way – would some rich-ass family hire her as housekeeper/nanny for $40,000 a year?

If her plan is to get married and take it as an early retirement, then you're in for a world of trouble. You want to marry a *capable* woman.

Ideally a Virgin

Plenty of studies show that the fewer sexual partners a woman has before marriage the higher her marital satisfaction and the sexual satisfaction she has within marriage. You very much want your wife to sexually imprint on sex with you and completely bond to you. The sex is just going to be that much better over the long term. Not to mention there's no ex-lovers lurking on Facebook, sexual diseases, bad experiences and regrets to worry about.

The harsh truth to the modern hookup girl is that yes indeed, every time you sleep with another man, you damage your long term wife potential. The best predicator of future behavior is past behavior and highly promiscuous women before marriage are far more likely to, have lower happiness, cheat during marriage, or divorce.

For the record I also believe the man should ideally be a virgin too. I say this not from a current religious perspective – in my teens and early twenties I was an evangelical Christian but am a quite firm atheist now – but simply from the perspective that while this was horribly hard in my life before Jennifer, the sexual payoff and trust between us is outstandingly good and on balance a significant part of our current happiness. I am laid like tile and have been for sixteen years now. But I will not lie and say it was anything other than torture at the time though.

Obviously not all women getting married will be virgins, so then it's largely a case of assessing whether her sexual history is concerning, or not too much to be worried about. Sex with a few serious boyfriends is one thing; dozens of one night stands is another. Likewise a woman that marries at age thirty is very likely going to have some sort of sexual history. At some age, though, the fact that she's had so little sexual history starts becoming concerning. A thirty-two year old virgin makes you wonder if they have any sort of sex drive at all.

Totally Into You Sexually

This is the counter point of sorts to the virgin one. Once we were engaged, Jennifer and I pretty much ran roughshod over "the rules" about no sex before marriage. We were still *each other's first* which is the essential point of the virgin thing, but so sexually activated on each other that we simply did not care what anyone else had to say or think on the matter.

My worry about a woman not willing to flex in the engagement period, is that she is simply not sexually interested enough in her man, or has a very low libido. You do need to see obvious sexual interest and eagerness in her for you. You don't want a used mattress, but you do want a wife that is sexually activated on you. *Chemistry matters, it really, really matters.*

I think during the engagement period, couples should experiment with each other to ensure there is a sexual compatibility there. Marriage is simply too long of a time to live together if you can't have an enjoyable sex life. I know of several couples who have discovered an appalling lack of basic sexual compatibility with one another on their wedding night and have had miserable and failed marriages because of it.

If you're only going to have one woman for the rest of your life, it's just too much to risk relying on blind luck that it's going to work out. Some spouses actively defraud the other by hiding vital sexual information from the other until after the wedding.

Emotion is Not Her Only Tool

Ideally your wife to be should be able to problem solve with something other than her emotion. If you're running into excess drama over minor issues, and the woman is using tears, anger or moodiness as a problem solving tool, this will not get better over time. Treat it like a Fitness Test a few times, but if you find it keeps coming back at you again and again, just move on. Who wants to spend fifty years with a screechtard whose hobby is giving you a colonoscopy?

She Has a Talent

I don't care what the talent is. All you need to see is that she has the willpower and interest to start something and master it. Maybe it's a musical instrument, maybe it's ice skating, maybe it's knitting or gardening or soccer or whatever... it really doesn't matter.

She may very well move from talent to talent over the fifty years together, everything has a season, you just don't want to get handcuffed to a couch potato that complains you never take her anywhere as her main form of entertainment. She needs to provide some of her own stimulation and interest. You'll find that you'll probably share an interest or two over the years that just develops at some point. But if her idea of fun just involves nothing but sitting around eating and drinking at twenty-five, don't complain about being married to an angry slug at forty-five.

That Thing You Really Need

There's usually something that you as a man really need from your wife that you can't flinch on. Maybe you're all about politics and are a dyed in the wool Republican and intend to seek office – it really helps if she is Republican too. Maybe you're Jewish and you just really want a Kosher home – it's really going to help if she's Jewish too. Maybe you're a military guy and will be deployed often – it really helps if she can tolerate being apart and knows what she's getting into.

Whatever it is that you're really about, if you're compromising yourself to have her in your life, it's never going to work. The idea of marriage is not to give up what's important about you in order to try and mesh together something mediocre together. If you give up what you're really about to be with her, you're giving up all your personal power and nerfing your Alpha down to nothing. In time, she will despise you for it.

So she should have that compatibility with that one thing you're really about. Cut her no slack on that issue... and cut a lot more slack on everything else that you really don't care about.

If you're a man of any worth, you're a man about something. It really helps a great deal if she can be on board with that.

Almost Good Enough Isn't Good Enough

I had a relationship in college with a girl I badly wanted as my future wife. She was beautiful, smart and we got on great. We hung out all the time, studying in the library every day, lunch every day, coffee, church. I was much less skilled with women at the time, so I mired myself in the Friendzone with her, while every other girl I knew gave me a wide berth because everyone knew how smitten I was with this girl.

One day we had started discussing sex, and the frequency of each other's sexual impulses and horniness came up.

Me: *"About five or six times"*

She: *"I dunno once or twice."*

We just stood there looking at each other, waiting...

Me: *"...a day."*

She: *"...a month."*

Me: *"Really?"*

She: *"Really."*

I never considered her again as a possible wife. All done, sorry, you are not the wife I am looking for. I've never really figured out if she just wasn't interested in me, or couldn't really be interested in anyone anyway. I just sure as hell wasn't wasting my one shot at sexual happiness on her.

Later I met Jennifer and I made it clear very early on that I was all about the sex. She agreed. We married, it's been great.

Don't settle.

Know That Beauty Fades

At some point, her beauty will fade and all that will truly matter is her personality and ability to love. Her character and kindness matter a very great deal over the long term.

Shut your eyes and listen to the tone of voice she uses with other people when she thinks you aren't listening. It can be very revealing...

Isn't In Debt

A college loan for a degree that's related to her job is one thing. Mindless dragging debt she has no hope of paying off is quite another. The same woman that can't handle money before getting married will likely bankrupt you after getting married.

Don't Marry a Quitter

If she has any sort of a pattern of giving up on completing important tasks like her education, keeping a job, or doing major projects simply because they are hard or require effort...

...she'll probably quit on *you.*

Chapter 29
Marriage 2.0

Wife Choice is Critical

Your choice of wife is the biggest decision of your life. Who you marry will shape your life forever in ways you can't yet imagine.

Also for men, the ugly truth is the way marriage law and family court currently work, getting married puts you in a very vulnerable position. Your trust in the character of your wife and your ability to maintain her positive interest in you, amount to your best, and perhaps only, defense against some very nasty outcomes.

Unless you are completely confident in your choice of wife and ability to maintain your relationship, I advise you not to get married at all.

Waking Up to the Marriage Matrix

Take the blue pill – Continue your belief that simply being married will make everything work out for the best and that divorce is something that happens to other people.

Take the red pill - If you're ready to know the truth about modern marriage, read on. But understand that you can never go back to not knowing. Some of this chapter may be quite disturbing.

Law Defined What was Marriage 1.0

Back when my grandparents married, marriage was a fairly well understood thing. Apart from your partner exhibiting provably horrid behavior, like cheating, insanity or murder, marriage was for life. Sex was assumed as a husbandly right that wives were required to submit to. Adultery was illegal and pre-marital sex was not exactly illegal, but carried significant social sanction as it risked pregnancy. In general she stayed home and raised the kids, while he went out to work and pulled a paycheck for the family. Most couples just never even thought about splitting up, because essentially you couldn't. That was "Marriage 1.0."

While all that is becoming ancient history, it's important to understand that Marriage 1.0 was not just a social creation, but a legally defined structure that spelled out what "marriage" was.

With modern marriage, a.k.a. "Marriage 2.0", nearly all the legal rules of Marriage 1.0 have changed. In some ways these changes are good and valuable, in other ways there have been a mess of unintended consequences that undermine the very institution that marriage law is meant to define and support. Marriage 2.0 is the era of no-fault divorce law, adultery laws repealed, marital rape laws added and a divorce industry that profits off of protracted legal battles.

If the downside of Marriage 1.0 was that it shackled couples together regardless of happiness and enjoyment of each other, at least it used sex as an enticement to become and stay married. The downside of Marriage 2.0 is that what is intended as a permanent arrangement is becoming increasingly temporary. Plus as the possibility of having sex is very clearly no longer confined to married couples, marriage is slowly stripped of its innate eroticism. There should be little wonder that divorce is so common now.

Seeing the Reality of Modern Marriage

The trap for people getting married today is that they are going into a Marriage 2.0 relationship, but they often have the romantic illusion that they are going into a Marriage 1.0 relationship. Personally I'm no different. When Jennifer and I married, I just assumed we would be together until one of us died...that we would be each other's only sexual partner forever. For us that has worked out great, but if either one of us had decided to call it quits, our Marriage 1.0 fantasy would have instantly turned into a Marriage 2.0 reality with heartbreak steak and a side serving of lawyers.

While I do believe in love, experience romantic feelings and am pleased at the idea of my friends falling in love getting married, I don't look at marriage with a pair of rose colored spectacles. There is good in Marriage 2.0, but also a lot of potential very bad as well. Increasingly the way most men lose their marital rose colored spectacles is by having them smashed off their face by (1) her initiating a divorce, (2) discovering her infidelity, (3) the endless clamping of her legs in the shut position or (4) her becoming unhappy about everything he does and undergoing a transformation into a screeching pterodactyl. The unlucky man experiences all four as Marriage 2.0 schools him into reality. *This is what can happen when you take the blue pill.*

Importantly, men are very much taught to respect and place women on a pedestal when it comes to relationships and many simply cannot comprehend their wives ever struggling with issues of commitment and fidelity. Many men have simply no idea that what they see as a "happy marriage" is a hair's breadth away from her simply walking away. When she leaves, they are emotionally shattered with raw disbelief that such a thing could even be happening to them.

Accept reality, bid Marriage 1.0 a fond farewell and learn about what Marriage 2.0 really is all about. Take the red pill. Adapt and become stronger.

The Law Defines Marriage 2.0

Making our job of understanding marriage both easier and harder is marriage law. Please bear in mind that laws do vary from state to state and that I am talking in *very* general terms and not offering legal advice here.

There are strong biological hormones that create a pair bonding between a man and a woman. A couple can do all sorts of things to forge a relationship together - living together, having children together, buying property together and joining a social network as a couple - but none of that means they are married.

Modern marriage is a legal creation, legally defined and constructed by the process of law. The way you are married and what being married means was decided by your local politicians and signed into law. You just happened to agree to abide by whatever it was they decided marriage is. Marriage law does vary from state to state, but typically it requires a state authorized marriage celebrant, a statement of mutual agreement to be married, and a small amount of paperwork. It is remarkably easy to become married with what amounts to a do-it-yourself legal filing and is less complicated than getting new license plates for your car.

Marriages are also dissolved by legal process called divorce, as I'm sure you know, and divorce is where any romantic and idealistic notions end as the cold legality of the actual agreement comes to light. Divorce stands in stark contrast to the mood of a wedding, not only because of the joy of the occasion, but because weddings can have a fantasy experience at their core while divorce is reality based.

Weddings 2.0 are a Marriage 1.0 Fantasy Day

At the wedding, what both the bride and groom say to each other about marriage, think about marriage, believe about marriage and hope about marriage, is at best simply a verbal agreement. A couple can make their own vows and say them to each other, but while this is an emotionally touching experience, the vows are a mere fantasy of what the actual marriage agreement is. The actual marriage agreement the couple makes is what is defined as the agreement by marriage law. The vows are just some sort of conversation you had before you signed the marriage certificate; not admissible in court. To put it in plain English, a couple can pledge to each other *"until death do us part"*, but if they married in a no fault divorce state, the true agreement is, *"until someone files for divorce."*

It doesn't matter if you were married with an Elvis impersonator in Las Vegas, the Town Clerk, or Moses popped down for a bit to marry you. It doesn't matter if your vows are in the original Latin, you make up your own, or you sing "Puff the Magic Dragon" to each other. Your marriage agreement is whatever marriage law says it is.

Even more sobering is that if marriage law changes during the course of your marriage, the legal agreement between you and your spouse also changes retroactively. For example, my grandparents married when divorce was only allowable for provable fault. So their real marriage agreement was *"until death do us part or provable fault."* Some decades later no fault divorce was signed into law, so their marriage agreement was changed on them to *"until death do us part, or provable fault, or for no good reason... just whatever, I'm tired of this."* Their consent was not required in order to have their marriage agreement changed on them.

Marriage Law is Vague

Marriage law is kind of odd in that it usually doesn't really define what marriage is for. I live in Connecticut and my research into Connecticut Law suggests that being married allows you to enjoy the *"rights, benefits and privileges"* of being married. Though what those *"rights, benefits and privileges"* are, aren't actually defined under marriage law. The legal benefits and responsibilities of being married are defined across hundreds of other laws rather than within marriage law itself.

If for example a marriage license was a fishing license, it wouldn't actually spell out things like when you could fish, or what size fish was too small, or what the daily limit was. It would just say *"This is a fishing license. Please enjoy your fishing license."* Then in a law about use of public waterways, there could be a clause that stated *"People with fishing licenses may fish."* It's a very odd way of organizing things.

Even more bizarre is that in marriage law there is minimal reference to having sex. Despite the fact that for centuries marriage has been seen as the socially legitimate context to have sexual relations, marriage law doesn't actually say that a marriage license allows you to have sex with your spouse. Unless of course it falls under that *"rights, benefits and privileges"* thing, but even that seems a little hazy.

Your Legally "Open Marriage"

Many older laws also had adultery defined as a criminal act, meaning having sex with someone else's spouse was illegal, so by implied default this meant your spouse was required to be sexually faithful to you. Now that adultery laws have been largely removed from law in every state, all that is left is merely a *social expectation* of sexual fidelity, but not a *legal* requirement of sexual fidelity.

So in one sense, all marriages are "open marriages" whether you want them to be or not. Your wife can have sex with another man and she very likely wouldn't have broken any laws or the legal marriage agreement by doing so. She could have a long torrid affair and when you file your taxes together, the IRS isn't going to kick them back to you because she voided the marriage agreement by cheating on you. It's just up to you to decide whether or not you want to continue on with the marriage or file for divorce.

Unless your state defines infidelity as a reason to apply for an "at fault" divorce, there are no additional legal consequences for a wife being unfaithful to her husband other than risking divorce if caught. In a legal sense she would not have broken the marriage agreement seeing as sexual exclusivity doesn't seem to be even mentioned in marriage law. It's like that fishing license that says nothing about fish.

No Guarantee to Have Sex

Another change in marriage law is the addition of marital rape as a potential charge. For centuries it was ruled that it was impossible for a husband to rape a wife because sexual consent was always assumed. A woman becoming a wife had legally agreed to a lifetime of sexual availability, so if he had to get physical with her and force sex to get his "rights, benefits and privileges," then so be it.

Obviously being raped is a terrible thing for a woman to suffer through and the ruling that a woman can be raped by her husband has serious merit. However the unexpected consequence of marital rape law was the undoing of the concept that generally ongoing sexual relations were always implied as a requirement of marriage.

Thus a wife could decline sex to her husband... once, twice, or perhaps permanently. So a man may have very well married with the idea that a lifetime of sexual compatibility lies ahead of him, but there's no requirement that she has to perform that role unless she wants to. As many men learn to their anguish, a wife can simply say "No"... forever.

So once again... marriage law is like that fishing license that says nothing about fish.

Oops! You got Married by Accident

Depending on the state, there can also be cohabitation laws that kick in after a certain number of years living together. After that, the cohabitation law may essentially backdoor you into a de facto marriage agreement without you being fully aware of the law.

So for example, if your state has a cohabitation law that after five years of living together as a purposely unmarried couple, you are granted what amounts to the same legal rules as being married... then congratulations to the happy couple. Now your girlfriend can divorce you! You don't look excited by that...

Marriage Creates a Financial Team

Primarily what legal marriage allows is to file your taxes together and gain access to a wide variety of financial benefits, health related access, shared information and wealth transfer after death. This is all the sort of thing that Gay Rights activists seek as they are real benefits with value. It's not so much that gays and lesbians want the ability to be in sexual relationships with another person and live together – they can already do that – but they want access to things like joint health insurance and to be able to visit each other in the hospital more freely. They want to file their taxes together and when they die they want their loved ones to get the majority of their money and not have their estate gutted by the government. These are all the same things that heterosexual people want from marriage as well; to be turned into a financial team.

The downside to this creation of a financial team is that in situations where one partner provides the vast majority of the income, the other partner becomes increasingly regarded as a dependent. Should the marriage fail, the state tends to not want to increase its own costs by having to support the dependent. So the state looks to the partner with income to continue to support the dependent partner even though the marriage agreement is broken. This is called alimony and it varies greatly from state to state as to how much is required to be paid and for how long.

Obviously there is reasonable argument to be made that a stay at home wife has supported her husband's career success and by assisting him to make vast sums of money, she has damaged her own ability to make money; therefore she should be supported into the future. The argument is that domestic support has been traded for greater income generation. While there is indeed some merit to this argument, the obvious complaint that goes along with alimony payments is that while income is still being transferred from the husband to the wife, she no longer is required to continue to provide that domestic support. She doesn't make him any more sandwiches or do his laundry, but he keeps having to pay for the sandwiches and laundry she handled before they divorced.

Each state has its own alimony law and some seem reasonable and some seem appalling. I can only advise readers to look into their local alimony law for themselves. I'm simply raising it as a potential issue that can occur as a result of divorce. Bear in mind that you will lay the groundwork for an alimony judgment many years before that judgment will be made. If you agree that your wife should become a stay at home mother in your second year of marriage and you divorce in the fifteenth year of marriage, then you decided to set yourself up for alimony payments all the way back in your second year of marriage. There are clearly some wonderful stay at home mother's that do creatively support their families and help advance their husbands' career paths, but some appear to have successfully conned a man into becoming his dependent via the stay at home and/or alimony approach. Alimony laws do vary wildly from state to state, with some favoring alimony payments over a few years, while some still have lifetime alimony.

The creation of a financial team can result in ridiculous results such as in Massachusetts where there have been well documented cases where the *lifetime* alimony for the first wife, is based on the income of her ex-husband, *plus the income of his second wife!*

Divorce and Moral Hazard

Furthermore, the financial team becomes jointly responsible for any children the wife has during the marriage. For the most part this proceeds without too much hassle; most dads do love their kids and want to support them. However, thanks to the no fault divorce law the marriage can end to the great surprise of the husband, whereupon the custody of the children can be split between the husband and wife or with solely one partner after divorce. Then the state will step in and ensure that income continues to flow from the parent with less custody (usually the husband) to the one with more custody (usually the wife). All of this can happen essentially without the consent or desire for a split family on the husband's part. If the wife wants out of a marriage, the Family Court machinery just starts up and the husband is fairly powerless to affect the outcome. Sometimes the father does get primary custody of course, but around 80% of divorces are started by women and the courts award on average far greater custody to mothers.

For the most part this all makes sense from the perspective of the state, which is all that really matters as far as it is concerned. The emotional pain of an individual man is not an issue for the state. Say for example another man actively sets out to seduce a man's wife, she sleeps repeatedly with the other man and she starts divorcing her husband. Her first move would be to allege that her husband threatened to hit her, which forces him out of the family home (by automatic arrest in some states), then keeps him out via restraining order and she retains full custody of the children while things are being looked into by the authorities.

It only takes a few angry verbal outbursts for a man to be regarded with extreme suspicion as a potential danger to his family and it can take months of costly legal effort to prove that he isn't. Of course none of this hurts the state's feelings, and the husband may very well be forced to pay both child support and alimony, and only get to see his children for a few hours a week as a result. Then if the other man moves into his former family home, he is forced to watch helplessly as all of this perfectly legal.

For a wife there can be a perceived incentive to kick her husband out of the house as she would still be "getting paid" via the court process. If the main factor about her husband that attracted her was his money, she can retain a fair percentage of it via divorce and simply cut him out of the picture. This is especially dangerous to her current husband if she has an affair partner who is also willing to bring his income into her home. She could thereby secure her half of the assets of the marriage, gain potential alimony and child support from her ex-husband, plus be supported by her new man as well. Of course almost all divorced women will tell you that being divorced is not something they ran at a profit, but there is the potential to take advantage of things if she is truly evil.

The Husband is Responsible to Support Her Children

The other potential downside for a husband is that he becomes financially responsible for any children his wife has during the marriage, even the ones he does not want her to have. Say a couple has two children and agree that they don't want a third one. If the wife flushes her birth control pills down the toilet and becomes pregnant again, the husband is still on the hook for supporting the child. He can use condoms of course and try and cover himself that way, but you really shouldn't flush condoms and women have been known to fish them out of the trash and complete the job of getting pregnant that way.

Even worse is that studies show that roughly 8-10% of all children have their biological fathers misidentified. In other words, if your wife cheats on you and gets pregnant by another man, you're on the hook for supporting the child. Considering that the wife is very well aware of her extra-marital sex, without protection, without contraception or use of the morning after pill, becoming pregnant by another man should be regarded as a deliberate act on her part and as the most outrageous fraud of her husband. Discovery of paternity fraud will have an enormously high chance of ending the marriage.

Depending on state law and time elapsed, the husband may still have to pay child support for a child proven by DNA testing *not* to be his.

This isn't a men's rights book, but an awareness of the harsh realities of what can happen when marriage goes bad isn't a bad thing. For female readers, I hope this goes some way towards an explanation of why many men are "afraid of commitment" and the increasing popularity of prenuptial agreements.

Summarizing Marriage 2.0

Marriage doesn't guarantee that she will have sex with you, be faithful, or stay with you. Marriage legally creates a financial team that may result in ongoing financial support after a divorce and very likely support for any children she has during the marriage.

So Why Marry Anyway?

After reading all this you might have the shakes if you're a man and rightly so. Marriage is a risk and you stake a lot on having found a good woman to marry. Correct that. You stake *everything* on having found a good woman to marry.

There are large upsides though. As I mentioned before, marriage creates a family unit as a financial team and that team can do better than two single people alone can. An accident or injury that might bankrupt a single person may only be a setback for a couple. It's easier coping with the death of a family member as a couple than as a single. While it sounds unromantic to say that a woman sells "wife" and a man sells "husband", if both make a fair trade it can provide a lifetime beneficial interpersonal economy to each other. Sometimes 2 + 2 really does equal 5.

Another added benefit is that many women have a deep need for security and safety in order to feel safe enough to fully embrace their sexuality. Most women feel an intense desire to have children at some point in their life, but they also desire a stable environment for those children. As many long time boyfriends have experienced, fertile girlfriends can bring considerable pressure to bear on the concept of getting married. It's possible to lose out on a very high quality woman permanently by failing to marry her. If your gorgeous sweet-tempered girl moves out for lack of an engagement ring, the next girl in your bed may not be so appealing. The male "shelf life" differs from the female one, but you do have one. A woman leaving you for failure to marry can markedly damage your ability to attract a new partner, especially in a smaller community.

When marriage works well, it works *very* well for men. Study after study suggests that married men are happier and healthier than unmarried men. Plus married men have on average more sex than unmarried men. It's always possible to point to sexless marriages as a pitfall, but on balance married men typically have longer, happier and sexier lives than those that don't marry.

After a certain age the unmarried or never married man increasingly starts looking like damaged goods. The perception is that it's not so much that he chose not to be married, but that he is incapable of a serious relationship or unable to attract anyone interested in being with him.

Marital sex isn't always automatically excellent, but with a lifetime of practice with a partner you can become increasingly proficient at providing each other sexual pleasure. One of the most common statements from cheating spouses is that while the sex with the lover was novel and emotionally addictive, it wasn't actually as physically good as sex with their spouse.

Also a shared history together can create a depth of love and understanding that short term relationships and hook ups simply cannot come close to approaching. Seeing your kids growing up, having family vacations and Christmas mornings together, there's a lot to love and experience as a committed couple.

The Good News

The very good news about Marriage 2.0 for a man is that your wife is freer than any generation of women before her. That can translate into her happiness, energy and sexual enjoyment with you. If it's working well, the sexual connection is fantastic and better than any form of marriage before now.

Marriage 2.0 Requires Endless Courtship

The key point to take away here is that marriage is vastly changed from what most people expect it to be. In the old version of marriage, men and women jostled for position to marry the best member of the opposite sex, in their small community that they could. They actively courted one another and displayed themselves as attractively as they could. Once they married though, they just settled down to the business of starting a family, raising kids and going to work. Essentially they had minimal concern that their spouse would be unfaithful, or that their marriage would ever end aside from death or serious abuse.

In the new version of marriage though, it can end at any time. It can end simply because your partner doesn't want to be with you, or would rather be with someone else. You can be a "good" husband or "good" wife and be suddenly dispossessed of your spouse by court order simply because they announce, *"I love you but I'm not in love with you."* Plus half your shared stuff goes as well and maybe the kids too.

The new marriage requirement is one of endless courtship. Spouses must, on an ongoing basis, display personality, behavior and appearance that increase the sexual and romantic interest their partners have in them. *You have no option about choosing to do The MAP or not, failure to do it risks your demise.* But if you court her in a manner that turns her on, the consequence is exceptional sexual excitement and freedom to explore that enjoyment together...

...which was what this book was all about.

Finishing Up

Chapter 30
Ten Things to Do Right Now

What happens now is up to you

One possible trap is to get caught up in thinking about everything I've written about and not do anything about it. This is not a book about thinking; this is a book about doing. Male sexuality is active and energetic, so simply sitting on your ass and thinking about the contents of this book is the exact opposite of what the book says to do.

You don't have to understand everything I've written in order to make it work for you. You don't even have to believe what I've said is true for it to work. You just have to get up off your ass and start trying it out. Your results will usually happen pretty quickly. I've had people thank me for turning their relationship around within two months. I'll take your belief that it works *after* it works for you.

So to get you up into action and doing, he's a list of things to immediately get started on right now. These are the most critical and simple pieces of doing The MAP.

1. Start exercising with weights.
2. Do the Ten Second Kiss move at least daily.
3. Stop letting her get away with nonsense.
4. Pick one thing from the Alpha chapter to work on.
5. Pick one thing from the Beta chapter to work on.
6. Switch out the soda and coffee for a protein shake in the morning.
7. Learn her menstrual cycle.
8. *"Instigate, Isolate and Escalate."*
9. Try a rough sex experiment on her.
10. Tell her what kind of sex you want before you go into the bedroom.

Once you get that up and running, you can always come back and reread the book and fine-tune things. Don't give up!

Chapter 31
Spread the Word

Ladies...

I know you've been reading the whole time. As I said in the beginning of the book, this is all a bit of a magic trick to get you a better man. I truly hope you are getting the man you have wanted him to be all along.

Also, you know how difficult women can get with their men. If you have sons, brothers and nephews who need my help, it's okay to meddle a little and send them a copy. Except according to the Rationalization Hamster it's not really meddling... it's *caring!*

Making Love

Also, do have sex more with your husbands. They really need that from you. It's not even really just about the sex itself. Remember when it used to be called "Making Love?" Considering how having an orgasm floods you with oxytocin, and his orgasm floods him with vasopressin, *having sex really is making love* together.

Every time you have sex isn't going to be a show stopper that you wished you had taped. A lot of the sex you have is going to be pretty average sex, but it's always going to renew the bonds of love between you. The way to a man's heart isn't through his stomach, it's through your vagina.

Be Wary of the Divorce Industry

The Facebook status updates of forty-year-old divorced women seem to be largely about getting pumped and dumped by men objectively worse than their husband was. You may still get lucky, but the dating market is a harsh place and glass slippers are in short supply. Just sayin'.

Guys...

The odds are that you know a guy that really needs this book. If so, don't be quiet about it. Worst case scenario, he's out $20 if he buys it. Best case scenario, his marriage turns around and he thanks you for it.

I get emails nearly every day from men and women who say that my blog saved their marriage somehow. This book is vastly better than the blog, so I can only hope that it's more effective at saving marriages.

Why *wouldn't* you tell them?

Help Me Out

And hey I'm not going to lie. Book sales put money in my pocket and that's part of the reason I write. But it's a quality book and I'm not charging $49.99 for a sixty page eBook which is usually the way this sort of information is dished out.

The Married Man Sex Life Primer

I'm planning on being around a long time. Currently my goal is to revise and review The Primer every year for the next thirty years, before retiring at age seventy and hopefully passing it on to my daughters and future sons-in-law to continue the work.

Life is what you make of it; this is my life's work.

I most sincerely hope that I have been of service.

About the Author

Athol Kay is an innovative thinker, humorist and family man with a one track mind.

He is a "Mixed Marital Artist" combining a variety of relationship approaches from evolutionary psychology, Pickup Artist "Game", sociology, biology, life experience, romance novels, crappy women's magazines, far too many books, blogging, behavior modification and cheap porn. He has distilled all this research into a few outstandingly effective tactics for gaining happiness and sex in marriage.

Athol was born in New Zealand and met Jennifer nine days before he was due to fly home after working on a summer camp in Maryland in 1991. Long distance for three years, they finally married in 1994. Married for 16 years, they have two daughters and live in Connecticut. They have a carefully balanced relationship where Athol dreams up all kinds of weird shit, and Jennifer doesn't leave him.

The author is also aware that has painted himself into a corner by writing a book on monogamy. At around 112,500 words, it is the longest chastity belt in existence. It only chafes a little.

Athol usually posts daily at **www.marriedmansexlife.com**

He can also be contacted via email at **Athol.Kay@Gmail.com**